KU-642-179

CHANGING SCOTLAND

Evidence from the British Household Panel Survey

Edited by John F. Ermisch and Robert E. Wright

First published in Great Britain in July 2005 by

The Policy Press
University of Bristol
Fourth Floor
Beacon House
Queen's Road
Bristol BS8 1QU
UK

Tel +44 (0)117 331 4054
Fax +44 (0)117 331 4093
e-mail tpp-info@bristol.ac.uk
www.policypress.org.uk

© John F. Ermisch and Robert E. Wright 2005

British Library Cataloguing in Publication Data
A catalogue record for this book is available from the British Library.

Library of Congress Cataloging-in-Publication Data
A catalog record for this book has been requested.

ISBN 1 86134 593 3 hardcover

John F. Ermisch is Professor of Economics at the Institute for Social and Economic Research, University of Essex, UK.
Robert E. Wright is Professor in the Department of Economics, University of Stirling, UK.

The right of John Ermisch and Robert Wright to be identified as editors of this work has been asserted by them in accordance with the 1988 Copyright, Designs and Patents Act.

All rights reserved: no part of this publication may be reproduced, stored in a retrieval system, or transmitted in any form or by any means, electronic, mechanical, photocopying, recording, or otherwise without the prior permission of The Policy Press.

The statements and opinions contained within this publication are solely those of the editors and contributors and not of The University of Bristol or The Policy Press. The University of Bristol and The Policy Press disclaim responsibility for any injury to persons or property resulting from any material published in this publication.

The Policy Press works to counter discrimination on grounds of gender, race, disability, age and sexuality.

Cover design by Qube Design Associates, Bristol.
Front cover: photograph © Scottish Parliamentary Corporate Body 2005.
Printed and bound in Great Britain by Hobbs the Printers, Southampton.

Contents

List of tables and figures

Tables

Figures

Foreword

This volume is published at a time when the big ideological claim that social justice and economic efficiency are two sides of the same coin has largely been won in advanced societies. However, if the ideological heights have been scaled, sound evidence-based policy making has not always followed!

Too often, the 'New Scotland' hesitates, unsure of its future. The 20th century may have gone, but its death throes reverberate, thrusting its deep tentacles into our present. This volume provides emerging route maps for moving towards realising that New Scotland. However, Scotland will only be able to build a consensus for change if that change is firmly rooted in a serious analysis of Scottish society. For example, acknowledging that despite the professed commitment of Scottish society to greater equality, Scottish citizens have frequently endured deeper and more intransigent levels of poverty than elsewhere.

Citizens of the 21st century look to government to improve the links between economic and social priorities, to better balance the demands of competitiveness and cohesion, and to renew the social contracts of the past for today's purposes. Governments may have less power over currencies, technologies and the flow of information, but modern government is also better able to shape vital aspects of our lives – eliminating childhood poverty, winning the war against crime and delivering better health. The volume looks forward to the challenges of balancing work, life, leisure and pleasure. It demonstrates how the New Scotland could grow in solidarity, hospitality and compassion.

Wendy Alexander, MSP

Preface

The Scottish Parliament opened in 1999. This devolution of powers has created a mechanism by which public policy may become more responsive to the needs of the Scottish people, and over time it is likely to create major differences in policy relative to the rest of the UK. One aspect of the evaluation of the impacts of these new policies is comparative research, with the developments in Scotland being compared with those in other areas of the UK.

The main aim of this book is to demonstrate how data from the British Household Panel Survey (BHPS) can be used to examine, on a consistent basis, a variety of social, economic and political differences between Scotland and other regions of the UK that are relevant for policy evaluation and formulation. The comparative studies in this book provide an important 'baseline' for analysing the impacts of subsequent differential developments in policy arising out of devolution. They allow us to address the question of whether Scots behave differently despite similar policy regimes in Scotland and the rest of the UK, or the same, despite some pre-existing differences in policy. If you are going to assess the impact of devolution in the future you need an empirical baseline showing how Scotland and England differed on many dimensions before devolution.

Identification of these differences is also crucial if policy is going to be pursued by the Scottish Executive aimed at narrowing those differences that represent 'disadvantage'. Hitherto, we were in the dark about the nature and size of these differences, in part because of the lack of good comparative data. The data gap has been filled to a significant extent by the 'booster samples' of the BHPS for Scotland, which has produced a representative sample of about 3,500 Scots who have been interviewed annually since 1999. Most of the studies in the book use the first two 'waves' of this enhanced sample – 1999 and 2000 – in conjunction with data from the rest of Britain from the main BHPS. However, the chapters are not only indicative of what can be done with the BHPS and of the policy baseline; they are also thorough empirical investigations of topics of interest to many researchers in a wide range of disciplines, and each emphasises Scottish–English differences.

The initial chapter briefly describes Scottish devolution, its broad impact on public policy and the role of evidence-based policy research.

The next seventeen chapters are organised into four sections, with each section representing a broad theme:

- families and households;
- inequalities;
- labour market issues;
- social and political behaviour.

Each section is introduced by a discussion of the policy and research issues related to that theme, particularly those raised by Scottish devolution, and the contribution of each chapter to these issues. The book ends with a brief conclusion highlighting the main objectives of the book and some of the policy questions raised by the findings.

List of contributors

Wendy Alexander, Member of Scottish Parliament and Visiting Professor, Strathclyde Business School, University of Strathclyde, Glasgow.

Harminder Battu, Senior Lecturer, Department of Economics, University of Aberdeen.

David Bell, Professor, Department of Economics, University of Stirling and Co-director, Scottish Economic Policy Network.

Nicole Bourque, Senior Lecturer, Department of Sociology and Anthropology, University of Glasgow.

Alex Christie, Research Fellow, Scottish Economic Policy Network, Universities of Stirling and Strathclyde.

John Curtice, Professor, Department of Government and Deputy Director, Centre for Research into Elections and Social Trends, University of Strathclyde, Glasgow.

Carolyn Davidson, Business Manager, Assessment, Research and Development, Scottish Qualifications Authority, Glasgow.

Robert Elliott, Professor, Department of Economics and Director, Health Economics Research Unit, University of Aberdeen.

John F. Ermisch, Professor, Institute for Social and Economic Research, University of Essex, Colchester.

Jeanette Findlay, Senior Lecturer, Department of Economics, University of Glasgow.

Patricia Findlay, Senior Lecturer, Management School and Economics, University of Edinburgh.

Anne Gasteen, Senior Lecturer, Division of Business Economics and Enterprise, Glasgow Caledonian University.

Vernon Gayle, Lecturer, Department of Applied Social Sciences, University of Stirling and Research Fellow, Longitudinal Studies Centre, University of St Andrews.

Vania Gerova, Research Officer, Institute of Education, University of London.

John Houston, Senior Lecturer, Division of Business Economics and Enterprise, Glasgow Caledonian University.

Gregor Jack, Research Fellow, Westminster Business School, University of Westminster, London.

Lynn Jamieson, Professor, Department of Sociology and Co-director, Centre for Research on Families and Relationships, University of Edinburgh.

Rannia M. Leontaridi, Honorary Research Associate, Welsh Economy Labour Market Evaluation and Research Centre, University of Wales Swansea.

Anne Ludbrook, Senior Research Fellow, Health Economics Research Unit, University of Aberdeen.

Cecilia MacIntyre, Head of Demographics, General Register Office for Scotland, Edinburgh.

Nicola McEwen, Lecturer, Department of Government, University of Strathclyde, Glasgow.

John H. McKendrick, Lecturer, School of Law and Social Sciences, Glasgow Caledonian University.

Kostas G. Mavromaras, Senior Lecturer, Department of Economics and Senior Research Fellow, Health Economics Research Unit, University of Aberdeen.

James Mitchell, Professor, Department of Government, University of Strathclyde, Glasgow.

Euan Phimister, Reader, Department of Economics, University of Aberdeen.

John Rigg, Research Officer, Centre for the Analysis of Social Exclusion, London School of Economics and Political Science.

Peter J. Sloane, Professor, Department of Economics and Director, Welsh Economy Labour Market Evaluation and Research Centre, University of Wales Swansea.

Mark Taylor, Chief Research Officer, Institute for Social and Economic Research, University of Essex, Colchester.

Ioannis Theodossiou, Professor, Department of Economics, University of Aberdeen.

Robert E. Wright, Professor, Department of Economics, University of Stirling and Research Coordinator, Demography and Social Justice Programme, Scottish Economic Policy Network.

ONE

Devolution, policy and evidence

John F. Ermisch and Robert E. Wright

What is devolution?

For many centuries prior to 1707, Scotland had its own government, with a Parliament that met in different geographic locations before settling in Edinburgh in 1633. However, the Act of Union of 1707 abolished the Scottish Parliament and merged the Scottish and English Parliaments into a single institution based in London. On 11 September 1997, a referendum was held in which residents of Scotland were asked to vote on two questions relating to their political future. The first was simply whether a Scottish Parliament should be re-established. The second concerned whether this Parliament should have tax-varying power.

The outcome of this referendum was a majority (74%) voting in favour of re-creating the Scottish Parliament, with a smaller majority (64%) voting in favour of allowing it to have tax-varying powers. In 1998, the Scotland Act was passed by the Westminster Parliament, which 'devolved' a range of responsibilities and powers to the new Scottish Parliament. On 6 May 1999, a General Election was held, with the first 129 Members of the Scottish Parliament (MSPs) being elected by a process that combines both first-past-the-post and proportional representation voting principles (technically referred to as an 'Additional Member' system). The Scottish Parliament formally opened in Edinburgh on 1 July 1999, with a Labour–Liberal Democrats coalition, led by the former Labour Cabinet Minister, Donald Dewar, as First Minister, and the pro-independence Scottish National Party as the official opposition. The 2003 election generated a similar outcome, with ex-Labour Councillor Jack McConnell as First Minister.

The chapters of this book are revised versions of papers presented at a conference held at the University of Stirling in October 2002. We are grateful to the Scottish Economic Policy Network (University of Stirling) and the Institute of Social and Economic Research (University of Essex) for financial support for this conference.

Central to the understanding of the way in which the Scottish Parliament operates is the distinction between 'devolved' and 'reserved' issues. In a nutshell, 'devolved' issues are the responsibility of the Scottish Parliament while 'reserved' issues are the responsibility of the Westminster Parliament. As there is still considerable confusion concerning the division of the responsibilities between the two institutions, it is useful to catalogue each. Devolved issues include:

- health, education and training;
- local government;
- social work;
- housing and planning;
- tourism, economic development and financial assistance to industry;
- certain aspects of transport, including the Scottish road network, bus policy and ports and harbours;
- law and home affairs, including most aspects of criminal and civil law, the prosecution system and the courts;
- police and fire services;
- environment;
- natural and built heritage;
- agriculture, forestry and fishing;
- sport and the arts;
- statistics, public registers and records.

Reserved issues include:

- constitutional matters;
- foreign policy;
- defence and national security;
- fiscal, economic and monetary system;
- immigration and nationality;
- energy, electricity, coal, gas and nuclear energy;
- common markets;
- trade and industry, including competition and customer protection;
- some aspects of transport, including railways, transport safety and regulation;
- employment legislation;
- social security;
- gambling and the National Lottery;
- data protection;
- abortion, human fertilisation and embryology, genetics, xenotransplantation and vivisection;
- equal opportunities.

It is also worth noting that the Scottish Parliament has the right to increase the basic rate of income tax by up to three percentage points. What is clear from the list of devolved issues is that the Scottish Parliament has direct responsibility for a range of matters that affect the lives of Scottish people. It is not unrealistic to assume that the process of devolution will generate differences in public policy since this is what it is meant to do in the first place. It is assumed that the Scottish Parliament will pursue policies more in tune with the desires and priorities of its electorate. In principle, this should lead to more effective government and reduce the resentment that many Scots have about being 'governed from London'. Devolution, however, has also created a new set of problems. In certain areas, the distinction between devolved and reserved issues is not as clear-cut as it may first seem. This has led to confusion in terms of who is actually responsible for what. Likewise, there is a constant debate on what issues *should* be devolved. The Scottish National Party is the only party with a clear answer to this question – 'Everything!'.

Public policy in a devolved Scotland

Devolution has generated the 'potential' for Scotland to pursue public policy that is considerably different to that pursued in other areas of the UK. In order to understand this potential, it is necessary to briefly outline how the Scottish government is organised. The Scottish government – or, more correctly, the 'Scottish Executive' – is divided into a set of 'departments'. Although this simplifies matters considerably from a public policy point of view, there are seven departments that are particularly relevant. Each is responsible for a set of devolved issues, although there is considerable overlap. The departments are:

- Education
- Enterprise, Transport and Lifelong Learning
- Health
- Justice
- Environment and Rural Affairs
- Development
- Finance and Central Services.

An examination of the specific responsibilities of each of these departments provides some information relating to the scope to which policies can be pursued that diverge from those followed at Westminster.

Department of Education

The main responsibility of this department is policy relating to pre-school education and primary and secondary schooling. It develops and administers policies for children's rights, support for families, child protection, regulation of childcare centres, children-in-care, and a host of social work issues affecting children and young people. It also has responsibility for policy relating to tourism, the arts, film, architecture, cultural heritage, sport, Gaelic and liaison with the UK government on broadcasting and the Lottery.

Department of Enterprise, Transport and Lifelong Learning

The main responsibility of this department is to assist in the generation of economic growth through policies aimed at supporting business, encouraging enterprise and entrepreneurship, fostering trade and inward investment and improving skills and employability (through such agencies as Scottish Enterprise and Highlands and Islands Enterprise). It is also responsible for further and higher education, the science base, lifelong learning, training, 'New Deal', and some aspects of tourism. In 2003, the task of developing an effective transportation and communications infrastructure (including information technology) was added to the responsibilities of this department.

Department of Health

The main responsibilities of this department are the National Health Service and the development and implementation of health and community care policy. The department plays a key role in the formation of social work policy and policy aimed at promoting positive attitudes towards health and healthy lifestyles. It is also responsible for setting and monitoring clinical standards and for the Scottish ambulance service.

Department of Justice

The main responsibility of this department is 'Home Affairs', which includes civil law and criminal justice, social work services group (except community care), police, fire, courts and prisons, law reform, land reform policy, freedom of information, drugs policy and the General Register Office for Scotland.

Department of Environment and Rural Affairs

This department's main responsibility is policy aimed at promoting rural development. This includes agriculture, fisheries, forestry, research, the environment, natural heritage, sustainable development, strategic environmental assessments and land-use planning.

Department of Development

Housing and construction are among this department's main responsibilities. The main policy aim is to ensure an adequate supply of housing with choice by assisting owner occupation and promoting the development of a diverse rental sector. The department is also responsible for land-use planning and building control. It also pursues social justice policies including area regeneration projects and economic, social and environmental improvement of disadvantaged urban areas.

Department of Finance and Central Services

The main responsibilities of this department are the Scottish Budget, local government finance, European structural funds and resource allocation. This includes the development and administration of policy on local government, such as structure, powers, conduct and finance. It is also responsible for media and publicity services for the Scottish Executive.

It is important to note how the overall budget of the Scottish Executive is determined. In most nations with sub-national governments, a 'need-based' approach is used. That is, the amount of funding received in devolved regions is based on variations in the level of demand for public services and differences in the costs of providing these services. In contrast, a population-based approach, usually referred to as the 'Barnett Formula', is used in the UK. This allocates increases in expenditure set by Westminster mainly on a per-capita basis. In this sense, the Barnett Formula determines the total size of the budget to be received by Scotland, and then the individual departments within the Scottish Executive 'compete' for their shares of this total.

Perhaps the most important outcome of devolution in Scotland is the considerable flexibility that the Scottish Executive has in the way it can spend the money it receives from the centre. For example, if the Scottish Executive decides to spend more on health and less on education it is 'allowed' do to so. In this sense, the Westminster Parliament decides the size of 'pie', but the Scottish Parliament decides how it is 'sliced'. This flexibility in the way public money can be spent has already led to the introduction of policies that are considerably different to those in place in other regions of the UK. Three concrete examples are worth mentioning:

- the so-called 'free personal care for the elderly' programme;
- the firm commitment not to introduce tuition fees in the higher education sector for Scottish students;
- the decision not to pursue in the health sector the pseudo-privatisation programme of 'foundation hospitals'.

The big policy issues

One area where there is a major difference between Scotland and the UK as a whole is demographic change. The current demographic situation in Scotland can be described as a population with below replacement-level fertility (that is, deaths exceed births), gradually decreasing mortality (increasing life expectancy) and zero net migration. If there are no major changes in these factors, particularly fertility, the Scottish population will decrease in size from its current level of about five million to 4.5 million over the next four decades. In addition, and perhaps more importantly, the Scottish population will continue to age rapidly. Population ageing is a redistribution of relative population shares away from the younger to the older age groups. Population projections carried out by the Governments Actuary's Department suggest that the share of the total population aged 65+ could reach 30% by 2042.

The ageing of the Scottish population will lead to an increase in the number of individuals of pension age and a decrease in the number of individuals of working age. This will lead in turn to a large increase in the demand for state-supplied health care, residential services, housing, pensions and other services consumed by older people. Unfortunately, at the same time, the base expected to pay for this increase – essentially people of working age – will become progressively smaller both in absolute numbers and in relative population share. That is, those 'demanding' will increase while those 'supplying' will decrease. It is not hard to imagine that such a situation of increasing imbalance is unsustainable in the long run and some will argue that 'cracks' caused by population ageing in Scotland's 'pay-as-you-go' welfare system are already starting to show.

There is a growing consensus that the Scottish Executive will soon find itself without the necessary resources to accommodate the changes in the expected demand for public services and other welfare benefits targeted at the elderly caused by population ageing. Nevertheless, it will be expected to increase expenditure in these areas in order to insure that the living standard of this numerically increasing segment of the population does not fall. As a population ages so does its electorate, and older people compared to younger people have much higher rates of participation in elections at all levels of government. The dilemma facing politicians is that if they do not (or cannot) accommodate the demands of their ageing electorate they will suffer dearly at the ballot box. A 'greying electorate' will not vote in mass for politicians who they believe are ignoring their interests. It is perhaps not surprising, therefore, that the current cohort of politicians have not only recently started to comment in public that Scotland may have a 'population problem' but they are also exploring a range of potential policies aimed at addressing this growing demographic imbalance. The recently announced Fresh Talent Initiative (a policy aimed at increasing immigration to Scotland) is an example.

There is little disagreement that over the past three decades or so, the rate of economic growth in Scotland has lagged behind that of the UK as a whole. The Scottish Executive is committed to a 'Growth Agenda', where the aim is to pursue policies that create an environment more conducive to long-term and sustainable economic growth. Most of these policies fall under the remit of the Enterprise, Transport and Lifelong Learning Department, and are executed through such initiatives as Smart Successful Scotland, Enterprise Networks and Local Economic Forums. These policies "should create a business environment which actively encourages innovation, entrepreneurialism and high skill levels, helping to encourage the creation, growth and transformation of businesses". It is clear that the Scottish Executive believes that the efficient creation of wealth by the private sector is not only the key to continued growth but is also critical if Scotland is going to 'catch up' with the wealthier regions of the UK.

The Scottish Executive also recognises that if Scotland is to compete more competitively in the global economy, generating a labour force with the 'right' skills is critical. Skilled workers are productive workers, who are able to adapt, change and innovate. One important lesson that human capital theory has taught us is that inequality in skills is the main determinant of inequality in earnings and the experience of unemployment, which in turn are the main determinants of social inequality. Social inequality generates 'social problems' and it is these social problems that the bulk of policy is aimed at 'solving'. However, addressing social inequality 'after the fact' has proven to be very difficult, as witnessed, for example, by the failure of many very expensive 'training' programmes aimed at re-skilling older workers displaced by technological change or by the decline of traditional manufacturing.

In most industrialised countries, governments still play a large role in the production of skills through the formal education system. Scotland is no exception to this general statement, with the majority of children and young adults being schooled at the expense of the state. However, there is broad agreement that an 'education policy' and a 'skills policy' are not one and the same policy. Formal schooling is only one component of the skills formation process, and is a component that many believe is becoming less effective in producing the type of skills that are needed to generate economic growth. To a certain extent, Scotland has an advantage over other regions in the UK since the responsibility for education is a 'devolved' matter. Furthermore, the importance that the Scottish Executive places on the links between education policy, skill formation and economic growth is apparent when you remember that the responsibility for further and higher education falls within the remit of the Department of Enterprise, Transport and Lifelong Learning and not the Department of Education.

It is worth remembering that skills are both cognitive and non-cognitive in nature. It is important to stress that there is a growing body of research that suggests strongly that much skill formation occurs within the family unit, with the process beginning well before children enter school. Empirical research is consistently showing that the interaction between children, parents and other family members is central to establishing the preconditions necessary for the successful acquisition of skills, not only in school, but also later on in the labour market. Unfortunately, this research is also showing that if this interaction is lacking (for whatever reason), a disadvantage is established at a very early age that persists and is very difficult to correct later on in life. Although it might be too pessimistic to conclude that 'the die is cast' before a child enters school, this research does suggest that important cognitive and non-cognitive skills are formed when children are very young. It follows that policies that 'invest' in these early years could have a profound impact on reducing social inequality before it 'starts'. In this sense, the integration of family policy, education policy and skills policy (which is happening in Scotland) is potentially a very positive development. If managed properly, such a holistic policy approach could not only provide a significant boost to economic growth, but could also lead to lower social inequality that finally breaks the vicious circle of disadvantage breeding disadvantage.

Life expectancy in Scotland is not only significantly lower than in England, Northern Ireland and Wales, but it is also the lowest in the European Union (EU). Relative to most industrialised countries, Scotland has a very poor record on health and health-related matters. Men and women in Scotland live shorter lives on average than those in almost any country with a comparable material standard of living. Mortality rates are higher across the complete range of ages for almost all causes of death, including heart disease, cancer and accidents. Even after known correlates of mortality are 'held constant' (such as average income), there is still a sizeable unexplained residual, usually attributed vaguely to the 'unhealthy Scottish life-style'.

The Scottish Executive acknowledges that there is much room for improvement. The provider of health services in Scotland, like the rest of the UK, is the National Health Service (NHS). Arguably, the NHS does not rank highly in terms of efficiency or value-for-money when compared to the systems in place in other welfare states. It is often viewed as a 'black hole' where taxpayers' money is wasted, with the bulk of the health budget being spent on the provision of medical services and hospital care rather than on preventative medicine and education.

Health policy is a devolved responsibility, including how the NHS is structured and managed. The Scottish Executive is committed to improving the health of the Scottish population. In 2001, it introduced a policy, *Our national health: A plan for action, a plan for change*, which outlines a quite radical set of reforms relating to the structure of the NHS and in the way in which health services are delivered. Central to this policy is an increased emphasis on the prevention of poor health rather than the treatment of ill health. Such a policy is in contrast to what is being pursued outside of Scotland where the emphasis is almost exclusively on providing medical services at lower costs through the introduction of competition and the injection of private investment in the health sector. It also worth noting here that, since Scotland has a separate legal system, it is easier to introduce laws that may generate health benefits, such a banning smoking in public places such as restaurants and the workplace. Nevertheless, shedding Scotland's image as the 'sick man of Europe' is a serious policy challenge.

Scottish-specific public policy research

Devolution has created a mechanism by which public policy may become more responsive to the needs of the Scottish people. It has also generated the potential for the elected government of Scotland to pursue a programme of public spending that is very different to what is pursued in other regions of the UK. However, for this potential to be realised, evidence-based research aimed at informing the rich policy debate that has arisen post-devolution needs to be carried out. Such research, which has been sadly lacking in the past, is crucially needed by the various departments of the Scottish Executive in order to design and execute effectively their policies. While it may be the case that Scottish-specific public policy research was not of much interest to researchers in the past, devolution has increased the demand for social science research focusing on Scottish-specific issues, and the Scottish Executive has provided new sources of funding for such research. One example of this increased expenditure is the Scottish Economic Policy Network.

The Scottish Economic Policy Network – or 'Scotecon' for short – was established in 2000 and is a network of economists based in Scotland's 12 universities. Its main aim is to stimulate academic research on the Scottish economy, particularly in those areas of concern to the Scottish Executive. The network concentrates on increasing the quality and quantity of evidence-based research to inform policy in areas such as education, enterprise, the environment, exclusion, health, rural affairs, training and transport. The Scottish Higher Education Funding Council funds the network under its Research Development Grant Scheme. The Universities of Stirling and Strathclyde are physical locations of the network. However, it has a strong virtual presence through its website, www.scotecon.net, which is being developed into a major focus for intelligence on the Scottish economy. The chapters in this book are revised versions of papers presented at a conference held at the University of Stirling in 2002, and sponsored by Scotecon and the Institute for Social and Economic Research (ISER) at the University of Essex.

'Evidence-based' policy research by its very nature implies that rich and detailed data sources, both at the micro and macro level, are available. It is a stated goal of both the UK and Scottish governments to increase both the quantity and quality of data available to researchers in order to facilitate the understanding of the likely impact of a whole array of public policy initiatives. Analysis of policy impacts often calls for research that is comparative in nature, with the situation in Scotland being compared to the situation in other areas of the UK (with England being the prime candidate).

Such research is needed now for at least two reasons. The first is simply that little empirically grounded comparative research of this type has been carried out in the past and there is a gap in our knowledge of what the 'big' differences between Scotland and other regions of the UK are. Such knowledge is required to provide a 'baseline' for analysing the impacts of subsequent differential developments in policy arising out of devolution. The second is that the identification of these differences is crucial if policy is going to be pursued by the Scottish Executive aimed at narrowing those differences that represent 'disadvantage'. Since all the chapters in this book use the British Household Panel Survey (BHPS) in their analyses, we conclude this chapter by describing briefly this valuable source of data for policy research.

The British Household Panel Survey

In 1989, the Economic and Social Research Council (ESRC) established the Research Centre on Micro-social Change (recently subsumed into the ISER) at the University of Essex, whose main purpose was to collect the data for the BHPS. The BHPS is a multipurpose study that has a variety of unique characteristics that makes it well suited for examining a variety of issues. It follows the same representative sample of individuals over a period of years; that is, it has a true 'panel' element. It is household-based, interviewing every adult member of the sampled households. It also contains sufficient cases for meaningful analysis of certain groups such as the elderly or one-parent families. Finally, it allows for the linkage of data both from other surveys and from local area statistics. Detailed socioeconomic, work history and attitudinal information is collected. Data for the first wave was collected in 1991 and consisted of some 5,500 households and 10,300 individuals drawn from 250 different areas of Britain, including Scotland and Wales (Northern Ireland was not included until the 2001 wave). To date (September 2004), 12 waves are available for analysis. There is little doubt that the BHPS is the most comprehensive dataset available to social scientists interested in examining British-specific issues through the use of household and individual-level survey data.

Unfortunately, there is a problem with the BHPS and this mostly explains why it has not been widely used by Scottish researchers interested in Scottish-specific issues. Currently the population of

Scotland is about five million, which is about 8.5% of the total British population. This suggests that a survey of 5,500 households, which aims to be 'nationally representative' (and does not over-sample), will contain a sub-sample of about 400–500 Scottish households. Such a survey may be representative of 'Britain as a whole' and the Scottish sub-sample may be representative of 'Scotland as a whole'. However, if one is interested in analysing more specific sub-groups, such as Scottish single parents or Highland households or children in Glasgow, such a sample is too small to be of much practical use.

Following the report of its Devolution Committee, the ESRC requested that the ISER should develop extensions to the BHPS in Scotland and Wales. There were two main aims of the extensions. The first was to increase the relatively small Scottish and Welsh sub-samples (to about 2,000 households) in order to permit independent analysis of the two nations. The second was to facilitate analysis of the two nations compared to England in order to assess the impacts of the substantial public policy changes that were expected to follow political devolution. A consultation period in the early part of 1999 established the requirements of the Scottish (and Welsh) user communities. In particular, it stressed the over-riding importance of the second aim, and hence the need as far as possible to use identical questionnaires and fieldwork arrangements. There are currently four waves of these 'enhanced' samples available to researchers, who can obtain them direct from the Data Archive at the University of Essex.

It is clear that the BHPS is not the only dataset that could be used for policy relevant to Scotland in general and to examine the issues considered in this book in particular. Over the past two decades, the use of panel data has become increasingly popular among applied researchers in the social sciences, particularly in the areas of economics and sociology. It is our view that the BHPS has some clear advantages for evidence-based policy research. Two are worth stressing. The first is that the same individuals, families and households are observed repeatedly at different points and therefore it is possible to measure actual changes in behaviour that occur over time, some of which may be in response to policy changes. The second is that with repeated observations it is possible to control for factors that are not measured but are likely to influence the outcome under study.

Section 1:
Families and households

For the past 20 years, birth rates have been lower in Scotland than in England. For instance, in 2000 the total fertility rate in Scotland was 1.47 children per woman compared with 1.66 in England. Births outside marriage have increased rapidly in both countries, but more so in Scotland. By 2000, 43% of Scottish births were outside marriage compared with 39% of English births. Also, Scotland has persistently had higher death rates. At 1999 age-specific mortality rates, the expectation of life at birth for women (men) is 78.2 (72.8) in Scotland, compared with 80.2 (75.4) in England. Differences in these vital rates contribute to differences in household and family structure, as well as population age structure. The chapters in this section deal with behaviour within families, the formation of families and households, their residential movement and their housing.

As noted in Chapter One of this book, a growing body of research suggests that the interaction between children and parents in the home is important for achievements in school and subsequent success in the labour market. In this light, the present integration of family policy, education policy and skills policy in Scotland has considerable potential. It is, however, important to establish 'baselines' of differences in family interactions between England and Scotland and in their impact on important decisions such as staying on at school. Such baselines help us evaluate the impact of the new Scottish policies as they evolve.

The first two chapters of this section do so using the British Youth Panel (BYP), which is administered to children aged 11-15 in British Household Panel Survey (BHPS) households. Lynn Jamieson and John McKendrick (Chapter Two) find, for the most part, that young people's reported interactions with their parents and friends are similar in Scotland and England. However, there are some potentially important differences. In particular, Scottish young people's parents appear to monitor their behaviour less than their peers in England. For instance, the minority of adolescents who do not 'always' or 'usually' tell parents where they are was twice as large in Scotland. Also, a larger minority of Scottish than English young people reported having been out after nine o'clock at night without parents knowing their whereabouts and having played truant. On the other hand, Scottish youth are more likely to bring friends 'round to the house'. There also appears to be a greater difference between the monitoring of children from one-parent and two-parent households in Scotland than in England, suggesting that that there may be something distinctive about the circumstances of lone parents in Scotland, such as poverty of money and/or time.

Vernon Gayle (Chapter Three) describes the various ways in which the BYP can be used to examine a number of key life changes (or 'transitions') that young people may or may not make. He illustrates one way the data can be used, in an analysis of the expectation to leave education at age 16 among youth aged 13-15. There are large existing differences between Scotland and England in the nature of their education systems, and local labour market conditions are also likely to affect the decision to remain in school. A simple comparison indicates that one third of the young Scots expect to leave school at age 16 compared with only one quarter of young people from England and Wales. Despite this difference, the analysis indicates no significant difference in the expectation to leave education at age 16 between the two countries after controlling for family background, thereby suggesting that the difference in expected staying-on rates is primarily due to the different population composition in Scotland relative to England and Wales.

Another key transition for young people is movement out of their parental home. It is likely that the difference in educational systems means that this process differs between Scotland and England, with attendant implications for housing and social welfare policies. John Ermisch (Chapter Four) shows that independent living is much more common in Scotland than England, particularly among young people. Scottish young people leave their parental home earlier than their counterparts south of the border, even after taking account of the higher rates of participation in post-compulsory education in Scotland, and they primarily leave to live in arrangements other than cohabiting unions or marriages. For example, among those who are not full-time students, 58% of English youth aged 18-26 lived with their parents compared with 39% of Scottish youth of these ages. Nine per cent of Scots aged 16-34 lived in households with two or more unrelated adults in 1999-2000, compared to 3% of their English counterparts.

Independent living is also more common among Scottish than English older people. This is not only because of higher mortality rates in Scotland, because even among those without a spouse, relatively more Scottish people aged 55+ live alone. The country differential is even larger for widows. Country differences in the income distribution of older people do not account for the differential. The greater incidence of living alone in Scotland has implications for the delivery of social care.

Residential mobility is not only important for effecting these different living arrangements and the efficient allocation of housing, but also for labour market flexibility and economic growth. Most research in this area focuses on the UK as a whole, and there are a few studies that consider mobility in Scotland, and these use cross-sectional data. Harminder Battu, Vania Gerova and Euan Phimister (Chapter Five) remedy this situation. They find that residential mobility is lower in Scotland than England, 12% per annum compared with 13%, and this difference persists after controlling for a number of attributes of people and their household that are known to affect mobility, such as a person's housing tenure. There are mainly similarities in the direction and size of the influence of these attributes between the two countries. For example, movers in both nations are young, highly educated and predominately reside in private rented accommodation. However, they do find that while Scottish outright-owners are more likely to move, the non-employed in Scotland are significantly less likely to move house than their counterparts in England. Although this latter difference is not large, it may reduce the flexibility of the Scottish labour market.

The process of earlier household formation among young Scots and of independent living of older Scots has implications for the volume and profile of types of accommodation required, and so it is relevant to the main housing policy aim of the Scottish Executive: to ensure an adequate supply of housing with choice. This policy objective is to be achieved by assisting owner-occupation and promoting the development of a diverse rental sector. Jeanette Findlay and Cecilia MacIntyre (Chapter Six) examine the existing similarities and differences in a number of aspects of housing between Scotland and the rest of the UK. They explore patterns of ownership, the physical characteristics of homes, the costs of housing (including fuel costs) and changes in housing tenure. They also relate some of the recent housing policy initiatives of the Scottish Executive to the current housing situation in Scotland. For instance, the Scottish Executive's review of local authority and housing association rent-setting arrangements is near the top of the housing policy agenda. Comparison with the rest of the UK indicates, however, that, on average, housing affordability (in terms of the proportion of income spent on housing) is not a more acute problem in Scotland, although still an important one. On the other hand, the Scottish Executive's initiatives aimed at tackling fuel poverty address a particularly Scottish problem, with Scottish households paying considerably more of their income on fuel.

TWO

Teenagers' relationships with peers and parents

Lynn Jamieson and John H. McKendrick

Introduction

In the 1990s, researchers seriously began to investigate children's views (Hill and Tisdall, 1997; Christensen and James, 2000), complementing earlier research on young people aged 16+ (Hutson and Jenkins, 1989; Wallace, 1989; Banks et al, 1992). With the exception of a few pioneering studies (Mitchell, 1985), this was the first time children's views of parenting, families and family life had been investigated. In a number of studies, researchers found that many children defined 'family' fairly flexibly and inclusively, and that the overwhelming majority saw parents as crucial to their well-being (Brannen et al, 1994, 1999, 2000; O'Brien et al, 1996; Borland et al, 1998; Morrow, 1998; Douglas et al, 2000; Dunn et al, 2001; Smart et al, 2001). This period was also a time of new studies of children's friendship and school-based peer relationships (Mac an Ghaill, 1994; Griffiths, 1995; Hey, 1996; Connolly, 1998), demonstrating that friendship was a major focus in most children's lives and also central to their well-being (Criss et al, 2002).

Interest in listening to children and young people has been stimulated by changes in how we think about children and childhood (Jenks, 1996; James and Prout, 1997). The new 'social studies of childhood' approach conceives of the child as a knowledgeable social agent with the ability to comprehend, reflect upon and effect change in his or her social world. Concern to investigate children's views of their families was an attempt to understand children's experience of widespread changes in family life and to begin to document children's perspective on the impact on their wider social world of events such as a family household regrouping from two parents to one parent. In this chapter, we explore the insight into family and friendship in the lives of 11- to 15-year-olds offered by the British Household Panel Survey (BHPS).

The BHPS is one of the few quantitative data sources in Britain to incorporate young people under the age of 16 into an otherwise adult study. Since 1994 (wave D), the British Youth Panel (BYP) has provided insights into young people's lives. In that year, all children aged 11-15 in the 605 BHPS households with children of this age (as of 1 December) were asked to participate in the BYP; an 89% response rate produced an original sample of 773 young people. Young people completed the survey on their own by writing their response on an answer grid to questions that were asked of them through a personal stereo system; in this way the interview could be delivered in the presence of adults, without adults being aware of the young person's responses. Since wave J (2000), the Scottish and Welsh samples of the BYP have been sufficiently large to enable comparative analysis of young people within Britain, allowing us in Scotland to consider whether there is anything distinctive about family life and friendship of young people in Scotland. This chapter presents a cross-sectional analysis of young people's relationships with peers and parents using these data; it serves to indicate the potential the BYP will afford once additional waves of boosted samples allow longitudinal analysis[1].

Quality of parent–child relationships

Young people typically want their families to give help and support when things go wrong, and to provide a basic level of love, security and enjoyment (Borland et al, 1998). In their Scottish study, Moira Borland and her colleagues (1998) found that the overwhelming majority of the children aged 8-12 interviewed were happy with, and felt supported by, their family situation. The most common complaints children made were that parents did not always have enough time for them or that parents were too quick to be dismissive of their problems, usually difficulties with friends. The BYP contains a number of questions that provide insight into the general quality of parent–child relationships and family life from the young person's point of view. These include asking young people how they feel about their family, how often they talk to their mother and father about 'things that matter', and how often they quarrel with their mother and father.

There are no differences between the national regions in terms of the children's views about their family life (Table 2.1). Only a small minority of about 15% of young people report feeling less than 'completely' or 'very' happy about their family. There are no significant differences between the three countries on any of the measures of quality of relationships with parents. On the whole, young people experience a more 'intense' relationship with their mother, being more likely to talk to her regularly about 'things that matter' and to quarrel

Table 2.1: Quality of family life by national region (%)

Weighted data	Scotland	Wales	England
Feel 'completely' or 'very' happy about family	84	84	85
Talk to mum about 'things that matter' at least once a week[a]	49	60	53
Talk to dad about 'things that matter' at least once a week[b]	31	28	30
'Hardly ever' quarrel with mother	49	47	52
'Hardly ever' quarrel with father	55	63	60

Notes: [a] Excludes the small number who have no mothers. [b] Excludes about 20% who have no fathers.

with her rather than with their father. Young people in Scotland talked to their mothers about 'things that matter' slightly less, while less likely to 'hardly ever' quarrel with their fathers than their peers in England or Wales. Young people in Wales seemed to express the most difference between their relationship with their mother and father. However, all national differences are small and do not approach statistical significance.

More marked are the differences in the quality of family life between 11- to 15-year-old boys and girls. While only the minority of children talked to fathers about 'things that mattered' once a week, boys were more likely to do so than girls. Although more talked to their mother about 'things that mattered' once a week, this was true for more girls than boys. Girls also reported more quarrelling with both their father and their mother. However, these gender differences were not as marked in Scotland and appear to be modified by social class. In Scotland, to a greater extent than in England and Wales, the degree of difference between boys and girls varied with the social class background of young people. For example, in Scotland, girls with working-class fathers were the most likely to quarrel with their fathers while boys with working-class fathers were the least likely to quarrel with them. Only 41% of working-class daughters reported that they 'hardly ever' quarrelled with their father compared with 53% of middle-class daughters, 50% of middle-class sons and 75% of working-class sons.

In and out of parental monitoring

Some social commentators have debated whether in many Western countries parent–child relationships are becoming more democratic, with parents wanting to be more like friends to their children rather than bosses (Giddens, 1992). A more negative view of this perceived change is that parental authority has collapsed, and, along with other departures from conventional family life, created moral disorder (see Jamieson, 1998, pp 62-74, for a review of these arguments). However, the empirical research has repeatedly identified parents who want both a 'good relationship' with their children and believe that it is in children's interests if they monitor and steer children's behaviour (Backett, 1982; Walkerdine and Lucey, 1989; Brannen et al, 1994; Ribbens, 1994; Borland et al, 1998).

However, it should also be noted that there are variations by class and ethnicity in notions and practices of 'good parenting'. For example, Brannen et al's (1994) research suggested that middle-class mothers were more concerned than working-class mothers to monitor the movements of their older teenage children. This work also indicated that some minority ethnic parents felt that there was no need to closely question children whom they believed to be guided by a clear set of religious rules of conduct. The BYP asks young people questions that provide some insight into young people's visibility to parents and their cooperation with parental monitoring, including whether young people let parents know where they are going, and whether time is spent at home, by bringing friends home and having shared family meals at home.

Young people in Scotland may experience less monitoring of their behaviour than their peers in England and Wales (Table 2.2). Although the majority (73%) of young people in Scotland, as elsewhere, reported 'always' or 'usually' telling parents where they are going, the minority who did not (27%) is larger than in Wales (18%) or England (14%). Similarly, a larger minority of Scottish rather than English young people reported having been out after nine o'clock at night without parents knowing their whereabouts in the last month and having played truant. Less direct parental monitoring of young people in Scotland is also suggested by the fact that a clear majority reported having been 'out with friends' more than three times in the past week. This was true for just over half of young people in Wales and less than half in England. However, it is not the case that young people in Scotland are typically beyond their parents' gaze. There is no statistically significant difference

Table 2.2: Parental monitoring by national region (%)

Weighted data	Scotland	Wales	England
'Always' or 'usually' tells parents where going	73	83	86
'Never' out after nine in the last month without parents knowing whereabouts	68	71	81
'Never' played truant	75	78	86
'Out with' friends less than three times in past week	45	49	57
Had an evening meal together with family 6-7 times in the past week	43	33	40
Parents have stopped them from watching a TV programme	55	56	62
Had friend round to house three or more times in past week	40	32	28

in the likelihood of young people in Scotland than in England and Wales eating an evening meal with their family and many young people in Scotland do so virtually every night of the week. Nor are there big differences of the likelihood of parents stopping children from watching a TV programme at some time between young people in the different national contexts. Also young people in Scotland were slightly more likely to bring friends round to their home three or more times in the past week. There is, therefore, no reason to assume that the majority of parents in Scotland typically saw less of their children but it seems that a larger proportion of Scottish-based parents were giving more freedom to young people.

However, the picture is again modified slightly by class and gender. While the majority of children from all backgrounds 'always' or 'usually' tell parents where they are going, a larger minority of working-class rather than middle-class young people said that they only do so 'sometimes' or 'not usually'. Boys were slightly less likely to tell parents where they were going than girls. Similarly, working-class young people were more likely than their middle-class counterparts to be out late without their parents knowing where they were and a slightly larger minority of working-class young people had played truant. In general, boys were slightly more likely to be out late without parents knowing their whereabouts than girls. Finally, working-class children and girls reported higher rates of frequently having friends round to their home, compared to middle-class children and boys.

It should be noted that Scotland's slightly larger working-class population is not in itself the explanation for the larger minority of children in Scotland whose parents were giving them more freedom. Controlling for class and gender confirms distinctive experiences of parental monitoring in Scotland: only 29% of working-class boys in Scotland report 'always' telling their parents where they are going (compared to, for example, 49% of working-class boys in England); 23% of working-class boys in Scotland report being out after nine o'clock in the evening at least thrice in the last month without their parents knowing (compared to, for example, 9% of working-class boys in England) and only 6% of working-class girls in Scotland report *not* 'having friends around to their house in the last week' (compared to, for example, 24% of working-class girls in England).

Expectations of gender roles in mothers and fathers

Some researchers have documented that young people hold different expectations of mothers and fathers and that expectations differ between young people and the parents themselves. For example, Warin et al's (1999) study of family households in Rochdale found differences in expectations of fathers from sons and daughters. Mothers and fathers themselves also had contrasting answers to the question, 'What do people expect of fathers these days?'. Fathers were much more likely to stress the traditional role of father as provider and then as an authority figure, rating involvement with children lower than both of these. Sons, daughters and mothers were all more likely to put involvement first. However, while over half of mothers and daughters stressed involvement, less than 40% of sons ranked involvement first. The BYP study does not explore these issues in detail. It has already been noted that young people are more likely to talk to mothers than fathers about 'things that matter', but it is not clear whether this reflects access or different ideals of and expectations of fathers and mothers. However, the questions put to young people in wave 10 of the BYP did include two items that directly canvassed opinions about gender and parenting roles.

A broadly similar pattern of views of young people is held across England, Wales and Scotland (Table 2.3). A substantial majority of girls do not support the traditional division of labour between parents into the husband-father-provider and the wife-mother-family carer roles, although opinion is more divided among boys. The majority of boys in Scotland concur with the traditional view. Similarly, more girls than boys disagree with the statement that family life suffers when women have full-time jobs but disagreement is less pronounced. For example, 60% of girls in Scotland disagree that 'family life suffers' when women work full time, compared to 76% of girls in Scotland who disagree that husbands should earn, while women 'look after home and family'. Interpreting how people understand this statement

Table 2.3: Percentage answering 'strongly disagree' and 'disagree' to the following statements

	Scotland		Wales		England	
	Girls	Boys	Girls	Boys	Girls	Boys
A husband's job is to earn money: a wife's job is to look after the home and family	76	47	67	52	75	53
All in all, family life suffers when the woman has a full-time job	60	47	57	46	60	45

about family life and women's full-time work is difficult. The statement is not clearly seeking views about ideals concerning gender roles – what men and women should and should not do as men and women. It can be read as inviting an interpretation of practical matters of fact. The statement does not make it clear whether it should be taken for granted that, in a two-parent family, if mothers are working full-time, any father will also be in paid employment. In practice, this is often the case (McRae, 1999). Borland et al (1998) found that children sometimes feel that they would like more time from parents and it is quite likely that children have their own awareness of the time famine demonstrated by recent research on employed mothers with children of school age (Backett-Milburn et al, 2001). Given children's desire for parents to have more time for them, it is perhaps surprising that so many young people disagree with the statement. The fact that more girls than boys repudiate the statement may mean that girls see less hardship in having no full-time mother at home. Alternatively, it could reflect a more acute sense of unfairness in expecting women to forego full-time work and a greater willingness to take a stand against such traditional gender inequalities.

Comparing family life in two-parent and one-parent households

The social change impacting on children and young people that has had the most research attention is the high incidence of divorce and separation resulting in the regrouping of many family households with children from two-parent households to one-parent households (see, for example, Kiernan et al, 1997; Ford and Millar, 1998; Rowlingson and McKay, 1998; Duncan and Edwards, 1999). Since the end of the 20th century, it has been estimated that over one quarter of children born to married parents in the UK experience the separation of their parents by the age of 16 (Clarke, 1996; Haskey, 1997). Difficulties in and failures of communication between children and parents are often an aspect of the upheaval of divorce and separation (see, for example, Simpson et al, 1995; Walker and Hornick, 1996; Simpson, 1998; Anderson et al, 2000; Dunn and Deater-Deckard, 2001; for an overview, see Pryor and Rogers, 2001). A large minority of the children involved lose all contact with the non-residential parent, usually the father, or have strained and complex parenting relationships following family regrouping (Simpson, 1998; Bradshaw et al, 1999a; Smart and Stevens, 2000; Smart et al, 2001).

In the BYP wave 10 data, 24% of the young people interviewed in

Scotland lived in one-parent families, compared to 23% of those interviewed in Wales and 21% of those interviewed in England. This provides a sufficient sample size to compare the responses of young people from one-parent and two-parent households to questions about the quality of their relationship with their parents and their satisfaction with family life.

Differences between the pattern of answers of young people in one-parent and two-parent families were often small. For example, young people from one-parent families were no more likely than young people from two-parent families to argue with their mother. However, differences were often slightly more marked in Scotland than in England. Table 2.4 suggests that a parent in Scotland was rather less likely to know where their children were in one-parent than in two-parent families. Higher proportions of children from two-parent households 'always' or 'usually' told parents where they were going, had never played truant and were never out after nine without parents knowing their whereabouts.

A number of questions suggested a greater difference between the experiences of children from one-parent and from two-parent households in Scotland than in England and Wales. For example, when asked how they feel about their family, in Scotland there was a larger difference between children from one-parent and two-parent families, in the minority who chose to describe their feelings as less than 'completely' or 'very' happy (26% of children from one-parent households and 11% of children from two-parent households). In Wales, the equivalent differences were negligible and in England it was 22% and 12%.

There was similarly a larger difference in the proportion of children saying that they frequently talked to their mother 'about things that matter'. In Scotland, 55% of children from two-parent families talked about matters deemed important at least once a week in comparison to 30% of children from one-parent families and 26% of children from two-parent families 'hardly ever' talked to their mother about

Table 2.4: Scottish one-parent and two-parent family households (%)

	One parent	Two parent
'Always' or 'usually' tells parents where going	65	75
'Never' played truant	63	78
'Never' out after nine in the last month without parents knowing whereabouts	54	71

Table 2.5: Percentage of young people saying that they 'hardly ever' talk to their mother about 'things that matter'

Weighted data (unweighted data)	Two-parent families	One-parent families
Scotland	26 (26)	41 (40)
Wales	20 (20)	29 (32)
England	25 (26)	35 (30)

'things that matter' in comparison to 41% from one-parent families (Table 2.5).

Differences in the responses of young people from one-parent and two-parent households are less marked in England and Wales. These findings suggests that it may not be the type of household in itself that is making the difference but something distinctive about the circumstances of lone parents in Scotland, such as poverty of money and/or time. Indeed, lone-parent households in Scotland are poorer, being more likely to be without a car and to live in local authority rented housing; 56% of the BHPS lone parents in Scotland have no car compared to 41% in Wales and 37% in England. Seventy-seven per cent rent their home rather than own it in comparison to 58% of lone parents in Wales and 55% in England.

Friendship and social inclusion

Friendship is a major concern for children and young people. A great deal of interaction at school is focused on making and maintaining friends; falling out with, and feeling excluded by, friends can be a major source of unhappiness (Medrich et al, 1982; Griffin, 1985; Griffiths, 1988, 1995; Rizzo, 1989; Hendry et al, 1993; Thorne, 1993; Hey, 1996; Gordon et al, 2000).

The overwhelming majority of young people were as happy with their friends as they were with their family. However, and as is the case for family life, a minority were less than 'completely' or 'very' happy with friends (Table 2.6). However, only a very small number of young people (about 3%) have the misfortune to feel unhappy with both family and friends. There are few statistically significant differences in friendship experiences between young people in England, Wales and Scotland. Indeed, the only difference that can be observed with confidence is that young people in Scotland are less likely to 'feel left out' when they are with friends (Table 2.6). More generally, the pattern of young people's responses suggests that larger minorities of young people in England and smaller minorities of young people in Scotland experience unhappiness in friendship, with young people in Wales

Table 2.6: Friendships: percentage giving the following responses

Weighted data	Scotland	Wales	England
Has four or more close friends	75	80	74
Has a girlfriend/boyfriend	31	35	30
Feels 'completely' happy about friends	52	51	48
Less than 'completely' or 'very' happy about friends	13	15	18
'Hardly ever' feels lonely	66	62	60
Feels left out when with friends	13	18	23
No friends 'round to your house' in the last week	21	26	31
Not out with friends in the last week	12	14	17
Worries about bullying at school	27	36	38
Fought with someone in the last month	33	26	30

situated in between. For example, larger minorities of young people in England had neither had friends round to their house, nor had been out with friends in the last seven days (Table 2.6). Larger minorities in England feel less than 'completely' or 'very' happy about friends, feel lonely some of the time, worry about bullying at school and feel left out when with friends. However, it is important to stress that the differences are not great.

Some experiences of friendship are gendered and some are 'classed'. Girls were less likely than boys to have fought with somebody in the last month. Answers to this question are highly gendered: 45% of boys in Scotland had fought with somebody in the last month, compared to 20% of girls. Class differences in the numbers reporting getting into a fight were negligible. Boys' greater propensity to fight was also reflected in the answers in Wales, 36% of boys compared to 17% of girls, and in England, 38% of boys compared to 22% of girls. While boys were significantly more likely than girls to have taken part in fights, girls were slightly more worried about being bullied than boys. Gender differences on this item were particularly marked in England where 45% of girls worried about bullying at school in comparison to 32% of boys.

Class seems to matter with regards to the likelihood of having a boy/girlfriend and overall satisfaction with friends, with working-class young people more likely to have a boy/girlfriend and to be satisfied with their experience of friendship. Both gender and class appear at first to be associated with the frequency with which young people go out with friends and feel lonely. Across all the countries, more girls than boys felt lonely enough of the time to answer something other than 'hardly ever' and reported feeling left out when with their friends. The 'independent' effect of class and gender on 'going out' is confirmed on further analysis. However, for 'feeling lonely', on closer analysis class differences are less evident when the effect of gender is controlled (for example, the same proportion of working-class and middle-class boys 'hardly ever' feel lonely). On the other hand, the difference between boys and girls is particularly marked in middle-class families, with 66% of boys reporting being 'hardly ever' lonely, compared to 48% of girls (chi square [χ^2], 16.34915: Sign. 0.00028). It is interesting that class and/or gender differences were sometimes exaggerated in particular national contexts. As already noted, levels of unhappiness with friendship were highest in England. There, 48% of girls felt lonely some of the time compared to 33% of boys, and 27% of girls and 19% of boys felt left out when with their friends.

Conclusion

The majority of young people report satisfaction with their family and their friends. However, minorities of young people do record various forms of unhappiness. Differences between the three national regions are often modest but the overall pattern is suggestive of some differences in the tenor of families and relationships. In Scotland, more young people (albeit a minority) do not talk to their parents, argue with them and are likely to be out and about without them knowing where they are. This is in spite of a slightly higher incidence of bringing friends round to the house. Differences in indicators of parental control were most marked between Scotland and England, with Wales taking an intermediate position.

Gender and class differences may play out slightly differently in the three countries. Class differences in monitoring children may be more marked in Wales. Gender differences in attitudes to parenting seem to be particularly acute in Scotland, the only country in which the majority of boys failed to disagree with the statement, 'A husband's job is to earn money: a wife's job is to look after the home and family'.

Slightly larger minorities of young people in one-parent households than two-parent households record dissatisfaction with their family life and lack of communication with their parent. The differences were most marked in Scotland where young people from one-parent households, for example, were significantly more likely to be out after nine o'clock in the evening without their parent knowing where they were.

The majority of young people have numerous friends and are happy with them but friendship also causes minorities (sometimes quite large minorities) considerable worry. Larger minorities of young people in England, and more girls than boys, are unhappy about aspects of their friendship. Boys in Scotland seem the most relaxed about friendship but a larger minority also lives up to a more conventional gender stereotype by being involved in fights.

Although comparable experiences of family life and friendship are evident for young people across Scotland, England and Wales, there does appear to be less monitoring of young people in Scotland. The differences are nuances that can be discerned through careful analysis of specific issues. This analysis yields many interesting observations of unique or more intense experiences in Scotland:

- boys and girls are equally likely to discuss 'things that matter' with their mother;
- fewer girls and children of working-class backgrounds quarrel with their father;
- only 29% of working-class boys 'always' tell their parents where they are going;
- as many as 23% of working-class boys report that they stayed out after nine o'clock in the evening without their parents' permission on at least three occasions in the last month;
- only 6% of working-class girls did not invite friends round to their home at least thrice in the last week;
- and 95% of working-class boys report that they never feel 'left out' when with their friends.

Further analysis of the BYP utilising its longitudinal function will permit analysis of the point at which these experiences and conditions emerge in the lives of young people. This should help inform policy and practice. Indeed, these BYP data raise many issues that will be of concern for those who are involved in shaping Scotland's future. It seems that levels of truanting are higher in Scotland than in England and Wales, a significant number of children of middle-class one-parent families are dissatisfied with family life (and perhaps are in need of support) and, for those who are concerned with the 'problem of unruly youth', the evidence of a 'lighter touch' in parenting may give cause for concern. Above all, these data require to be interpreted cautiously. In addition to affording multiple interpretations of the same conclusions (it would be perfectly reasonable for some to conclude that the aforementioned 'lighter touch' in parenting is evidence of a more realistic and mature approach to parent–child relations), there is a need to resist grand theories that speak to the 'nature of family life and friendship in Scotland'. What transpires is a complex array of experiences that requires careful and issue-by-issue analysis and interpretation.

Note

[1] It should be acknowledged that while 303 of the 1,414 young people in the sample reside in Scotland, when a weighting is applied this reduces the working sample size of the Scottish population to 120. Weighting reduces the sample of Scottish children to 8.5%, a proportionate share of the 11- to 15-year-olds in Britain. Weighting should not be required when comparing separate samples for England, Wales and Scotland rather than speaking about Britain. Nevertheless, weighted data are generally used in this chapter. The pattern of difference has been checked against unweighted data. Unweighted data are used when doing three-way cross-tabulations resulting in perilously small numbers with weighted data, for example when looking at the national samples by gender and class.

References

Anderson, M., Tunaley, J. and Walker, J. (2000) *Relatively speaking: Communication in families*, London: BT Future Talk.

Backett, K. (1982) *Mothers and fathers*, London: Macmillan.

Backett-Milburn, K., Cunningham-Burley, S. and Kemmer, D. (2001) *Caring and providing: Lone and partnered working mothers in Scotland*, Bristol/York: The Policy Press/Joseph Rowntree Foundation.

Banks, M., Bates, I., Breakwell, G., Bynner, J., Emler, N., Jamieson, L. and Roberts, K. (1992) *Careers and identities*, Milton Keynes: Open University Press.

Borland, M., Laybourn, A., Hill, M. and Brown, J. (1998) *Middle childhood: The perspectives of children and parents*, London: Jessica Kingsley.

Bradshaw, J., Stimson, C., Skinner, C. and Williams, J. (1999a) *Absent fathers?*, New York, NY: Routledge.

Bradshaw, J., Stimson, C., Skinner, C. and Williams, J. (1999b) 'Non-resident fathers in Britain', in S. McRae (ed) *Changing Britain: Families and households in the 1990s*, Oxford: Oxford University Press, pp 404-26.

Brannen, J., Hepinstall, E. and Bhopahl, K. (2000) *Connecting children: Care and family life in later childhood*, London: Falmer Press.

Brannen, J., Hepinstall, E. and Bhopahl, K. (1999) *Children's views and experiences of family life*, London: Thomas Coram Institute.

Brannen, J., Dodd, K., Oakley, A. and Storey, P. (1994) *Young people, health and family life*, Buckingham: Open University Press.

Christensen, P. and James, A. (eds) (2000) *Research with children: Perspectives and practices*, London and New York, NY: Falmer Press.

Clarke, L. (1996) 'Demographic change and the family situation of children', in J. Brannen and M. O'Brien (eds) *Children in families: Research and policy*, London: Falmer Press, pp 66-83.

Connolly, P. (1998) *Racism, gender identities and young children: Social relations in a multi-ethnic inner-city primary school*, London: Routledge.

Criss, M.M., Pettit, G.S., Bates, J.M., Dodge, K.A. and Lapp, A.L. (2002) 'Family adversity, positive peer relationships, and children's externalizing behavior: a longitudinal perspective on risk and resilience', *Child Development*, vol 73, no 4, pp 1220-37.

Douglas, G., Butler, I., Fincham, F., Murch, M., Robertson, L. and Scanlon, L. (2000) 'Children's perspectives and experiences of divorce', *Children 5-16 Research Briefing*, no 21.

Duncan, S. and Edwards, R. (1999) *Lone mothers, paid work and gendered moral rationalities*, Basingstoke: Macmillan.

Dunn, J. and Deater-Deckard, K. (2001) *Children's views of their changing families*, York: Joseph Rowntree Foundation.

Dunn, J., Cutting, A.L. and Fisher, N. (2002) 'Old friends, new friends: predictors of children's perspective on their friends at school', *Child Development*, vol 73, no 2, pp 621-35.

Ford, R. and Millar, J. (1998) *Private lives and public responsibilities*, London: Policy Studies Institute.

Giddens, A. (1992) *The transformation of intimacy: Sexuality, love and eroticism in modern societies*, Cambridge: Polity Press.

Gordon, T., Holland, J. and Lahelma, E. (2000) *Making spaces: Citizenship and difference in schools*, Basingstoke: Macmillan, pp 110-35 (esp ch 7).

Griffin, C. (1985) *Typical girls*, London: Routledge.

Griffiths, V. (1987) 'Adolescent girls: transition from girlfriends to boyfriends', in P. Allat, T. Keil, A. Bryman and B. Bytheway (eds) *Women and the life cycle: Transitions and turning points*, New York, NY: St. Martin's Press.

Griffiths, V. (1995) *Adolescent girls and their friends: A feminist ethnography*, Aldershot: Avebury.

Haskey, J. (1997) 'Children who experience divorce in their family', *Population Trends*, vol 87, pp 5-10.

Hendry, L.B., Shucksmith, J., Love, J.G. and Glendinning, A. (1993) *Young people's leisure and lifestyles*, London: Routledge.

Hey, V. (1996) *The company she keeps: An ethnography of girl's friendship*, Buckingham: Open University Press.

Hill, M. and Tisdall, K. (1997) *Children and society*, London: Longman.

Hutson, S. and Jenkins, R. (1989) *Taking the strain: Families, unemployment and the transition to adulthood*, Milton Keynes: Open University Press.

James, A. and Prout, A. (1997) *Constructing and deconstructing childhood: Contemporary issues in the sociological study of childhood* (2nd edn), London: Falmer Press.

Jamieson, L. (1998) *Intimacy: Personal relationships in modern societies*, Cambridge: Polity Press.

Jenks, C. (1996) *Childhood*, London: Routledge.

Kiernan, K., Land, H. and Lewis, J. (1997) *Lone motherhood in twentieth century Britain*, Oxford: Oxford University Press.

Mac an Ghaill, M. (1994) *The making of men: Masculinities, sexualities and schooling*, Buckingham: Open University Press.

McRae, S. (ed) (1999) *Changing Britain: Families and households in the 1990s*, Oxford: Oxford University Press.

Medrich, E.A., Roizen, J., Rubin, V. and Buckley, S. (1982) *The serious business of growing up: A study of children's lives outside of school*, Berkeley, CA: University of California Press.

Mitchell, A. (1985) *Children in the middle: Living through divorce*, London: Tavistock.

Morrow, G. (1998) *Understanding families: Children's perspectives*, London: National Children's Bureau.

O'Brien, M., Aldred, P. and Jones, D. (1996) 'Children's constructions of family and kinship', in J. Brannen and M. O'Brien (eds) *Children in families: Research and policy*, London: Falmer Press, pp 84-100.

Pryor, J. and Rogers, B. (2001) *Children in changing families: Life after parental separation*, Oxford: Blackwell.

Ribbens, J. (1994) *Mothers and their children*, London: Sage Publications.

Rizzo, T. (1989) *Friendship development among children in school*, Norwood, NJ: Albex.

Rowlingson, K. and McKay, S. (1998) *The growth of lone parenthood*, London: Policy Studies Institute.

Simpson, B. (1998) *Changing families: An ethnographic approach to divorce and separation*, Oxford: Berg.

Simpson, B., McCarthy, P. and Walker, J. (1995) *Being there: Fathers after divorce*, Newcastle: Relate Centre for Family Studies.

Smart, C. and Stevens, P. (2000) *Cohabitation breakdown*, London: Family Policy Studies Centre.

Smart, C., Neale, B. and Wade, A. (2001) *The changing experience of childhood*, Cambridge: Polity Press.

Thorne, B. (1993) *Gender play: Girls and boys in school*, Buckingham: Open University Press.

Walker, J. and Hornick, J.P. (1996) *Communication in marriage and divorce: A consultation on family law*, London: BT Forum.

Walkerdine, V. and Lucey, H. (1989) *Democracy in the kitchen: Regulating mothers and socialising daughters*, London: Virago.

Wallace, C. (1989) *For richer for poorer: Growing up in and out of work*, London: Tavistock.

Warin, J., Solomon, Y., Lewis, C. and Langford, W. (1999) *Fathers, work and family life*, London: Family Policy Studies Centre for the Joseph Rowntree Foundation.

THREE

Youth transitions

Vernon Gayle

Introduction: existing sources of British youth data

The inherently dynamic nature of the 'youth phase' implies that longitudinal data is needed to study it. A number of important sources of longitudinal data exist in Britain that can be used to study young people. The most notable of these resources are the birth cohort studies. The National Survey of Health and Development (NSHD), the National Child Development Study (NCDS) and the British Cohort Study (BCS70) are birth cohorts of children born in 1946, 1958 and 1970 respectively. The logic behind these surveys was to provide broadly comparable nationally representative birth cohorts for every generation after the Second World War. (However, it is debatable as to whether 12 years is the appropriate age gap between generations.) The birth cohort that should have commenced in 1982 never took place. These three birth cohort studies initially had a medical/health orientation (for example, perinatal mortality, neonatal morbidity and child development), but as they progressed they included more data appropriate to social science inquiry.

The NCDS and the BCS70 are more widely known than the NSHD within the British social science community. These three datasets suffer the usual problems associated with birth cohort studies. I suggest that they also suffer the major limitation that their data is of decreasing relevance to contemporary youth research, although they are still being analysed (see Bynner, 2002).

The light at the end of the tunnel is the Millennium Cohort Study (MCS). This new study will fill the gap of 30 years in the British birth cohort portfolio (see Smith and Joshi, 2002). It is proposed that the MCS will maintain the essential features of the earlier birth cohort studies. However, it has a different design and sampling strategy, so I remain sceptical about how easily the MCS data could be used in research projects designed to make comparisons with data from the earlier birth cohorts.

The Scottish Young People's Survey (SYPS) and the Youth Cohort Study (YCS) of England and Wales both began in the 1980s. It is sometimes suggested that they help to fill the gap left by the missing 1980s birth cohort study. Both studies provide longitudinal data but this is mostly at the level of the individual young person. Some information on the young person's parents and their family is provided, but there is almost no information at the household level. The individual-level focus places a heavy constraint on the type of analyses that can be undertaken with these two sources of data.

The design and content of the SYPS and the YCS have both been altered at various times. This is problematic for any researcher wishing to compare cohorts of data or to undertake analysis that compares English and Welsh data with Scottish data (see Raffe et al, 1999; Gayle, 2000). In addition to the absence of household-level information, another limitation of the SYPS and the YCS is that they comprise very few waves of data and do not track young people very far into their adult lives. This precludes more comprehensive analysis that either locates young people within the context of family life, or attempts to understand their behaviour in terms of the lifecourse.

To remedy some of the limitations of the current YCS design, the Department for Education and Skills (DfES) plans to develop a new survey. Its working title is Longitudinal Survey of Young People in England (LSYPE). However, as its name suggests, it will be restricted to England.

The British Youth Panel (BYP) was introduced into the British Household Panel Survey (BHPS) in 1994. Although the Scottish extension to the BHPS, Living in Scotland, began in 1999, the Scottish extension to the BYP did not begin until 2000 The BYP is not widely known within the British youth research community. The BYP is currently under-analysed but Brynin (1999), Bradshaw (2001) and Scott (2002) have used it in recent analyses.

The BYP is an important resource for youth researchers because it is representative of Britain, now has a reasonably long run of data (1994-2000; that is, annual waves 4-10 of the BHPS), locates the young person's experience within the household and tracks the young person into adult life. It is important to note that these features would make the BYP an important survey in it own right. However, the BYP also plugs an important gap in the existing portfolio of British youth data.

The British Youth Panel (BYP)

There are currently seven waves of the BYP available. The survey includes young people aged 11-15 in the BHPS sample households[1]. The Health Education Authority initially funded this extension to the BHPS.

The BYP uses a novel data collection strategy. The questions are tape-recorded and delivered through use of a personal stereo system. The use of the personal stereo system helps to ensure confidentiality even where family members might be present. Only response categories are printed on the questionnaire forms. Therefore, if any household member were able to scan the young person's responses, confidentiality would still be preserved. Using the personal stereo, the young person can therefore control the pace of the interview and complete the questionnaire while adult members of the household are being interviewed.

The questions on the youth survey are different from those on the adult survey. A core set of questions has been retained throughout the life of the BYP and the non-core questions are replaced or rotated. Reflecting the interests of the funding agency, in 1994 the main focus was health. The survey explored the health, health behaviour, psychological well-being and the aspirations of the young person as a tool to explore how these issues were associated with family relationships. The adult questionnaire contained a small number of new questions for parents of eligible children that were designed to match key questions in the BYP questionnaire. In later waves of the BYP, the focus shifted from health towards social networks.

The BYP is effectively a variant of the standard rotating panel. A core group remains within the panel for a maximum of five waves (Figure 3.1). Every wave the oldest year group is lost to the adult survey but is replaced by a new group of young people who have

Figure 3.1: Structure of the youth survey – age cohorts A–E

	wave			
Youth survey	4	5	6	7
Age 11	A			
Age 12	B	A		
Age 13	C	B	A	
Age 14	D	C	B	A
Age 15	E	D	C	B
Adult survey		E	DE	CDE

Figure 3.2: New age cohorts of 11-year-olds F–H enter the youth survey

Youth survey	wave			
	4	5	6	7
Age 11	A	F	G	H
Age 12	B	A	F	G
Age 13	C	B	A	F
Age 14	D	C	B	A
Age 15	E	D	C	B

Notes: A–E original age cohorts from wave 4; F–H new age cohorts from wave 5 to 7.

reached the minimum age (Figure 3.2). These new entrants are sometime referred to as 'rising-11s'.

In 1994, there were 605 households containing eligible, cooperating young people. In wave 4, there were 773 youth interviews. In the next wave (1995), 75% of the original group were interviewed, 17% of the young people had become part of the adult survey and 8% were non-respondents[2].

The data from the BYP are available in the wYOUTH file (or its equivalent). The wYOUTH file contains key identifiers; the household identifier (wHID) and the person number (wPNO) but, at the current time, *not* the cross-wave identifier (PID). wYOUTH contains an individual weight (wYPWGHT) specific to the youth responses.

A simple strategy to analyse the data is to treat a single wave in a cross-sectional fashion (Figure 3.3). Another simple strategy is to pool waves of data, although here data analysts should be extra vigilant in choosing appropriate statistical procedures.

It is also possible to construct a 'synthetic' panel by analysing pooled aged cohorts of the data (Figure 3.4). The panel will be unbalanced, however, since there are four waves of 14-year-olds and only three waves of 13-year-olds. Another approach moves towards a full panel design (Figure 3.5). Here, the individual young people in the age cohort, in this case young people in Group A who were aged 11 in 1994, are tracked and measured at each wave. Overall, the BYP design

Figure 3.3: Cross-sectional analysis of age cohorts A–E in wave 4

Youth survey	wave 4
Age 11	A
Age 12	B
Age 13	C
Age 14	D
Age 15	E

Figure 3.4: Pooled cohort analysis of youth survey cohorts aged 13 and 14

	wave			
Youth survey	4	5	6	7
Age 13	C	B	A	
Age 14	D	C	B	A

Figure 3.5: Full panel approach following an age cohort A

	wave			
Youth survey	4	5	6	7
Age 11	A			
Age 12		A		
Age 13			A	
Age 14				A
Age 15				

facilitates the investigation of age, cohort and period effects should this be required, although at present there is only one wave of data with the enhanced Scottish sample (2000).

The data collected in 2000, which includes the extension sample of young people living in Scotland, contains information on a broad range of questions. These include individual characteristics (such as gender), patterns of daily life (for example, how many hours the young person spends watching television on a school day), family relations (for example, quarrelling with parents), friendship, relationships (boy/girlfriends), pocket money, paid work, smoking, drugs, health/wellbeing, general attitudes, politics, school and school life, and questions about how the young person perceives their future.

BYP (2000 wave)

The 2000 wave of the BYP contains information on 1,414 young people. It is split more or less equally with 714 males and 700 females. There is about one fifth of the sample in each of the five age groups. As we would expect the majority of the sample are from original BHPS (living in Britain) households. There are 303 young people living in Scotland; 228 young people are from new Scottish households, and 75 are from exiting Scottish BHPS households. Figure 3.6 maps the geographical location of the BYP young people living in Scotland in terms of post-1996 local authorities. A synoptic analysis suggests that there is reasonable coverage across Scotland. Possible geographic bias within Scotland in the BHPS has been a long-standing concern. It appears that this is less of a concern in wave 10 of the BYP.

Figure 3.6: Gazetteer of BYP young people living in Scotland

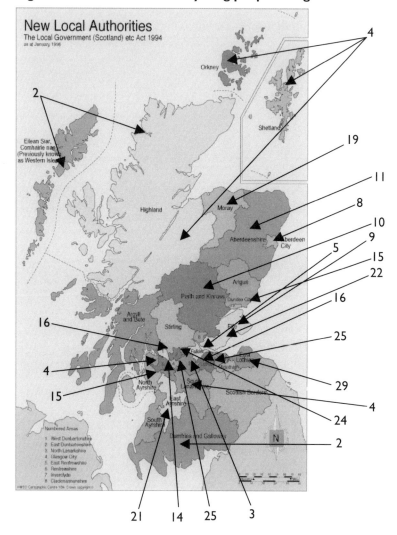

The characteristics of the Scottish young people

The Scottish young people are distributed reasonably evenly across the five age groups:

- 19% aged 15
- 24% aged 14
- 17% aged 13
- 20% aged 12
- 20% aged 11.

There are 158 young men and 145 young women. The largest family has five children and the modal number of children in each household is 2 (mean = 2.1; sd = 0.9). Sixteen per cent of the young people were in households with nobody in employment, 27% were in households with one person in employment and 57% were in households with two or more people in employment. The youngest father was aged 28 and the oldest father aged 72 (mean = 43; sd = 6.8). The youngest mother was aged 28 and the oldest mother aged 53 (mean = 39; sd = 5.3). There were 63 Scottish households with two young people and one household with three young people in wave 10 of the BYP.

Matching files

A new user to the BHPS might experience some difficulties matching the youth data with other BHPS data. An initial problem is that the wYOUTH file, at the time of writing, does not contain the cross-wave person identifier (PID). This is due to be rectified in future releases of the data. A solution to this is that the youth data can be matched with the data in the wINDALL file, which contains the cross-wave person identifier (PID), using the household identifier (wHID) and the person number (wPNO). Household data from the HHRESP file can also be matched to the youth data.

The wINDALL file contains a father's PNO variable (wHGFNO) and a mother's PNO variable (wHGMNO), which can be used to match the relevant parental information from the wINDRESP files to the youth data. Figure 3.7 illustrates the process of matching files with the BYP data[3]. I was able to match the individual data for 166 mothers and fathers, 122 mothers only and 13 fathers only to the youths in the wave 10 dataset (JYOUTH). It was not possible to match data from either parent to 12 young people.

Figure 3.7: Matching the youth data and other BHPS information

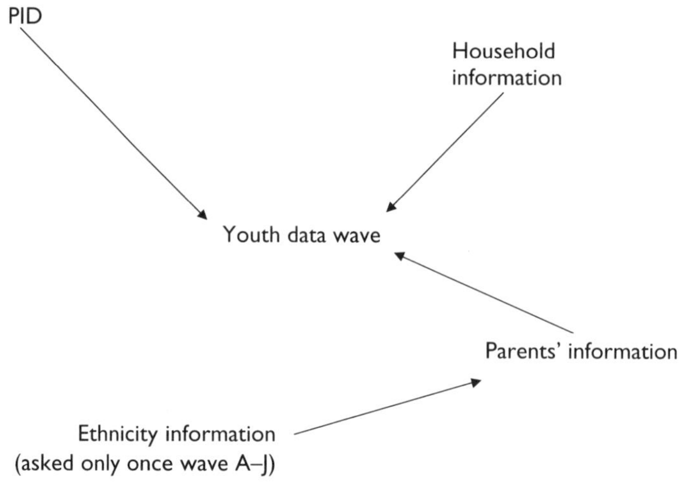

Youth transitions: an example using the BYP

Unfortunately, at the time of doing this analysis, only the 2000 wave of the BYP included the new Scottish households. This presents a heavy restriction at the current time. Therefore, in providing an example of using the data, I have to commit what I consider as a cardinal sin and undertake cross-sectional analysis on BHPS data. The example that I develop in this chapter is slightly artificial given the restriction of limited data; however, it is indicative of the type of analysis that the BYP data will facilitate in the future. It is restricted to a single wave of BYP data and the overall sample size is small ($n=840$). Despite this caveat, the results are substantively plausible and are broadly similar to the results of the model for staying on at school aged 16 derived from analysis of the YCS (Gayle et al, 2000).

Youth transitions are a strong theme in British youth research (Gayle, 1998). Traditionally researchers have been interested in key transitions, for example when young people leave school, leave home and when they either get married or form permanent relationships. Young people's aspirations are another aspect of their experience that is routinely examined and often interwoven with youth transitions within British youth research.

It is undeniable that remarkable similarities exist for all young people across Britain. However, young people from England and Wales and young Scots participate in two education systems that are organised differently and have their own qualification structures. Post-compulsory education and employment training is organised slightly differently in Scotland than it is in England and Wales. Local and regional labour markets affect young people's choices and opportunities. The Scottish extension to the BYP will allow the examination of a wide range of substantive hypotheses that comprise comparative intra-Britain analyses.

The BYP contains an important question that asks the young person if they intend to stay in education or leave education. I have restricted the analysis of the expectation to remain in education to young people aged 13-15. This is because this age group has usually begun to make choices about their education (for example, choosing school subjects) and begin to become aware of the choices and options available after they reach the minimum school leaving age.

In the first stage of the analysis, I explored the relationship between the young person's expectations; that is, leaving or staying in education at age 16, and a set of variables that are comparable to the factors identified in Gayle et al (2000). The data indicate that 33.5% of the young Scots expect to leave school at age 16 compared with only 25.3% of young people from England and Wales. Table 3.1 indicates that this difference is statistically significant, and it also reports the results of other bivariate exploratory analyses. In the second stage of the analysis, the significant variables were entered into a standard cross-sectional logistic regression model using data from the BYP matched with BHPS data. Table 3.2 reports the results of this model.

Despite the overall difference, when we control for family background in the multivariate analysis in Table 3.2, young Scots and young people from England and Wales are not significantly different in their expectations about leaving education. Overall, the facility to make such intra-Britain comparisons is a major step forward for youth researchers. Since the creation of the Scottish Parliament, there is a political motivation to undertake intra-Britain research but a strong scientific case can also be made.

Table 3.1: Young people aged 13-15 wave 10 BYP who expect to leave education aged 16

Variable	Sig
Country	$p=0.027$
Social class	$p<0.001$
Gender	$p=0.003$
Parental education	$p<0.001$
Ethnicity	$p=0.151$
Home ownership	$p<0.001$
Number of children in household	$p=0.062$

Note: n=840.

Table 3.2: Logistic regression model – young people aged 13-15 wave 10 BYP who expect to leave education aged 16

Variable (significance)	Odds
Country (p=0.499)	
England and Wales	–
Scotland	–
Social class[a] (p=0.045)	
Professional and intermediate	1
Manual	1.7
Gender (p=0.019)	
Males	1
Females	0.56
Parental education[b] (p<0.001)	
Non-graduate parents	1
Graduate parents	0.21
Ethnicity (p=0.165)	
Family not from a minority ethnic group	–
Family from a minority ethnic group	–
Home ownership (p=0.439)	
Parents own home	–
Parents do not own home	–

Notes: [a] Highest Registrar General social class category father or mother.
[b] Either parent has a degree.

Social class is important and young people from families in the manual social class group have higher odds of expecting to leave education aged 16. A crude measure of social class based on the Registrar General's Classification and derived from the present occupation of one or both parents has been operationalised (see Erikson, 1984). The facility to match household and parental information is vitally important. Within the British youth research and within government circles there is growing interest in examining the effects of social exclusion on participation in post-compulsory education. The BHPS contains more elaborate occupation based social class measures that could be utilised in full-scale analyses.

Young women had lower odds of expecting to leave education. This finding is consistent with existing results and the current explosion in female participation in post-compulsory education. Young people with graduate parents had lower odds of expecting to leave education aged 16. This is consistent with other findings on the effects of parental education on filial educational participation (for example, see Gayle et al, 2002) and supports the theoretical claim that 'educational capital' is transferred from parents and influences young people's expectations.

In Britain, there are marked differences in educational participation across ethnic groups and the overall educational disadvantage suffered by young people from minority ethnic backgrounds has been well documented (see especially Drew et al, 1992). The problems of researching the effects of ethnicity on young people's transitions have also been documented (Drew and Fosam, 1994). The general message that comes out of the sociology of youth is that ethnicity effects are complex. Overall, coming from a minority ethnic family was not significant in this analysis. I am cautious to point out that we are using a very simple measure of ethnicity because there are only 13 young Scots in this analysis from minority ethnic families.

At the present time, constructing ethnicity measures from the BHPS requires some familiarity with the BHPS protocols and data handling expertise. The ethnicity question (like some others) is only asked once, where appropriate, in the BHPS. The logic behind this, I assume, is that it is a time-constant measure. Consider, for example, we might be matching youth data in wave 10 with wave 10 parental data. However, the ethnicity measure for the parent might be measured in the wave 1 data file rather than in the wave 10 data file. At the time of writing, there is a proposal to append the ethnicity measure at each wave.

The housing tenure variable, home ownership, was not significant in this analysis. This is a proxy measure of household wealth. The BHPS provides a raft of very detailed household measures that could be operationalised in a full-scale analysis. The linking of this type of household information is vital for analyses attempting to map the effects of social disadvantage in the lives of young people.

Conclusion

The results presented here are constrained by the data currently available. However, they demonstrate that more thoroughgoing intra-Britain comparative youth research will be possible with BYP data. The analysis above explored young people's expectations but the BYP has the facility to support analysis of both expectations and actual behaviour. This has obvious appeal in the analysis of youth transitions. With additional waves of data the BYP will become an important resource for British youth researchers. The main weakness of the BYP is that researchers must be familiar with using BHPS data and an outlay of erudition is required before the data can be constructed for analysis.

On the other hand, there is a clear set of strengths that can be attributed to the BYP design. The survey begins with 11-year-olds. This is very much earlier in the 'youth phase' than existing datasets (such as YCS and SYPS) and will provide researchers with more comprehensive data on the youth phase. Currently, there are 12 available waves of data for young people living in Britain; this makes the BYP a precious resource. Over time this will be enhanced with the new Scottish data.

Since it is located within the BHPS structure the BYP offers fantastic possibilities for matching information and augmenting data at the level of the individual young person with both household-level information and an individual-level information from other household members. The obvious example of this is matching parental information but it is also conceivable that research might expand to include siblings and other family members. The BYP is effectively a variant of the standard rotating panel and is refreshed at each wave with new young people. The jewel in the BYP crown is that young people are tracked into adulthood. This unique feature will allow key transitions such as entry into the labour market, leaving the family home and the formation of long-term relationships to be studied with full-scale longitudinal methods of analysis. Taken together, these features make the BYP an attractive data source for youth researchers.

Despite the requirement for longitudinal data that is implied by the inherently dynamic nature of the 'youth phase' and the existence of large-scale British datasets, far less longitudinal analysis is carried out within British youth research than one might expect. Davies (1994) suggests that something more than the glib claim that longitudinal data analysis permits insight into social change is required to convince researchers whose interests are substantive rather than methodological. When more data becomes available more advanced analysis of the BYP will be possible. I envisage that full-scale longitudinal analysis will be able to address a range of methodological issues familiar to longitudinal data analysts such as exploring directions of causality, providing increased statistical control for residual heterogeneity, state dependence and endogeneity and exploring age/period/cohort effects. In my view, the increased sophistication of such analyses will be a palpable and convincing advertisement for the necessity of longitudinal data and analysis.

Notes
[1] The age band is 11-15 inclusive but with slight alteration at each end of this range in line with the BHPS criterion for selection into the adult sample. Those 15-year-olds turning 16 by 1 December in the current wave are interviewed as adults rather than in the youth survey even if interviewed before then, while 10-year-olds turning 11 by this date are included.

[2] Non-response includes refusal, or non-contact with the household and with the respondent.

[3] Proposed changes to the structure of the information contained within the BHPS files will alter this and make matching information more straightforward.

References

Bradshaw, J. (2001) *Poverty: The outcome for children*, London: Family Policy Centre and National Children's Bureau.

Brynin, M. (1999) 'Smoking behaviour: predisposition or adaptation?', *Journal of Adolescence*, vol 22, pp 635-46.

Bynner, J. (2002) 'Changing youth transitions across time: an examination of processes and outcomes for three post-war generations born across the interval 1946-1970', *International Sociological Association*, XV World Congress.

Davies, R.B. (1994) 'From cross-sectional to longitudinal', in A. Dale and R.B. Davies (eds) *Analyzing social and political change*, London: Sage Publications.

Drew, D. and Fosam, B. (1994) 'Gender and ethnic differences in education and the youth labour market', British Sociological Association Annual Conference.

Drew, D., Gray, J. and Sime, N. (1992) 'Against the odds: the education and labour market experiences of black young people', *Youth Cohort Series 19 Employment Department Training Research and Development Series*.

Erikson, R. (1984) 'Social class of men, women and families', *Sociology*, vol 18, pp 500-14.

Gayle, V. (1998) 'Structural and cultural approaches to youth: structuration theory and bridging the gap', *Youth & Policy*, vol 61, pp 59-72.

Gayle, V. (2000) 'Youth transitions: a comparative study of Britain and Norway', *Final Report on Visiting Fellowship Norwegian Social Science Data Archive* (funded under the EU Training and Mobility of Researchers Programme).

Gayle, V., Berridge, D. and Davies, R.B. (2000) 'Young people's routes to higher education: exploring social processes with longitudinal data', *Higher Education Review*, vol 33, no 1, pp 47-64.

Gayle, V., Berridge, D. and Davies, R.B. (2002) 'Young people's entry to higher education: quantifying influential factors', *Oxford Review of Education*, vol 28, no 1, pp 5-20.

Raffe, D., Brannen, K., Croxford, L. and Martin, C. (1999) 'Comparing England, Scotland, Wales and Northern Ireland: the case for "home internationals" in comparative research', *Comparative Education*, vol 35, no 1, pp 9-25.

Scott, J. (2002) 'Teenagers at risk: a prospective study of how some youth beat the odds to overcome family disadvantage', *ESRC End of Award Report L134251027*.

Smith, K. and Joshi, H. (2002) 'The millennium cohort study', *Population Trends*, vol 107, pp 30-4.

FOUR

Comparison of living arrangements

John F. Ermisch

The modest objective of this chapter is to provide Scottish–English comparisons of aspects of household and family structure that are not readily available from other data sources, such as the census or General Household Survey. These include the proportion of young people living with their parents or the proportion living in a cohabiting union. It also aims to exploit the panel nature of the British Household Panel Survey (BHPS) to compare age patterns of people's household context taking into account unobserved person-specific influences on individual living arrangement decisions, and to compare key transition rates such as departure from the parental home. The comparison finds that independent living is much more common in Scotland than England, particularly among young people, but also among older people.

It is well known that birth rates are lower in Scotland than in England, and this has been the case for the past 20 years. For instance, in 2000 the total fertility rate in Scotland was 1.47 children per woman compared with 1.66 in England. Births outside marriage have increased rapidly in both countries, but in the past five years the percentage of births outside marriage has increased faster in Scotland than in England. By 2000, 43% of Scottish births were outside marriage compared with 39% of English births. Also, Scotland has persistently had higher death rates. At 1999 age-specific mortality rates, the expectation of life at birth for women (men) is 78.2 (72.8) in Scotland, compared with 80.2 (75.4) in England. Differences in these vital rates are likely to contribute to differences in household and family structure.

We first compare aspects of household structure between England and Scotland using data from 1999 and 2000, appropriately weighted to represent nationally representative samples from each country. The weights, available in the BHPS user database, reflect sampling design and non-response. For many of the aspects of people's household context, the weighting is very important.

Overview

Table 4.1 shows the distribution of adults in 1999-2000 according to the type of household in which they live. Scotland has a larger percentage of households containing a couple with dependent children than England, but relatively fewer couple households with non-dependent children. The latter difference is more clearly evident for persons aged 16-34 (Table 4.2), and here it is also clear that relatively more young Scots live in households with two or more unrelated adults. As shown below, these differences are related to differences in the patterns of leaving home between the two countries. Scotland also has a larger proportion of lone-parent households with dependent children. At the other end of the adult age distribution, among persons aged 55+, there is little difference in the distribution of adults by

Table 4.1: Distribution of adults by household type (1999-2000) (%)

Household type	Scotland	England
Single non-elderly	8.3	7.2
Single elderly	8.6	9.9
Couple no children	29.3	30.7
Couple: dependent children	28.1	26.8
Couple: non-dependent child	11.9	14.4
Lone parent: dependent children	5.3	4.1
Lone parent: non-dependent children	3.7	4.1
2+ unrelated adults	3.2	1.2
Other households	1.7	1.6
Total	100	100
Weighted *n*	6,647	25,177

Table 4.2: Distribution of adults by household type (1999-2000) (%)

Household type	Aged 16-34		Aged 55 and older	
	Scotland	England	Scotland	England
Single adult	9.5	9.8	32.3	30.5
Couple no children	17.0	16.0	51.9	52.2
Couple: dependent children	38.0	38.2	1.4	1.3
Couple: non-dependent child	11.7	18.8	8.6	9.5
Lone parent: dependent children	8.4	7.4	0.5	0.3
Lone parent: non-dependent children	4.3	5.3	3.4	3.7
2+ unrelated adults	8.8	2.8	0.4	0.6
Other households	2.3	1.8	1.6	1.9
Total	100	100	100	100
Weighted *n*	2,198	7,164	2,119	9,106

household type between Scotland and England (Table 4.2). A marginally larger proportion of Scottish people of these ages lives in one-person households, but this may reflect different age distributions within this older population, which are explored further later in this chapter.

Taking the adult population as whole, there are only small differences in the household size distribution. But among those aged 16-34, a larger proportion of Scots live in two-person households, and relatively fewer live in four- and five-person households than English people aged 16-34 (Table 4.3).

Relatively fewer Scots are married than the English (53.2% compared with 55.7%); more of them live in a cohabiting union ('living as a couple') or are never-married (and not living as a couple). These figures, however, conceal big differences between younger and older persons. Among people aged 16-34, relatively more Scots are married or are living in cohabiting union than the English (Table 4.4), in contrast to 1991, in which official statistics indicate that exactly the same proportion of people aged 15-34 were legally married (40.3%)[1]. The higher proportion married in Scotland partly reflects a steeper fall in the general marriage rate (marriages relative to the unmarried population) in England than Scotland. In 1981, the general marriage rate was higher in England than Scotland, but by 1991 it was lower, and it has stayed that way. Among those aged 55+, a smaller proportion of Scots than English are married (or living as a couple), with relatively more of these older Scots being widows or widowers than the English. This reflects higher mortality rates in Scotland than in England.

Table 4.3: Distribution of adults by household size (1999-2000) (%)

Household type	Aged 16-34		Aged 55 and older	
	Scotland	England	Scotland	England
1	9.5	9.8	32.3	30.5
2	27.4	21.0	55.0	55.5
3	26.1	26.2	9.0	10.0
4	22.8	27.5	2.6	3.1
5	10.1	11.4	0.8	0.5
6	2.3	2.4	0.2	0.3
7 or more	1.8	1.8	0.2	0.1
Total	100	100	100	100
Weighted *n*	2,198	7,164	2,119	9,106

Table 4.4: Distribution of adults by de facto marital status (1999-2000) (%)

Household type	Aged 16-34		Aged 55 and older	
	Scotland	England	Scotland	England
Married	28.0	26.5	60.5	61.6
Living as a couple	17.3	14.9	1.3	2.1
Widowed	0.2	0.1	25.1	23.9
Divorced	1.4	1.8	5.5	5.9
Separated	1.3	1.5	1.1	0.7
Never-married	51.8	54.5	6.5	5.7
Total	100	100	100	100
Weighted *n*	2,198	7,164	2,119	9,106

Young adults (ages 16-34)

We now consider the living arrangements of young people in greater detail, particularly focusing on age patterns. Figures 4.1–3 show age-specific, weighted, cross-sectional comparisons pooling the 1999 and 2000 data. What is very striking is the much smaller proportion of young Scots aged 18-26 who live with their parents compared with English young people of these ages (Figure 4.1). This may be related to the larger proportion of young Scots aged 18-23 who are in full-time education (Figure 4.2). At ages 16-17, relatively more English youth are in full-time education[2]. However, even among full-time students aged 18-26, 61% of English and only 39% of Scots live with their parents. The corresponding figures for those aged 18-26 other than full-time students are 58% and 39%. So student status does appear to account for these country differences in the percentages living with parents.

Figure 4.1: Percentage of persons living with parents

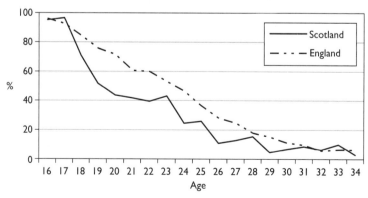

Figure 4.2: Percentage of persons in full-time education

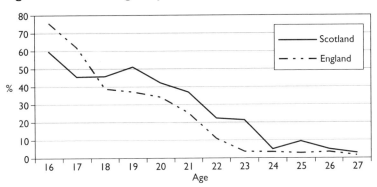

The stronger tendency for young Scots to be living apart from their parents is largely accounted for by the fact that a larger proportion of them are living apart from their parents but without a partner, as illustrated by Figure 4.3. Also, a slightly larger percentage of Scottish '20-somethings' are in a partnership. At ages 20-24, this is because relatively more Scots live in a cohabiting union, and at ages 25-27 it is because more of them are married.

The small sample sizes at individual ages for the Scottish sample make it difficult to make precise comparisons of the age patterns of living arrangements between the two countries, as indicated by the relatively 'saw-toothed' curves for Scotland in Figures 4.1-3. I adopt, therefore, a model-based approach to smooth these patterns using a flexible formulation of the age pattern. The models are 'latent variable' models of living arrangements that use the longitudinal aspect of the data. For the estimation of these, all of the data available in each country

Figure 4.3: Percentage of persons living in arrangements other than with a partner or with parents

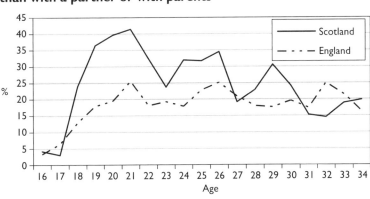

(that is, back to the 1991 wave) is used, but temporary sample members are excluded because they are not followed when they move out of a permanent sample member's household (weights are not used in estimating the models). This approach also allows statistical tests of differences in age–gender patterns between the countries.

The first type of model considered leads to a 'multinomial logit specification' for the set of living arrangement choices. Here it is applied to a set of four possible choices:

1) living with parents;
2) living in a married couple;
3) living in a cohabiting couple;
4) living in an arrangement other than the first three[3].

The parameter estimates indicate significant differences in the age–gender patterns of living arrangements between Scotland and England (chi square $[\chi^2]$ 12=36.33)[4].

Figure 4.4 illustrates the age pattern of the probability that a young man lives with his parents implied by the parameter estimates in each country, and Figure 4.5 illustrates the probability he lives in an arrangement other than with a partner or with parents. Scottish young men exhibit a much higher probability of living in this 'other' arrangement at ages up to their mid-20s, and a lower probability of living with parents throughout most of the age range. The probability of living in the 'other' arrangement is higher for Scottish than English women across the entire age range (results not shown), and the incidence of this living arrangement is higher for young women than

Figure 4.4: Proportion of young men living with parents, multinominal logit estimates

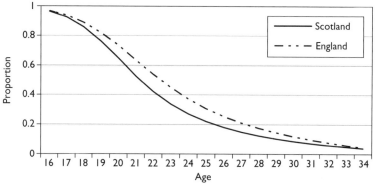

Figure 4.5: Proportion of young men living in an arrangement other than with a partner or parents, multinominal logit estimates

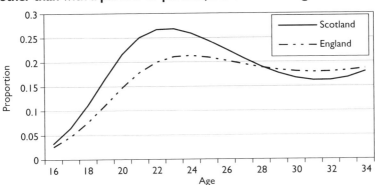

men in both countries. Young women in both countries are less likely to live with parents than young men.

The age patterns for being married and living in a cohabiting union are illustrated in Figures 4.6 and 4.7. Here it is clear that relatively more young Scotsmen live in a cohabiting union at ages 21-25, but more young Englishmen do so at ages 28-30 (Figure 4.6), by which time relatively more Scots than English are married (Figure 4.7). In both countries, young women are more likely to live in partnerships of either type than young men. The country differences for these two types of partnership arrangements are much smaller for young women of these ages (results not shown).

In order to see if the different pattern of full-time participation in education in the two countries can account for these differences, the model is re-estimated with an indicator variable for being a full-time student. Despite the strong impact of student status on living arrangements and the big difference between countries in age patterns

Figure 4.6: Proportion of young men cohabiting, multinominal logit estimates

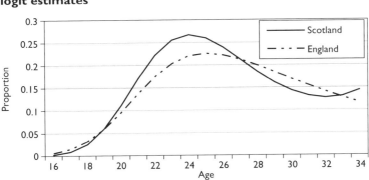

Figure 4.7: Proportion of young men married, multinominal logit estimates

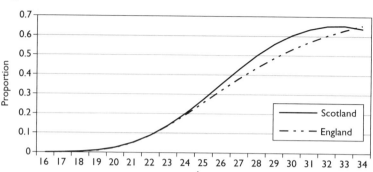

of full-time participation in education (for example, see Figure 4.2)[5], the age–gender patterns in living arrangements remain significantly different between the two countries (chi square $[\chi^2]$ 15=46.09). However, it is important to distinguish full-time students in higher education from other full-time students.

Full-time student status is now split into two variables, what are called 'university students', which are full-time students with at least an A-level equivalent qualification (or higher), and 'other full-time students'. In both countries, full-time university students are more likely to live in an arrangement other than with parents or with a partner, and less likely to live with parents and in partnerships than non-students. For instance, the probability of a full-time university student living in this 'other' arrangement at age 20 is 0.25 higher in England and 0.19 higher in Scotland than for non-students, while the probability of living with parents at 20 is 0.15 lower in England and 0.09 lower in Scotland. Other full-time students are more likely to live with parents and less likely to live in all other arrangements than non-students in both countries. Even allowance for this distinction in type of student does not eliminate the significant differences in age–gender patterns in living arrangements between the two countries (chi square $[\chi^2]$ 18=60.6). Using the estimated parameters to calculate the age patterns in living arrangements, these are very similar to those in Figures 4.4-7 for people who are not students after the age of 16 or for people who leave full-time education at age 18. If we simulate the age profiles for young men who are 'other students' when aged 16-18, then university students when aged 19-22, the age profile of the probability of living in an arrangement other than with parents or with a partner is very similar for the two countries. However, the probability of living with parents is higher in England from age 19 onwards, while the probability of being in a cohabiting union rises faster after his 18th birthday in Scotland than in England and stays above the English probability until 26. Finally, the probability of being married rises faster after age 23 in Scotland, and it remains above the English probability until 33.

The second type of model considered uses the panel nature of the data more efficiently. It allows for an unobserved, fixed 'person-specific' influence on young people's living arrangement choices in addition to age and gender[6]. This influence has a probability distribution in the population, which is taken to be logistic here. This is often called the 'random effects' model. This analysis examines the probability of a particular living arrangement compared with all others.

The parameter estimates for the probability of living with parents indicate significant differences between the two countries: the chi square statistic (χ^2, six degrees of freedom) is 91.9. Figure 4.8 illustrates the implications of these parameter estimates for the age profile of the probability that a young man lives with his parents in the two countries. It is drawn for a man with the mean person-specific influence (that is, zero). In both countries, young women are less likely to live with their parents at every age (the odds of living with parents are about 30% lower), and about 80% of the residual variance is accounted for by variance in the fixed person-specific influence.

Again, the influence of patterns of full-time participation in university or other education is explored. The parameter estimates are still significantly different (chi square [χ^2] 8= 99.9), and being a full-time 'university student' reduces the odds of living with parents much more in England than in Scotland (by 90% compared with 50%)[7]. This is

Figure 4.8: Proportion of young men living with parents, random effects estimates

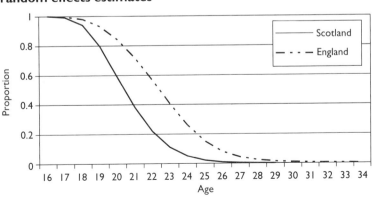

probably because many more Scottish students attend a higher education institution in their hometown.

As Figures 4.3 and 4.5 suggest, the 'random effects' model estimates confirm that there are significant differences in the age–gender pattern of living in arrangements other than with a partner or with parents (chi square [χ^2] 6=125.94). These estimates indicate that English women have a significantly larger chance of living in this 'other' arrangement than English men, but there is no significant gender difference in Scotland. The estimated age patterns are qualitatively similar to those in Figure 4.5, but the Scottish–English differential is much larger. When the student variables are included in the model, being a full-time university student is significant in both countries, with full-time university students being much more likely to live in this arrangement, particularly in England. Compared with non-students, the odds of living in this 'other' arrangement are 11 times higher in England and five times higher in Scotland[8]. However, there are still significant age–gender differences in the model including these variables (chi square [χ^2] 8=116.8).

In an analogous analysis of the age pattern of the probability of living with a partner (compared with not living with one), the parameters are not significantly different (chi square [χ^2] 6=7.86). There are, however, significant differences between the two countries in the age pattern of the incidence of cohabiting unions (chi square [χ^2] 6=16.52). These age patterns are similar to those in Figure 4.6. For neither country is there a significant difference between men and women in the probability of living in a cohabiting union. Estimation of a model with the student indicator variables indicates that, in both countries, the odds of cohabiting are much lower for full-time students of either type.

As a final exercise for this age group, a 'fixed effects' model is estimated for the probability of living with parents. In this model, the unobserved, fixed 'person-specific' influence on living with parents is treated as a person-specific parameter, and no assumptions about its distribution need be made. It may be correlated with any explanatory variables, and so a richer list of such variables can be plausibly included. In particular, a person's own income (during the past month before the interview) is allowed to affect the choice of whether or not to live with parents. The data from the two countries are pooled, constraining the impacts of age, gender, income and the two student statuses to be the same, but allowing for a difference in the probability of living with parents in the two countries. Identification of this difference in

Table 4.5: Fixed effects estimates of impact on the odds of living with parents[a], persons aged 16-34 (ratio of coefficient to standard error in brackets)

Age	−3.827	(5.03)
Age^2	0.112	(3.61)
Age^3	−0.00125	(3.01)
University student	−1.989	(14.25)
Other student	0.618	(2.24)
log (income)	−0.0968	(4.08)
England	0.698	(1.78)

Note: [a] This is the impact of a unit change in the variable on the logarithm of the ratio of the probability of living with parents to the probability of not living with them.

the context of the 'fixed effects' model comes entirely from people who move between the two countries (77 people in this case).

Somewhat surprisingly, this small number of 'country-switchers' is sufficient to identify a strong positive effect from residence in England on the odds of living with parents, as Table 4.5 shows. Why English residence should have this effect is not clear. The table also shows that higher personal income reduces the odds of living with parents, and university students are much less likely to live with parents while other full-time students are more likely to do so. These results are even stronger, particularly the income effect and the impact of being a university student, when the model is estimated on a sample of persons who do not have a partner. However, in this sample, we cannot identify the country effect (there are 46 'switchers').

Older people (aged 55+)

In comparison with English people aged 55+, Scots of these ages demonstrate more independence in the sense that a larger proportion of them in their sixties live alone, according to the weighted, cross-sectional comparisons from pooling the 1999 and 2000 data in Figure 4.9. Independence is partly forced upon them because, as a consequence of higher mortality in Scotland, relatively more of them are widows or widowers by these ages, and of course a smaller proportion are in partnerships than in England. Again, the small samples at individual ages suggest that a modelling approach can be helpful in understanding the differences.

Estimation of a simple logit model for the probability of living alone (for persons aged 55-80) indicates a significant difference between the two countries in the age pattern of this probability (chi square [χ^2] 3=18.12). The estimates indicate that the probability is higher in Scotland throughout the ages 55-80, with the differences being larger

Figure 4.9: Percentage of persons aged 55+ living alone

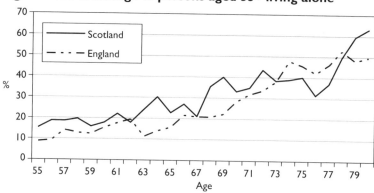

at younger ages. Even if we focus only on people without a partner (widowed, separated, divorced and never-married), differences between the countries remain (chi square [χ^2] 3=11.95), and these are illustrated in Figure 4.10. Significant differences still exist when the model also includes an indicator variable for whether or not a person is a widow(er) (chi square [χ^2] 4=36.85). Thus, even among persons without a partner, a larger proportion of Scottish people live alone (about 0.05 larger), and this proportion is estimated to be higher throughout the age range.

Controlling for a person's own income in the previous month also does not eliminate these differences between countries (chi square [c^2] 5=37.30), as Table 4.6 shows. The estimates indicate that the probability of living alone increases with a person's income in both countries, but the impact is lower in England than in Scotland. Also, being a widow(er) increases the odds of living alone by 84% in Scotland, but reduces them by 22% in England. Thus, the country-difference in the probability of living alone is much larger for widow(er)s, with

Figure 4.10: Proportion of persons without a partner living alone

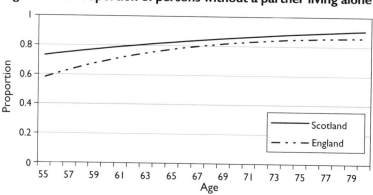

Table 4.6: Estimates of impact on the odds of living alone[a], persons aged 55-80 without a partner (ratio of coefficient to 'robust' standard error in brackets)

	Scottish impact		English impact	
Age	0.088	(0.26)	0.403	(2.51)
Age^2	−0.00028	(0.11)	−0.00248	(2.07)
Woman	0.327	(1.16)	0.056	(0.31)
Widow(er)	0.608	(2.37)	−0.244	(1.35)
Income (£100)	0.0598	(1.71)	0.0321	(1.95)
Constant	−4.35348	(0.40)	−14.6296	(2.75)
χ^2_5	19.21		52.01	
n	1,329		6,367	

Note: [a]This is the impact of a unit change in the variable on the logarithm of the ratio of the probability of living alone to the probability of not living alone.

Scottish widows being much more likely to live independently. This differential impact of widowhood is replicated in a 'random effects' model analogous to that in Table 4.6, although the effects of income are no longer significant in this model.

Transitions

It is also possible to use the BHPS data to study *movement* between different living arrangements in the two countries. However, here the comparisons begin to be limited by the relatively small number of panel observations for Scotland. For example, in studying the formation of first partnerships, there are only 141 Scottish first partnership formations observed in the 1991-2000 data. Comparisons of the age pattern of first partnership formation indicate no significant differences between the countries, but this could be because of the small number of 'events' observed in Scotland, which influences the standard errors of the estimates of the partnership formation rate. However, the similarity could be real. For instance, we find that in both countries about four of every five first partnerships are cohabiting unions.

Similarly, the estimates of age-specific departure rates from the parental home indicate no significant difference between the countries in the age pattern of departure rates, despite the fact that Figures 4.1, 4.4 and 4.8 indicate that young Scots leave home earlier. The inability to detect this in the estimates of the departure rate may reflect the small number of Scottish 'departure events' at each age. However, to illustrate the potential of the Scottish panel data as the panel continues, estimates of the rate of movement from the parental home to a particular

Figure 4.11: Young men's rate of departure from parental home to non-partnership living

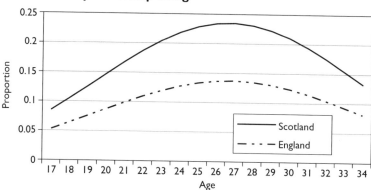

living arrangement, namely non-partnership living (that is, to the 'other' arrangement of Figures 4.3 and 4.5), are now presented.

At each age, we are estimating the rate of departure to non-partnership living among the persons who are still living with their parents. In practice, this is estimated as the proportion of people of a given age who were living with their parents last year who now live apart from their parents without a live-in partner. A model-based approach is again used to smooth the age patterns, and the parameter estimates are illustrated in Figure 4.11. It is clear that throughout the age range, Scottish men living with their parents are more likely to make this transition in the coming year. The estimates also indicate that at any age young women are 28% more likely than young men to move from their parents into this living arrangement in both countries[9].

Conclusion

The analysis in this chapter finds that independent living is much more common in Scotland than England, particularly among young people. Scottish young people leave their parental home sooner, primarily to live in arrangements other than cohabiting unions or marriages. They also appear to move into cohabiting unions sooner than English young people. Preliminary analysis here has indicated that these differences cannot be fully explained by country differences in patterns of participation in full-time education, even though these are substantial.

Independent living is also more common among Scottish than English older people. This is not only because of higher mortality rates in Scotland, because even among those without a spouse, relatively more Scottish people aged 55+ live alone. The country differential is even larger for widows. Country differences in the income distribution of older people do not account for the differential.

Further analysis is needed to explain why these differentials have emerged. What differences are there in institutions or markets (the housing market, for example) between the two countries that encourage Scottish people to adopt more independent living arrangements?

Notes

[1] In comparison with the General Household Survey (averaged over 1996-99), the BHPS indicates a higher proportion of non-married Scots aged 16-59 living in a cohabiting union (24% compared with 20%) and a lower proportion of non-married English of these ages (23% compared with 24%).

[2] This is line with official education statistics, which show 63% of Scottish 16- to 17-year-olds in full-time education and government-supported training schemes, compared with 74% of English youth of these ages. See *Regional Trends* (2001), no 36, table 4.8.

[3] Note that 0.9% of person–year observations are living in a cohabiting union and with their parents, and 1.5% are married and living with their parents. These observations have been categorised as living in a cohabiting union or married respectively.

[4] The 'pooled estimates' in the test allow for a different constant for the two countries in each equation. A cubic in age is assumed, and the gender of the respondent shifts the age pattern up or down.

[5] When estimating a model for the age–gender patterns for the probability of being a full-time student, the parameter estimates are significantly different (chi square [χ^2] 6=29.26).

[6] The model also allows for flexible age pattern, which in this case is taken to be a fifth-order polynomial.

[7] The positive effect on living with parents of being an 'other' full-time student is similar in the two countries.

[8] In England, the odds are lower for full-time 'other' students, but in Scotland being an 'other' student has virtually no impact on the odds.

[9] The model is the *complementary log-log* model. It was estimated for each country separately, but we cannot reject the hypothesis that quadratic age coefficients and the gender coefficient are the same for both countries, and they only differ by the constant (chi square [χ^2] 3=0.365). The coefficient for the variable indicating England is 0.565 (SE=0.056), which implies that this transition rate is 43% lower in England.

FIVE

Residential mobility

Harminder Battu, Vania Gerova and Euan Phimister

Introduction

In a dynamic economy, people are always moving residence. Having a child, getting married, separated or divorced, obtaining a job – these have all been identified as triggers in the mobility process. Regardless of the driving forces, residential mobility is generally regarded as being good for the economy and the prosperity of individuals. The basic argument is that mobility generates a convergence in incomes and employment. Regions experiencing strong economic growth will exhibit wage growth, encouraging a movement of labour into the region, raising labour supply and so forcing down wages. Depressed regions experience a movement out of labour, reducing labour supply and driving up wages.

However, the degree of residential mobility in Britain is regarded as low especially compared to the US (Gregg et al, 2004). According to recent research, around one in 10 households in Britain relocates each year (Hughes and McCormick, 2000). The removal vans, however, do not move far since only one in every 100 moves is inter-regional. At the same time, however, quasi-mobility has increased via rises in commute distances and times (Benito and Oswald, 1999).

This chapter represents an initial exploration of residential mobility in Scotland relative to England. At the outset, one would expect differences arising from differences in unemployment, earnings, occupational and industrial profile, education and also housing tenure across the two countries. The questions we seek to address are the following:

1) How much residential mobility is there in Scotland relative to England?
2) What types of moves do individuals make?
3) What factors drive such mobility?

In essence, we try to ascertain whether the types of regularities that have been found for Britain as a whole also hold for Scotland.

A brief review of the literature

The classical approach to migration argues that households will move away from regions that offer low wages and higher unemployment to regions or areas that offer high wages and lower unemployment. Most theoretical models assume that migration is determined by expected utility flows. Potential migrants make a comparison of the stream of expected future benefits from moving with the immediate costs. A household will move if the expected gains from moving net of transaction costs are greater than the expected utility from staying put. Potential benefits are clearly related to relative wage rates and also rates of employment growth. Transaction costs include the direct and psychic costs of moving and the costs involved in a diminution of location-specific human capital and information networks. Of course, the decision to migrate is dynamic and contingent upon the household's circumstances, including dissolving and creation of partnerships, the obtaining or loss of employment, the birth of a child or the departure of children from the parental home. This type of framework implies that private renters are more mobile since they have lower transaction costs and skilled professional workers are more mobile since they can afford to move.

What does the empirical evidence reveal? It is worth separating our discussion of the empirical findings into housing tenure influences, household composition and life cycle influences and other influences. As already mentioned, migration is low in Britain, with only 10% of households moving in any one year (Boheim and Taylor, 1999). One argument is that this stems from the nature of the housing market, particularly for the unskilled (see McCormick, in Bowen and Mayhew, 1991), due to the decline of the private rented sector and the constraints imposed by the subsidised council-house sector. Indeed, it has been found that local authority tenants exhibit lower mobility relative to those in other forms of housing tenure (Hughes and McCormick, 1981, 1987). More recent work (Oswald, 1996, 1998) has argued that it is now owner-occupation that is a barrier to mobility via the higher fixed costs of owner-occupation relative to renting.

Other literature focuses on the role of household change and in particular, childbirth and partnership dissolution and formation. Much of this research treats migration as a by-product of a shift in the structure of the household. Some studies focus on the young leaving the parental home (Murphy and Wang, 1998; Ermisch, 1999), and others examine household transitions in the middle years of life associated with cohabitation, divorce and separation (Warnes, 1992; Flowerdew et al, 1999). Buck (2000) finds that 46% of moves are associated with a change in household composition. Separations are involved in 6% of household moves, children leaving the parental home affect 12% of moves and childbirth is associated with 3% of moves.

Mincer (1978) highlights the potential problems that may arise where families have dual earners. Here, family gain rather than individual gain drives household migration. In a dual-earner family, the primary earner is pivotal in initiating moves but is also the chief beneficiary of a move. The secondary earner is constrained and is the tied mover in the sense that they move for the benefit of the family but bear an individual loss in doing so. Migration is then sub-optimal for the tied mover but optimal for the family. Females are seen as the secondary earners owing to their attenuated labour market participation with respect to their husbands (Mincer, 1978). There is some support for this hypothesis. Boheim and Taylor (2002) find that dual-earner families are less likely to move; Battu et al (1999) find that for married females their partner's employment is a more important factor than their own employment in driving migration.

Additional evidence reveals that migration is selective with the young (with a longer time period to recoup costs), non-manual professional groups and the highly educated and graduates exhibiting greater mobility (Cameron and Muellbauer, 1998; Gregg et al, 2004). The greater mobility of graduates is reflected in the fact that only 12% of graduates live in the same local authority district as they were born (relative to 44% of the population in general). This stems both from the fact that attending university breaks the link with the parental home and because the graduate labour market is national (Gregg et al, 2004). It has also been found that mobility among graduates is more likely to be regional. Indeed, Gregg et al (2004) find that regional mobility for graduates is more than double that for those without any qualifications.

Boheim and Taylor (2002) examine the relationship between labour market dynamics and residential mobility. Among their findings are that the unemployed are more likely to move than the employed. Gardner et al (2001) use the British Household Panel Survey (BHPS) to examine residential mobility for job reasons. They have two main findings:

- *Gender matters.* Females in relationships are less mobile than men for own job reasons and more mobile for partner's job reasons. Males living with a non-employed partner exhibit higher mobility.
- *Job-related moves and the nature of housing are closely related.* In particular, private renting is associated with higher mobility than other forms of tenure. Long-distance moves are primarily associated with the attraction of employment opportunities in distant labour markets. Short-distance moves are driven largely by attempts to improve housing and may be associated with changes in the composition of the household (birth of a child, divorce) (Buck, 2000).

Another factor that has been identified as a constraint on mobility are regional house price differences. High house prices in areas of high demand reduce the potential gains from a move and also discourage out-migration from areas since a move may imply a loss of prospective investment gains (Cameron and Muellbauer, 1998).

But what of the Scottish dimension and what factors might drive any differences across Scotland and England? There are a few studies that consider mobility in Scotland. However, the analysis uses cross-sectional data with limited retrospective information, and has focused on a narrow range of factors. For example, McCleery and Forster (1995) use the Migration and Housing Choice Survey and find that quality of life considerations rather than employment factors are critical to both short- and long-distance moves. Parkes and Kearns (2002) use the 1996 Scottish House Condition Survey and find that deteriorating perceptions of a neighbourhood increase the likelihood that individuals would consider a move.

There are a number of differences between Scotland and England that suggest that mobility may vary across the two countries. Scotland clearly has higher average unemployment, lower average earnings and a different occupational and industrial profile with tertiary employment making up just over 80% of jobs (Houston et al, 2001). Manufacturing now employs barely three out every 20 Scottish workers. The share of the workforce with high-level qualifications and the proportion of young people entering higher education are greater than in the rest of Britain (Peat and Boyle, 1999). In addition, the tenure profile of Scotland is quite different with social renting playing a larger role and owner-occupation a less prominent one. According to recent analysis Scotland also has a lower proportion of poor households in owner-occupation compared to Britain as a whole. Also, homeowner costs are less relative to incomes than in England and at the same time house values and negative equity are generally lower than in England (Bramley et al, 2001).

Despite these differences there is no empirical work that tries to decipher the differential impact of these factors on residential mobility in Scotland and England. Most research focuses on Britain as a whole with at best a cursory treatment of Scotland or focuses on Scotland or England in isolation without making a direct comparison between the two countries.

Data and methods

Given that residential mobility is a process, the most appropriate form of data has to be longitudinal, individual-level data. Given the Scottish extension to the BHPS it is now possible for the first time to undertake an examination of residential mobility in Scotland compared with England. The BHPS contains extensive information on residential status and mobility and asks respondents why they moved. At each date of interview, respondents were asked:

> Can I just check: have you yourself lived in this [house/ flat] for more than a year; that is, before September 1, 199[1, ... 2000]?

We use data from 1991 to 2000. Only in the last two waves (1999 and 2000) is the Scottish booster sample available. This increased the relatively small Scottish sample size from around 400-500 households in the initial BHPS sample.

Throughout our analysis, a 'residential move' is defined as where an individual changes residence in the preceding year. This refers to any move in place of usual residence regardless of distance. The BHPS allows us to identify local moves (moves within a local authority district), inter-district moves (but within a region), and moves that cross regional boundaries, of which there are 11. (Local does not strictly equate with local authority district [LAD] since LADs are aggregated in the BHPS to avoid small numbers in some cells.) A much richer set of information relative to other datasets is also available including information on household composition, household income, tenure, qualifications and labour market status.

Our analysis proceeds in three steps. First, we provide some descriptives focusing on the extent of residential mobility in the two countries and on why individuals say they move. We also discuss the characteristics of movers and non-movers in both countries and introduce a dynamic element into the analysis by investigating the coincidence of various economic and demographic events for movers and also the complete sample (movers and non-movers). Second, using a probit model we investigate the determinants of residential mobility and ask whether with the introduction of controls there is still a distinct effect for Scotland. Given the differences between Scotland and England in terms of tenure profile, educational qualifications, labour market status and occupation, we interact each of these terms with the Scotland dummy. The coefficients then measure whether the impact of these factors is different for Scotland. Third, we quantify the differences in mobility rates across the two countries.

Some descriptives

Table 5.1 provides some information on the extent of mobility. We have 6,892 movers in total. A slightly lower percentage of Scottish people move in one year (11.7%) compared to England (12.8%). These estimates are not markedly different from other studies. Boheim and Taylor (2002), using the BHPS (1991-97), find that 10% of the sample move house each year.

The BHPS also allows us to identify the main reason for moving through a set of retrospective questions. In particular, the BHPS asks whether the reason for a move was job related and, if so, the respondent is asked to expand:

> Did you move for reasons that were wholly or partly to do with your own job, or employment opportunities?

Only 13.3% of moves are for job-related reasons in England with a lower figure for Scotland at 11.3%. This compares with 12.3% for Britain in Gregg et al (2004). Respondents were then asked to expand on the employment reasons: employer relocated, new job (same employer), new job (new employer), closer to same job, start or relocate own business, salary increase (new home), to seek work and other employment reason. Given that some cells had very few cases, we do

Table 5.1: Overall mover incidence, BHPS waves 1-10 (%)

	Movers % (n)	n
Scotland	11.7 (786)	6,699
England	12.8 (6,106)	47,757
Total	12.7 (6,892)	54,546

Note: Data are unweighted.

not report these results here. Other evidence, however, does reveal that only a very small percentage of those who move for job reasons move to obtain employment (Gregg et al, 2004).

The respondents were also asked about their first and second non-employment reason for moving:

What were your (other) main reasons for moving?

It is worth noting that this question focuses on why people move and not on their preferences for moving (Boheim and Taylor, 2002). Table 5.2 tabulates these responses and there do exist differences across Scotland and England. The dominant reason given in both countries is housing and in particular a desire to obtain larger/better accommodation, wanting smaller/cheaper accommodation, wanting own accommodation, wanting to buy somewhere and desiring better accommodation. The least important reason given in both countries is employment with less than 5% in both countries citing this as their main reason for moving. The percentages citing partner (moving in with a partner or splitting from a partner) as the reason for moving are higher in England (19.3%) compared to Scotland (17.8%). The 'other' category is the third most cited reason for moving in both countries and this includes those who want a change and also health reasons. Education is seen as less important in Scotland, with only 8% citing this as their main reason for moving. The equivalent figure for England is 11.25%

Table 5.3 provides information on the mean characteristics of movers and the combined sample (movers and non-movers) for England and Scotland. Owner-occupation (both mortgage and outright) is lower for movers in both countries relative to non-movers and the incidence of private renting is higher. Public housing is found to be more

Table 5.2: Reasons for moving (%)

	Scotland	England	All
Job	4.47	4.77	4.73
Partner	17.80	19.30	19.08
Other family	7.09	7.75	7.65
Education	8.01	11.25	10.79
Eviction	9.72	7.44	7.76
Accommodation	33.05	29.96	30.40
Area	6.60	7.25	7.15
Other	13.26	12.29	12.43
Number of movers	1,410	8,598	10,008

Note: Data are unweighted.

Table 5.3: Mean characteristics of movers

	Scotland		England	
	Mover	**All**	**Mover**	**All**
Outright owner	0.085	0.104	0.081	0.158
Mortgage owner	0.425	0.550	0.430	0.580
Public rented	0.205	0.265	0.160	0.161
Private rented	0.277	0.079	0.313	0.097
Self-employed	0.059	0.072	0.072	0.088
Employed	0.601	0.611	0.586	0.630
Unemployed	0.056	0.055	0.068	0.050
Retired	0.023	0.054	0.016	0.045
Student	0.132	0.052	0.130	0.038
Other	0.130	0.156	0.127	0.148
No qualifications	0.082	0.176	0.111	0.204
O-levels	0.241	0.281	0.303	0.316
A-levels	0.241	0.180	0.201	0.132
Nursing	0.193	0.199	0.203	0.207
Degree	0.243	0.164	0.181	0.141
Age (years)	30.8	38.7	30.8	39.2
Manual	0.532	0.475	0.500	0.499
Male	0.429	0.440	0.484	0.467
Married and living together	0.548	0.686	0.546	0.720
Rooms per person (number)	1.388	1.552	1.473	1.743
Real household labour income (£)	16,317.9	17,141.6	18,181.1	19,083.4
Number of adults	2.383	2.296	2.402	2.378
Number of children	0.561	0.645	0.540	0.679
Commuting time (minutes)	21.7	22.2	24.2	23.0

Note: Data are unweighted. Unless otherwise stated all variables measured as a percentage.

important in Scotland relative to England (for both movers and non-movers). The owner-occupier rates, however, are a little higher than those reported in other studies (Henley, 1999). Given the existing empirical evidence, we would expect less mobility in Scotland because of the constraints arising through public housing. Indeed, we find that the incidence of public renting for movers is lower than that for the combined sample.

In terms of labour market status, we find that for England fewer movers are employed and more are unemployed. There is little difference, however, across movers and non-movers in Scotland in terms of labour market status. In both countries, fewer movers are retired and more are students relative to the complete sample. In particular, around 13% of movers are students compared to 3.8% and 5.2% of the combined sample for England and Scotland respectively.

The educational qualifications profile of movers vis-à-vis non-movers reveals that movers are more highly qualified. Around a quarter (24.3%) of Scottish movers possess a degree compared with only 18.1% of

English movers. Movers are also on average eight to nine years younger. With respect to occupation, the gap between movers and non-movers is greater in Scotland where higher percentages of movers are in manual occupations relative to the combined sample. Movers are also more likely to be single.

What is the relationship between household characteristics and mobility? Here rooms per person (capturing house quality) are lower for movers in both Scotland and England. Rooms per person are simply the number of rooms in the household divided by the size of the household. Since there is little discernible difference in the number adults across movers and non-movers this suggests that post-move there is a fall in the number of rooms associated with a residential change. Although the number of adults differs little across movers and non-movers the number of children is lower for movers in both countries.

Rather surprisingly movers are found to have a lower real household income in both countries. There is also a difference across Scotland and England when we examine commute times. Movers exhibit higher commute times in England but lower commute times in Scotland. This suggests that residential mobility in England is not necessarily a mechanism for reducing commute times.

In order to provide some insight into the possible trigger events, in Table 5.4 we examine the coincidence of various economic and demographic events with moves. Here an event is defined as a change in a particular characteristic over one year. A number of types of events are specified including change in housing tenure, in job status, in household income, in the number of adults, in the number of children, in household type, in commute times, in education and whether individuals had obtained a new job. Although this information does not tell us about the direction of change, the information is suggestive of the types of factors that might drive a move.

There are essentially two dimensions to the data in Table 5.4:

- *The differences in the incidence of an event between movers and the complete sample.* So, for example, the percentage of households experiencing a change in job status is greater for movers relative to all (movers and non-movers).
- *Any differences between the two countries.* To gauge whether there are any differential effects across the two countries, an examination of the ratio of movers divided by all across Scotland and England needs to be made.

Table 5.4: Coincidence of economic and demographic events with move (%)

	Scotland		England	
	Mover	**All**	**Mover**	**All**
Housing tenure change	0.414		0.399	
Job status change	0.209	0.175	0.220	0.159
Household income				
Up 10%	0.368	0.314	0.371	0.322
Same	0.298	0.432	0.283	0.416
Down 10%	0.334	0.253	0.346	0.261
Number of adults				
Up	0.128	0.067	0.148	0.080
Same	0.587	0.832	0.600	0.832
Down	0.285	0.090	0.252	0.089
Number of children				
Up	0.063	0.053	0.082	0.042
Same	0.902	0.916	0.881	0.916
Down	0.036	0.032	0.037	0.042
Household type change	0.394	0.132	0.400	0.136
Commute time				
Up 10%	0.401	0.291	0.396	0.288
Same	0.292	0.437	0.257	0.448
Down 10%	0.307	0.272	0.347	0.264
Education	0.056	0.033	0.060	0.032
New job (job tenure <1 year)	0.184	0.163	0.223	0.185

Note: Data are unweighted.

In terms of job status, we find that around a fifth of movers in Scotland and England experience a change in job status. However, taking ratios (mover:all) reveals a greater coincidence of job status changes with moves in England (1.38) relative to Scotland (1.19).

Around 41% of movers in Scotland experience a change in their housing tenure compared to just under 40% for those in England. The two cells for non-movers are empty since it is more unusual for non-movers to change tenure. This was more common during the 1980s when many council tenants took advantage of the 'right to buy' under the 1980 Housing Act and thereby moved from public rented to owner-occupier accommodation. Moves also tend to be associated with household income changes. Over 70% of English and Scottish movers experience a change in household income compared to fewer than 60% of the non-movers in both countries. Rises in income do dominate, although there are few differences across Scotland and England. For Scotland, 37% of movers experience an income increase of 10% and 33% of movers experienced an income fall of 10%. For a rise in income of 10% the ratio of movers to all is 1.15 for England and 1.17 for Scotland. Although a slightly lower percentage of Scottish movers experience a fall in income (33.4%) compared to English movers (34.6%), the ratios for moves to all are the same at 1.32.

There is also a tendency for the number of adults in the household to fall with moves. An examination of the ratios reveals a greater tendency for this to occur in Scotland. On the other hand, moves also seem to coincide with a rise in the number of children in the household and this effect seems to be stronger for England. Rather unsurprisingly, moves also coincide with changes in household type (single, married with children, married without children, and so on). There is little difference between Scotland and England in this regard.

In relation to commute times it is evident that higher percentages of movers experience a change in commute times relative to the complete sample. Around 40% in both countries experience a 10% rise in commute times associated with a move. This compares with the 31-35% in both countries who experience a 10% decline in commute times. The data for both countries suggest that residential moves are not necessarily a mechanism for moving closer to the place of work and that individuals do tend to move largely for non-employment reasons.

Finally, while movers are more likely to experience coincidental changes in educational qualifications and also are likely to have obtained a new job, the differences between movers and non-movers with respect to these variables are small. Taking ratios does reveal, however, a slightly stronger effect for England with respect to these two events.

Regression results

Here we examine the relationship between prior characteristics with the probability of subsequent migration. The dependent variable is a dummy variable coded 1 if the respondent moved residence. Here we do not distinguish between types of moves. The model is estimated using a probit model, and the results are provided in Table 5.5. The covariates include housing tenure (omitted category is owned with mortgage), labour market status (omitted category is employed), highest qualifications (no qualifications as reference group), age (in bands and with under-30 the reference group), manual, gender (male), married and cohabiting, household characteristics and region (southeast England is the reference spatial area).

It needs to be borne in mind that any examination of the impact of

Table 5.5: Estimation results from probit for moving residence

	Coef	t-stat	Coef	t-stat
Owned outright	−0.004	−0.15	−0.035	−1.19
Public rented	0.163	6.51	0.177	6.49
Private rented	0.901	36.57	0.896	34.37
Self-employed	0.099	3.24	0.106	3.26
Other labour market status	0.190	8.53	0.205	8.55
O-levels	0.071	2.40	0.070	2.19
A-levels	0.159	4.76	0.152	4.24
Nursing	0.135	4.32	0.132	3.93
Degree	0.271	7.92	0.259	6.99
Aged 30-39	−0.354	−15.73	−0.350	−14.33
Aged 40-49	−0.682	−26.50	−0.679	−24.41
Aged 50+	−0.855	−27.98	−0.841	−25.67
Manual	0.040	1.91	0.035	1.59
Male	0.029	1.62	0.033	1.71
Married or living together	−0.147	−7.52	−0.155	−7.3
Rooms per person	−0.089	−10.28	−0.091	−10.42
Real household labour income (£ 000)	0.003	4.59	0.003	4.72
Number of adults	−0.050	−5.71	−0.050	−5.41
Number of children	−0.085	−8.46	−0.093	−8.78
Scotland	−0.106	−3.85	−0.202	−1.32
South West	0.034	1.08	0.034	1.1
East Anglia	0.100	2.43	0.101	2.46
Midlands	−0.085	−3.26	−0.085	−3.24
North West	−0.015	−0.51	−0.015	−0.52
Yorkshire and North East	−0.017	−0.65	−0.017	−0.67
Owned outright *Scot			0.309	3.75
Public rented *Scot			−0.059	−0.87
Private rented *Scot			0.057	0.7
Self-employed *Scot			−0.085	−0.93
Other labour market status *Scot			−0.120	−1.81
O-levels *Scot			0.050	0.58
A-levels *Scot			0.088	0.91
Nursing *Scot			0.073	0.79
Degree *Scot			0.127	1.3
Aged 30-39 *Scot			−0.022	−0.35
Aged 40-49 *Scot			−0.016	−0.22
Aged 50+ *Scot			−0.103	−1.15
Manual *Scot			0.019	0.3
Male *Scot			−0.033	−0.64
Married or living together *Scot			0.057	1.03
Rooms per person *Scot			0.024	0.62
Real household labour income *Scot			−0.0025	−1.6
Number of adults *Scot			0.004	0.13
Number of children *Scot			0.061	1.87
Constant	−0.749	−15.18	−0.744	−14.29

Number of observations = 54,075
Wald χ^2_{25} = 4,203.6
Prob > χ^2 = 0.00
Log likelihood = −17,411.4
Pseudo R^2 = 0.1514

Number of observations = 54,075
Wald χ^2_{44} = 4279.7
Prob > χ^2 = 0.00
Log likelihood = −17,394.0
Pseudo R^2 = 0.1523

Note: t-statistics robust to intra-individual correlations.

economic factors on residential moves could suffer from an inability to separate causality. We can argue that changes in labour market circumstances (losing a job, obtaining a job, and so on) influence residential location. It is also well established that residential location influences labour market outcomes (Gabriel and Rosenthal, 1996; Ihlanfeldt, 1997).

One way to disentangle the direction of causality would be to employ appropriate instruments. Without these we proceed by examining the relationships using a reduced form modelling approach.

The results are, on the whole, plausible. The housing tenure variable coefficients behave as expected and support existing evidence. Those in rented accommodation (either public or private) are more likely to move relative to those who own with a mortgage. The lower mobility of owner-occupiers can be assigned to their greater commitment to the neighbourhood, higher moving costs and greater flexibility in modifying the current dwelling. The coefficient on private renting is larger and better determined than that for public renting.

The self-employed are somewhat more mobile relative to the omitted category of employed. This is rather counterintuitive since we would expect the self-employed, who have greater local capital (connections with suppliers and customers) to be less mobile. Furthermore, the self-employed are less likely to receive financial assistance in moving from employers relative to the employed. Those in the other labour market status category (unemployed, the retired, students and the sick) display greater residential mobility. Other studies find a strong mobility effect arising through being jobless. McCormick (1997) states:

> All UK studies which examine the effect of individual unemployment ... find this has a strong positive effect on out-migration.... (p 587)

One, however, needs to be careful in interpreting this. Since we do not make an allowance for why people moved, we cannot interpret this as individuals changing location in order to improve their labour market opportunities.

Educational qualifications increase the propensity to migrate perhaps by increasing employment opportunities and providing greater access to better information about other areas (Sandefur and Scott, 1981). This is clearly evident in our results, with the strongest effect being evident for those with degree qualifications. This partly reflects the fact that significant numbers of students do not study in the parental region (Gregg et al, 2004). In essence, students become movers at an early age, making it easier for them to move in the future. As Gregg et al (2004) acknowledge, there are important regional dimensions to this in terms of a willingness to study in the parental region. Scotland stands out with 80% of Scottish students studying in Scotland compared to around 50% of South East students who study in the South East of England.

The young are more mobile – there is a significantly higher probability of moving residence for those below the age of 30. Although there is not a statistically significant effect for manual workers in Scotland, in England manual workers have a greater probability of moving residence. This is somewhat surprising since most British evidence finds that there is an occupational dimension to residential mobility with managerial, professional and non-manual workers exhibiting greater mobility than manual workers (Hughes and McCormick, 1987).

Marital status is an important feature of theories about migration behaviour, with evidence that married individuals are less likely to migrate. We find that marriage acts as a restraint upon residential mobility. School-age children create important ties to an area, and the fear of disrupting children's education may inhibit migration (Long, 1972). A rise in the number of children hinders moves by increasing the costs of a move. Higher real household income encourages moves perhaps by reducing the financial costs of moving.

The results for housing density (capturing housing quality) are in line with previous evidence given the definition of the variable. As stated earlier in this chapter, rooms per person are simply the number of rooms divided by the number of individuals in the household. If this rises (density falls), we find that there is a smaller probability of moving. We would then expect increased density (poor housing quality) to encourage moves.

The estimated value of the dummy variable for Scotland provides a simple measure of whether mobility is different between Scotland and the omitted category, that is, the southeast of England. This suggests that even after controlling for differences in characteristics, living in Scotland is associated with a lower probability of moving relative to the southeast region. In terms of the English regions, only in the Midlands is there a comparable and statistically significant difference in mobility.

The results in Columns 2 and 3 of Table 5.5 assume that the effects of all the covariates are identical across the two countries. Given our early discussion on possible differences in the two countries, this may be rather restrictive. To test this, we estimate separate mobility equations for the two countries by interacting the Scotland dummy with the explanatory variables used. The results are given in Columns 4 and 5 in Table 5.5. The coefficients and the associated t-values reported therefore provide an indication of the extent to which a particular variable has a different effect in Scotland (and its statistical significance). For example, the positive impact of real household labour income on the probability of moving is estimated to be slightly less in Scotland but this apparent Scotland–England difference is just short of statistical significance at the 10% level.

The results also suggest that the structure of mobility differs across Scotland and England. Statistically, the assumption that all the coefficients on the explanatory variables have identical effects on the probability of moving in both countries is rejected at less than 1%, ($\chi^2(20)=49.32$, $p=0.0003$). Furthermore, although few of the coefficients on individual interactions are statistically significant there is some evidence that the structure of the effects of various variables differs across the two countries. First, outright owner-occupiers in Scotland are more mobile relative to the base category of mortgage owner-occupiers. Although none of the other tenure interaction terms are individually statistically significant, the joint significance test that the structure of the effects of the housing tenure variables are identical is rejected at the 1% level ($p=0.0004$). Second, although the estimated coefficient on other labour market status is positive, interacting it with Scotland generates a negative coefficient (significant at the 10% level). This may indicate that the unemployed in Scotland have gathered or possess a greater amount of local capital thereby hindering mobility relative to the base category of employed in England. However, the joint test that the overall effects of labour market status are the same cannot be rejected at the 10% level ($p=0.164$). The interaction terms for education are all insignificant and do not indicate important differences between Scotland and England in terms of the effect of educational qualifications. The results also do not indicate important significant differences between Scotland and England in the effect of occupation.

In other regressions we investigated the effects of commute times. The arguments are that higher commute times generate a greater incentive to move. The costs of moving may also be higher for those with shorter commutes. Our results indicate that convenience to work plays little role since residential mobility is quite unresponsive to higher commute times. Similar findings were obtained by Henley (1998), suggesting that the direction of causation may be in the opposite direction. High levels of housing transaction costs may limit job search

Table 5.6: Probability of moving under various assumptions

Predictions	Scotland	England
Regression 1		
Own coefficients	0.121	0.133
Scotland coefficients	0.121	0.115
England coefficients	0.140	0.133
Regression 2 (with interactions)		
Own coefficients	0.121	0.133
Scotland coefficients	0.121	0.117
England coefficients	0.141	0.133

Note: Data are unweighted.

to the immediate travel-to-work area, putting upward pressure on commute times and distances.

In summary, the results of the regression analysis suggest some important differences across Scotland and England. To quantify these differences we calculated the predicted mobility rates for the two countries and compared these with the predicted values for the two countries using the estimated coefficients from the other country. In essence our approach is similar to a decomposition analysis where we split the differences in mobility rates into explained (differences in characteristics) and unexplained (differences in coefficients) components. The results are given in Table 5.6. The probability of moving in Scotland is around 0.12 with a slightly higher rate in England of 0.13. Furthermore, these results indicate that there are apparently significant quantitative differences in mobility across Scotland and England even after controlling for the effect of differences in the structure of housing tenure, employment status, education, and so on. For example, if mobility in Scotland was identical to England, the rate of mobility would increase from 0.12 to 0.14. Likewise, if mobility in England followed Scottish patterns, the mobility rate would decrease from 0.13 to 0.115.

Conclusion

This chapter has examined the extent to which mobility and the factors affecting mobility differ across Scotland and England. In general, the patterns of mobility by income, household type and economic activity mirror the patterns elsewhere in Britain. Movers in Scotland are young, highly educated and reside in private rented accommodation. However, there are also some notable differences with England, with a larger proportion of Scottish movers being in public rented accommodation, fewer in private rented accommodation, relatively more have degree-level qualifications, more are in manual occupations, more are female, they have lower average household income, and have relatively lower commute times.

In order to provide some insight into the possible trigger events we also examined the coincidence of various economic and demographic events with moves. This analysis reveals a number of important differences across Scotland and England. In particular, it appears that for Scotland there is a smaller coincidence of job status changes with moves, there is also a greater tendency for the number of adults in the household to fall with moves and moves tend to coincide less with lower commute times.

Finally, we consider the effect of various factors, such as housing tenure, employment status, and education level on the probability that an individual will move. The results indicate that there is a statistically significant difference in the way these factors affect the probability of a move in the two countries. The overall effect is small but significant, for example, if mobility in Scotland was identical to England, then the rate of mobility would increase from 12% to 14%.

References

Battu, H., Sloane, P.J. and Seaman, P.T. (1999) 'Are married women spatially constrained: a test of gender differentials in labour market outcomes', *European Research in Regional Science*, vol 9, pp 91-110.

Benito, A. and Oswald, A.J. (1999) 'Commuting in Great Britain in the 1990s', Unpublished, University of Warwick.

Boheim, R. and Taylor, M. (1999) 'Residential mobility, housing tenure and the labour market in Britain', Unpublished, University of Essex.

Boheim, R. and Taylor, M. (2002) 'Tied down or room to move? Investigating the relationships between housing tenure, employment status and residential mobility in Britain', *Scottish Journal of Political Economy*, vol 49, no 4, pp 369-92.

Bramley, G., Ford, T., Ford, J., Morgan, J. and Wilcox, S. (2001) *The future of owner occupation in Scotland: Issues of sustainability*, Edinburgh: Communities Scotland.

Buck, N. (2000) 'Housing, location and residential mobility', in R. Berthoud and J. Gershuny (eds) *Seven years in the lives of British families*, Bristol: The Policy Press, Chapter 6.

Cameron, G. and Muellbauer, J. (1998) 'The housing market and regional commuting and migration choices', *Scottish Journal of Political Economy*, vol 45, pp 420-46.

Ermisch, J. (1999) 'Prices, parents and young people's household formation', *Journal of Urban Economics*, vol 45, pp 47-71.

Flowerdew, R., Al-Hamad, A. and Hayes, L. (1999) 'The residential mobility of divorced people', in S. McRae (ed) *Changing Britain: Families and households in the 1990s*, Oxford: Oxford University Press, pp 427-44.

Gabriel, S. and Rosenthal, S.S. (1996) 'Commutes, neighbourhood effects and earnings: an analysis of racial discrimination and compensating differentials', *Journal of Urban Economics*, vol 40, pp 61-83.

Gardner, J., Pierre, G. and Oswald, A. (2001) 'Moving for job reasons', Unpublished, University of Warwick.

Gregg, P., Machin, S. and Manning, A. (2004) 'Mobility and joblessness', in D. Card, R. Blundell and R. Freeman (eds) *Seeking a premier league economy*, Chicago, IL: National Bureau of Economic Research, University of Chicago Press.

Henley, A. (1998) 'Residential mobility, housing equity and the labour market', *Economic Journal*, vol 108, pp 414-27.

Henley, A. (1999) 'The economics of the crazy British housing market', Inaugural lecture to the University of Wales, Aberystwyth, 10 November.

Houston, J., Gasteen, A. and Asenova, D. (2001) 'Labour market flexibility in Scotland and the new Parliament's income tax varying powers', *Regional Studies*, vol 34 no 4, pp 321-8.

Hughes, G. and McCormick, B. (1981) 'Do council housing policies reduce migration between regions?', *Economic Journal*, vol 91, pp 907-18.

Hughes, G. and McCormick, B. (1987) 'Housing markets, unemployment and labour market flexibility in the UK', *European Economic Review*, vol 31, pp 615-45.

Hughes, G. and McCormick, B. (2000) 'Housing policy and labour market performance', Report for the DETR, Unpublished, University of Southampton.

Ihlanfeldt, K. (1997) 'Information on the spatial distribution of job opportunities within metropolitan areas', *Journal of Urban Economics*, vol 41, pp 218-42.

Long, L.L. (1972) 'The influence of the number of children on residential mobility', *Demography*, vol 9, no 3, pp 371-82.

McCleery, A., Forster, E., Ewington, H. and Burnhill, P. (1995) 'Developing a Scottish migration monitor: a cooperative approach', *IASSIST Quarterly Journal*, vol 19, no 4, pp 12-22.

McCormick, B. (1991) 'Migration and regional policy', in A. Bowen and K. Mayhew (eds) *Reducing regional inequalities*, London: Kogan Page.

McCormick, B. (1997) 'Regional unemployment and labour mobility in the UK', *European Economic Review*, vol 41, pp 581-9.

Mincer, J. (1978) 'Family migration decisions', *Journal of Political Economy*, vol 86, pp 749-73.

Murphy, M. and Wang, D. (1998) 'Family and socio-demographic influences on patterns of leaving home in postwar Britain', *Demography*, vol 35, no 3, pp 293-305.

Oswald, A. (1996) 'A conjecture on the explanation for high unemployment in the industrialised nations: part 1', University of Warwick Economic Research Papers, no 475.

Oswald, A. (1998) 'A missing piece of the unemployment puzzle', Paper presented at CEPR/ESRC Workshop on Unemployment dynamics, London, 4 November.

Parkes, A. and Kearns, A. (2002) *Residential perceptions and housing mobility in Scotland: An analysis of the Longitudinal Scottish House Condition Survey 1991-1996*, Paper 3, Bristol: Centre for Neighbourhood Research.

Peat, J. and Boyle, S. (1999) *An illustrated guide to the Scottish economy*, London: Duckworth.

Sandefur, G.D. and Scott, W.J. (1981) 'A dynamic analysis of migration: an assessment of age, family, and career variables', *Demography*, vol 18, pp 355-68.

Warnes, T. (1992) 'Migration and the life course', in T. Champion and T. Fielding (eds) *Migration processes and patterns, Vol 1: Research Progress and Prospects*, London: Belhaven Press, pp 175-87.

SIX

How Scots live: housing and housing policy

Jeanette Findlay and Cecilia MacIntyre

Introduction

The housing system in the UK has undergone a number of significant changes over the last decade. More importantly, it is facing a series of new challenges in the future arising from demographic changes and the changing role of local authorities as they move away from their traditional landlord role. The aims of this chapter are:

- to describe the nature of the housing system in Scotland;
- to give an overview of the changing pattern and distribution of tenure;
- to look at the quality of Scottish housing and the nature of housing and housing-related costs such as fuel;
- to look at the residential mobility of Scots and the extent to which the existing pattern of tenure impacts on mobility.

There are a number of datasets in existence that serve to give us a picture of both the physical and social elements of housing in Scotland (Scottish House Condition Survey; Scottish Household Survey). These are repeated surveys, which allow us to look at aggregate changes over time in relation to housing choice, tenure structure, housing conditions, neighbourhoods, affordability, housing investment, housing-related expenditure and a whole host of other factors that are of interest to academics and policy makers. However, when it comes to trying to understand the motivation for such changes, the choices facing households and the way in which households make housing and related decisions we are forced to make a number of assumptions that are, for the most part, theoretical and lacking in empirical content. If, for example, we try to model housing choice, involving as it does a number of sub-choices (tenure, neighbourhood, house type, size, and so on), we must make some very strong assumptions about the order in which the choices are made (Meen and Andrew, 1999; Gibb et al, 2000). However, if we are able to track individuals (and their associated households) over time, as we can with the British Household Panel Survey (BHPS), then we can begin to put some empirical flesh on the bones of such models. Similarly, if we can track the attitude of individuals to their housing circumstances and then look at any changes they make and the reasons for their changes, then we can begin to build up an understanding of the process that takes place. This is vitally important for a number of policy areas ranging from the specifics of the legal and institutional arrangements relating to house buying and selling to much wider questions relating to urban regeneration and social inclusion.

Housing is an area that has been at the forefront of the policy agenda for many decades but the use of a panel survey of this kind (that is, a household panel as opposed to a dwelling panel such as contained in the Scottish House Condition Survey which we discuss later) will, over time, give us a much fuller understanding of the nature of housing and neighbourhoods in Scotland and give us much clearer evidence on which to base policy. This is doubly important given that housing is an area where there are quite distinctive institutional and other differences between Scotland and England. It should be noted, however, that there are only two waves (1999 and 2000) of the boosted Scottish sample in the public domain at this point. Most of the processes that would be of interest take place over longer periods than a year so any results derived from the current dataset cover too short a period for them to be much other than suggestive. This makes future waves of the BHPS Scottish booster sample vital to ensuring that we have an accurate picture of how Scots live in the 21st century.

Overview

A simple analysis of the most recent wave of the data gives a broad picture of housing in Scotland and the rest of Great Britain (RGB) in terms of, among other things, tenure, mobility, house type and problems with the local area. If we compare these results we can already see some distinctive differences emerge.

We can see from Table 6.1 that, despite the growth in owner-occupation throughout the UK, there is still a marked difference in the number of owner-occupiers between Scotland and the RGB. There is a corresponding difference in the number of social sector tenants also. In terms of movers (within the previous year), there is a clear difference between the tenures but very little difference across the

Table 6.1: Housing and households in Scotland and the RGB (2000)

	Scotland % households	RGB % households
Household tenure:		
Owner-occupiers	62	69
Social sector tenants	26	20
Private renters/others	10	9
Not known	2	3
Household structure:		
Single people	32	32
Couple no children	26	28
Couple with dependent children	23	21
Lone parent with dependent children	7	6
Other	12	13
	% households within tenure	
House type – owner-occupiers:		
Flats	25	6
Houses	74	93
Other	1	1
Social renters:		
Flats	53	30
Houses	45	67
Other	2	5
Private renters/others:		
Flats	52	31
Houses	42	54
Other	6	15
	% individuals who have moved	
Individuals moved in last year by tenure:		
Owners	8	8
Social renters	10	12
Private renters/others	42	43

UK. There also appears to be very few differences in household structure and this result stands in contrast to the results of the Survey of English Housing for 2001, the preliminary results of which suggest that the number of couples with no dependent children stands at 37% in England.

There does not appear to be huge differences overall between Scotland and the RGB in terms of the kinds of problems that people identify with their homes and neighbourhoods (Table 6.2). The most noticeable difference is a concern with noise in the street and pollution. Concern with pollution is small across the UK but is identified as a problem by nearly double the proportion of people in the RGB compared with Scotland. Concern with noise appears to be much greater in the RGB. There are clear tenure differences here. Table 6.3

Table 6.2: Problems identified with housing and neighbourhood (2000) (%)

	Scotland	RGB
Shortage of space	21	19
Noise: neighbours	12	11
Noise: street	13	17
Inadequate light	5	7
Inadequate heating	7	5
Condensation	10	13
Leaky roof	4	4
Damp walls etc	8	7
Pollution	5	9
Vandalism/crime	19	19

shows there are differences in Scotland in terms of accommodation problems identified by renters on the one hand and owners on the other. In Scotland, problems with crime, noise, light, condensation and pollution are about twice as much in the rented sectors. The differential seems to be even greater with heating and dampness, at around three to four times greater. The private rented sector does not

Table 6.3: Accommodation problems by tenure (2000) (%)

	Owner	Owner (with mortgage)	Social renter	Private renter/ other
Scotland				
Shortage of space	10	25	27	24
Noise: neighbour	5	12	20	17
Noise: street	8	11	21	17
Inadequate light	2	4	8	11
Inadequate heating	4	4	10	19
Condensation	7	7	18	14
Leaky roof	3	5	4	7
Damp walls etc	4	4	16	15
Pollution	4	4	7	7
Vandalism/crime	15	15	32	21
RGB				
Shortage of space	12	23	27	22
Noise: neighbour	7	10	19	16
Noise: street	14	16	21	25
Inadequate light	5	6	9	10
Inadequate heating	3	4	10	13
Condensation	9	13	24	22
Leaky roof	3	4	5	8
Damp walls etc	6	6	13	21
Pollution	9	8	11	9
Vandalism/crime	16	15	31	18

stand out in such contrast in the SHCS, other than possibly with issues such as inadequate heating.

Affordability

The question of affordability, its definition and the role that it plays in rent setting in the social sector, is one that has troubled economists and housing policy analysts worldwide. Most developed countries have their own definitions and approach the question of affordability in a way that matches their own institutional and welfare arrangements (Chaplin et al, 1997; Wilcox, 1999). The key distinction is whether housing subsidy is delivered either as a 'bricks and mortar' subsidy (which is delivered in terms of the rent attached to a particular dwelling) or as a personal subsidy (which is delivered through the benefits system) or, as in the UK, as a combination of both. Accurate measurements of affordability (under all definitions) are crucial to the development of policy in relation to rent setting. The recent changes in England with regard to rent setting in the social sector (Garnett, 2000; King, 2001) and the current interest of the Scottish Executive in reviewing local authority and housing association rent-setting arrangements indicate that this is near the top of the housing policy agenda. The recent wave of large-scale voluntary stock transfers, the largest of which is in Glasgow, also serves to focus attention of the question of rents in the social sector. Fundamental to the concerns of many tenants in the run up to the vote on stock transfer in Glasgow which took place in April 2002, was the question of future rent levels. The data contained in Table 6.4 give some indication of the position in Scotland and the RUK in 2000. The table gives the proportion of gross rent to income. A benchmark figure for the ratio of rent to income is usually between 20-30%. In almost no developed country is a figure above 30% considered affordable. From the table it is clear that the differences between Scotland and the RGB are marginal. Table 6.5, which breaks down affordability in Scotland by tenure, shows that the key issue

Table 6.4: Gross housing costs as a proportion of income (2000) (%)

	Scotland	RGB
<10%	52	51
10-20%	26	25
20-30%	10	12
>30%	12	13

Table 6.5: Scotland: gross housing costs as a proportion of income by tenure (2000) (%)

	Owner with mortgage	Social renter	Other renters
<10%	39	16	41
10-20%	42	27	21
20-30%	10	25	14
>30%	9	32	24

here lies in the differences between tenures. Social renters are clearly the worst off but again this result must be treated with caution given the very small number of private sector renters in the sample.

Housing and housing-related costs

There are many costs associated with housing beyond rent and mortgage payments. The dataset is also a rich source of information on the other expenditures that people undertake that relate to their housing circumstances. These are important for a number of reasons. Households can react in a variety of ways to specified problems with their housing circumstances. For instance, if a household is faced with a shortage of space (which we can see that around a fifth of all households do across the UK), then they may do one or more of the following:

• move to a bigger house;
• build an extension or undertake some other form of renovation, which will increase space in the areas required;
• rearrange their household structure – adult children may leave home earlier;
• do nothing, possibly due to income constraints, inertia or other reasons.

The dataset contains information on the reasons people gave for moving house (either as a whole family or as a process of changes in the family structure). It also gives information on other expenditures, which gives an indication of how particular families have invested in their current property. Unfortunately, the data only give this information where respondents have borrowed to finance the expenditure and it would be useful if future waves included questions on all investment and maintenance expenditure that people undertake. This would allow us to gain further insight into the way that people react to the mismatch between their perceived housing needs and their current housing circumstances. A further aspect of this, which goes beyond the remit of this chapter, but is touched on in Chapter Eighteen, and which the dataset would allow, would be to examine the activities that people engage in when they are unhappy with aspects of their neighbourhood.

Another reason why we have a particular policy interest in housing-related expenditure is in terms of expenditure on heating. The concept of fuel poverty is one that has been under discussion since the 1970s. It is clear that there is a gap between the expenditure required to comfortably heat different properties, which is dependent on both the physical characteristics of the property and the heating system that is used. If lower-income families are on average more likely to be living in badly insulated homes with more expensive heating systems then that is an issue that policy makers will want to address. The climate differences between Scotland and England may exacerbate this problem, with families in Scotland suffering more as a result.

There are a number of Scottish Executive initiatives underway that are targeted at alleviating fuel poverty. The Central Heating programme aims to have central heating and appropriate insulation installed in all local authority and housing association dwellings by 2005. The programme also provides grants of an average of £2,500 to install central heating in dwellings owned by elderly households.

The formal definition of fuel poverty that is most commonly used involves information on the dwelling as well as the circumstances of the household that happens to live there. In this respect, the BHPS is not necessarily the most suitable database, on its own, for this kind of study, lacking, as it does, the kind of detailed dwelling information that is contained in the House Condition Surveys for Scotland and England. However, what we can get from the BHPS is information on actual expenditure on fuel and if people feel they can adequately heat their home. Households can be formally in fuel poverty but actually be comfortable in their homes because they spend a larger proportion of their income on heating. It is akin, therefore, to the debates on the definition of affordability; that is, we might want to take a view on the maximum proportion of a household's income that should be spent on heating. Clearly this cuts across traditional economic theory, which suggests that expenditures reflect or reveal the differing tastes and preferences that people have and that a higher expenditure on an item is not in itself evidence of a policy problem. However, it is clear that expenditure on heating and other basic needs such as housing and food are regarded in a different way to other expenditures in a welfare-oriented society such as Scotland.

The tables reveal a distinct difference both between Scotland and the RGB, with Scottish households paying considerably more of their income on fuel. There are also clear differences in this regard between owners and renters. Table 6.7 indicates that, although there are no owners with mortgages paying more than 20% of their income on fuel, outright owners are paying high fuel costs in the same proportion as renters. Since outright owners are likely to be older couples or single people living on a pension, this is clearly a function of low income. This does not necessarily indicate overall poverty given that their housing costs are likely to be very small.

Residential mobility and tenure

Understanding mobility and the factors that determine it is an essential component of understanding key elements of both the housing and labour markets. The BHPS is a rich source of information on actual and intended moves and contains a wealth of information on the sorts of reasons that lie behind such moves and/or aspirations. This information has been analysed in some detail in the past at a GB level (Buck, 1994; Ford et al, 2001) and is examined further in Chapter Five of this book. At a Scottish level, some attempt has been made to use the Scottish House Condition Survey's longitudinal element to determine the extent to which the attitudes of respondents to their houses and neighbourhoods influence mobility (Parkes and Kearns,

Table 6.6: Fuel costs as a proportion of income: Scotland and the RGB (2000) (%)

	Scotland	RGB
<10%	88	94
10-20%	10	5
>20%	2	1

Table 6.7: Fuel costs as a proportion of income by tenure (2000) (%)

	Outright owner	Owner with mortgage	Social renter	Other renter
Scotland				
<10	91	96	79	81
10-20%	9	4	17	14
>20%	4	0	4	6
RGB				
<10	91	98	91	90
10-20%	7	2	7	8
>20%	2	1	2	2

2002). There is some evidence that, of all the reasons that people give for considering a move, some are much more likely than others to induce an actual move. These include health reasons (Buck, 1994) and deteriorating neighbourhood perceptions (Parkes and Kearns, 2002). Clearly, the boosted Scottish panel of the BHPS is an ideal means by which a clearer understanding of this process can be attained.

From Table 6.1, we can see that, not unexpectedly, there is considerably more mobility in the private rented sector. From Table 6.8 we can see that there is slightly more mobility in the RGB as compared to Scotland.

When we look at the expectations that people have in one year (Table 6.8), and then look to see what they actually do a year later, we find the following. Of the individuals who expressed a preference to stay in their current home, around 95% of those were still there after a year. Of those who said they would prefer to move, over 40% of them realised a move within the year. This varies considerably depending on the reason they gave for wanting to move. Most notably, there was much less likelihood of a move where the reason given was a desire to move to another area, for example, to a rural location or to a specific area rather than a dislike of the current area or dwelling. In Scotland, dislike of the area seemed to prompt more mobility than in the RGB.

Tenure changes

The BHPS allows a direct assessment of individual movements between tenures. In Scotland, owner-occupation is very stable, as one would expect, with 98% of owners still owning a property a year later (Table 6.9). Social renters are more likely to change, with approximately

Table 6.8: Individual moves – actual and preference (%)

	Actually moved in year	
	Scotland	RGB
Expect to move in next year:		
Yes	42	46
No	4	5
Don't know	12	12
Prefer to move:		
No	4	7
Yes – accommodation	19	23
Yes – to other area	7	11
Yes – dislikes area	17	14
Yes – other	19	19

Table 6.9: Individual tenure change

	% tenure in 2000		
Tenure in 1999	Owner-occupier	Social renter	Private renter/other
Scotland			
Owner-occupier	98	1	1
Social renter	6	91	3
Private renter	18	9	73
RGB			
Owner-occupier	98	1	2
Social renter	6	91	3
Private renter	17	8	75

6% becoming owners within the year and 3% moving into private renting. The private rented sector is the most volatile, with 18% and 9% moving into owner-occupation and social renting respectively. These last figures should be treated with some caution given the small number of private renters. The figures for the RGB reveal almost no difference in respect of tenure change.

Conclusion

The foregoing is no more than a flavour of the kind of housing and housing-related data that the BHPS contains, together with some suggestions as to the kinds of questions that might be answered once further waves of the Scottish boost become available. There is no doubt that the ability to track a panel of Scottish individuals (and the households to which they belong) over a period of time offers economists and housing policy analysts the opportunity to further understand the ways in which people make a myriad of housing and housing-related choices, and to understand them in the context of a distinctive set of institutional, economic and social arrangements. Scottish housing and related policy can then be clearly based on Scottish evidence and focused more directly on the issues of greatest concern to the Scottish people.

References

Buck, N. (1994) 'Housing and residential mobility', in N. Buck, J. Gershuny, D. Rose and J. Scott (eds) *Changing households: The British Household Panel Survey, 1990-1992*, Colchester: ESRC Research Centre on Micro-Social Change, University of Essex.

Chaplin, R., Freeman, A. and Whitehead, C. (1997) *A review of international literature on rental affordability*, Discussion Paper 88, Cambridge: Department of Land Economy, University of Cambridge.

Ford, T., Bramley, G. and Champion, T. (2001) 'The household impacts of migration', Paper presented at the 2001 BHPS Research Conference, Colchester, July.

Garnett, D. (2000) *Housing finance*, Chartered Institute of Housing.

Gibb, K., Mackay, D. and Meen, G. (2000) *Citywide needs and demand: The demand for social rented housing in Glasgow*, Report to Glasgow City Housing, Scottish Homes and the West of Scotland Forum of Housing Associations, Glasgow: Scottish Homes.

King, P. (2001) *Understanding housing finance*, London: Routledge.

Meen, G.P. and Andrew, M. (1999) *Spatial structure and social exclusion*, Discussion Paper in Urban and Regional Economics no 140, Reading: University of Reading.

Parkes, A. and Kearns, A. (2002) *Residential perceptions and housing mobility in Scotland: An analysis of the Longitudinal Scottish House Condition Survey 1991-1996*, Discussion Paper no 3, Glasgow: Centre for Neighbourhood Research, University of Glasgow.

Scottish House Condition Survey, 1991-96, Communities Scotland (formerly Scottish Homes), The Scottish Executive.

Survey of English Housing 2001-02 Preliminary Results (2002) *Housing Statistics Summary*, no 12, London: ODPM, National Statistics.

Wilcox, S. (1999) *The vexed question of affordability*, Edinburgh: Scottish Homes Research Paper.

Section 2:
Inequalities

Health policy is a devolved responsibility, and in 2001 the Scottish Executive initiated a set of reforms relating to the structure of the NHS and the way in which health services are delivered. Central to this policy, and in contrast to health policy in England and Wales, is an increased emphasis on the prevention of poor health rather than the treatment of ill health. Anne Ludbrook, Ioannis Theodossiou and Vania Gerova (Chapter Seven) examine present inequalities in health. Not only do they provide a Scottish–English comparison, their study is the first to use the superior SF-36 health status indicator in the British Household Panel Survey (BHPS). Their focus is on links between aspects of lifestyle and socioeconomic circumstances and self-reported measures of health. Despite Scotland's image as the 'sick man of Europe', they find that differences in average self-reported health measures between the Scots and English are not as great as in age-standardised mortality rates. While the correlates of health also seem to be broadly similar, some aspects of lifestyle and life circumstances appear to have different impacts in the two countries. Negative life circumstances, such as smoking and unemployment, produce worse health measures in Scotland than England, and positive ones produce better health outcomes. Thus, a simple comparison of 'average health' masks significant but offsetting differences at either end of the distribution, and these differences may provide important clues for prevention policies.

The Scottish Executive is committed to pursuing policies that create an environment more conducive to long-term and sustainable economic growth, emphasising the links between family policy, education policy and skill formation and between economic growth and the reduction of social inequality. Many studies contend that income inequality may be associated with poorer health, crime and social exclusion, and some argue that greater inequality may be associated with slower economic growth. The next three chapters document the existing differences in poverty and economic inequality between England and Scotland, thereby providing a baseline from which to assess the impact of these new policies.

Vernon Gayle, Gregor Jack and Robert Wright (Chapter Eight) employ an 'absolute' definition of poverty and a poverty line used in much comparative European Union (EU) poverty research. Absolute poverty was higher in Scotland in the 1990s than in England; for instance, in 2000 16% of Scots lived in poor households compared with 14% of English people. Their analysis suggests that the difference is in large part accounted for by differences in the factors correlated with poverty, such as the lack of qualifications and unemployment of the household head and the number of employed household members. Once they control for these, the odds of being in poverty are not significantly different in the two countries. Absolute poverty declined in both nations during this period, at a similar speed.

David Bell and Gregor Jack (Chapter Nine) conclude that Scotland is a highly unequal society with a substantial gap between high and low earners, but less so than the rest of the UK. Their analysis of New Earnings Survey data indicates that wage inequality increased less in Scotland than in the rest of the UK since the mid-1990s. Also, in contrast to the rest of the UK, wage differentials within occupations fell in Scotland since 1987 and wage differentials between occupations remained relatively stable since 1994. In line with this, evidence from the BHPS indicates that, by the end of the 1990s, earnings differentials *between* educational qualifications were smaller in Scotland than the rest of the UK, and earnings inequality *within* these qualifications was also lower. It is not clear what aspects of the Scottish labour market are responsible for these differences in the evolution of inequality, nor for their finding that both low and high incomes are less stable in Scotland than in the rest of the UK. Finally, they find that there has been an increase in income inequality among Scottish retired households. With an increasing older population, who are substantial consumers of public services, and several non-means tested policies aimed specifically at older people, the distribution of income among older people needs more research and policy attention.

Inequality often has a clear gender dimension. Kostas Mavromaras and Ioannis Theodossiou (Chapter Ten) examine male–female differences in the labour market in order to explore how patterns of work may be generating inequality. Their focus is on labour force participation rates, job tenure, occupational segregation and earnings. They find that in most occupations women represent a larger proportion of employees in Scotland than in England. The gender gap in pay is found to be higher in England than in Scotland, primarily because of much higher male earnings in England. Each of these differences may be related to the larger proportion of Scottish employment in the public sector and wider union coverage in Scotland (see Chapter Eleven), both of which act to provide more equal opportunities for women in terms of employment and earnings. While Scottish women have similar average job tenure to their English counterparts, Scottish men have much longer job tenure than Englishmen. This could be related to the lower residential mobility among Scots than English found in Chapter Five of this book.

SEVEN

Health and deprivation

Anne Ludbrook[1], Ioannis Theodossiou and Vania Gerova

Introduction

Scotland has an unenviable record as the 'sick man of (Western) Europe', with high mortality rates for most major diseases. The Scottish way of life, poor nutrition, smoking, alcohol consumption and lack of exercise are seen to contribute to this image. Other factors in terms of life circumstances, such as income, education, and employment status, are seen as contributing to poor health, particularly for lower socioeconomic groups. The Scottish Executive is committed to tackling the causes of ill health and reducing health inequalities (Scottish Executive, 2000).

To date, most of the research concerning health status and its determinants has been carried out in terms of mortality. This limits the analysis to negative outcomes and to outcomes that affect a minority of the population. On average, mortality rates for 15- to 39-year-olds in Scotland are 50% higher than in England. However, the cumulative mortality risk over 25 years of age is only 2.4% (Scotland), implying that the survival rate is 97.6%. Comparing this with the cumulative survival rate for England of 98.4% does not provide such a dramatic contrast. Among the problems in trying to refocus the analysis on health rather than death is the fact that in surveys most people declare themselves as having good health and suitable sources of health measures or morbidity data are scarce. This chapter explores the contribution that can be made by using data from the British Household Panel Survey (BHPS) and the extended Scottish sample.

The BHPS has not been widely used to explore health-related issues[2]. This limited use of the BPHS may be explained in part by the nature of the health measures that have been included. The General Health Questionnaire (GHQ-12), which is included in all waves of the BHPS and therefore both waves of the extended Scottish panel, was devised as a screening instrument for diagnosable psychiatric disorders. As such, it is restricted in its definition of health. Another recognised scale that is used, the Activities of Daily Living (ADL), is only asked of respondents aged 65+. All waves of the panel have included questions on specific health problems relating to a variety of clinical and functional issues, but these do not appear to be scaled in any way.

A number of other measures of health status are included in the BHPS. Questions about limitations that health places on activities are asked in all waves, questions on energy and activity are asked in some waves and a single question about health status in the last 12 months is asked in every wave. In 1999, these questions were asked in a slightly different format through the incorporation of the SF-36 generic health status indicator. This is a shortened form (SF) of a 245-item questionnaire (Medical Outcomes Study). Health status is measured on eight dimensions:

- *Physical functioning* (PF) relating to limitations on specific activities due to health.
- *Role limitations* (RLP) in the past four weeks due to *physical* health problems and relating to work or other regular daily activities.
- *Bodily pain* (BP) experienced in the past four weeks and its impact on work or housework.
- *Social functioning* (SF) based on the extent to which physical or emotional health has interfered with normal social activities in the past four weeks.
- *General mental health* (GMH) in the past four weeks.
- *Role limitations* (RLE) in the past four weeks due to *emotional* problems and relating to work or other regular daily activities.
- *Vitality, energy or fatigue* (VEF) in the past four weeks.
- *General health perceptions* (GHP).

The SF-36 measure has been extensively tested for reliability and validity. For self-reported health change (item 2 in the SF-36 questionnaire), end of scale problems have been reported (that is, reporting better health when it has worsened and vice versa). The SF-36 correlates well with a number of other established health measures and has been widely used in health service research and health economics. The eight component scores can be combined to produce two summary scores for physical (PCS) and mental (MCS) health.

The inclusion of the SF-36 data in the BHPS offers scope to explore the relationship between this measure of current health status and factors that have previously been demonstrated to be related to excess mortality. The aims of this analysis are to examine the extent to which lifestyle and life circumstances impact on current health status and to identify differences between Scotland and England.

Previous studies using BHPS health data

A search of electronic databases was carried out to identify studies that had used the BHPS[3]. None of the published studies retrieved had used SF-36 as an outcome measure, reflecting its relatively recent inclusion in the Panel, and none had used the extended Scottish sample.

Three studies had used mortality as the outcome measure, relating this to other data in the BHPS dataset, such as area of residence at birth and migration patterns (Brindlecombe et al, 1999, 2000), or income and the organisation of health care provision (Klein and Unger, 2001). Chandola (2000) compared different measures of social class for use in analysing social inequalities in mortality. Other studies have used the GHQ-12 data to examine the effects of unemployment and low pay (Theodossiou, 1998), and mortgage debt (Nettleton and Burrows, 1998), while GHQ-12 and other health measures have been used in relation to poverty and income (Benzeval et al, 2000; Benzeval and Judge, 2001). The most interesting findings were that long-term income is more important than current income, reductions in income appear to have more effect than increases and controlling for initial health status reduces but does not eliminate the association between income and health (Benzeval and Judge, 2001). A further study used both GHQ-12 and self-assessed health as independent variables, to explore their effect on wages (Contoyannis and Rice, 2001). Finally, there is a group of studies that has looked at smoking behaviour (Graham and Der, 1999a, 1999b, 1999c; Clark and Etilé, 2002) and the health risk behaviour of adolescents (Bergmann and Scott, 2001).

Methods

In this chapter, the data analysed are all from the 1999 wave of the BHPS, including the first year of the extended Scottish sample. The analysis was restricted to a single year, as SF-36 questions have only been asked in this one wave to date. Inclusion of data from previous waves relating to other items such as income was not possible for the extended Scottish sample.

Data were included for adults aged 18-65, excluding proxy responses. The basic sample sizes were 2,641 (Scotland) and 6,849 (England), although non-responses to particular questions will reduce the sample in specific instances. The age range was selected to provide in terms of an analysis focused on health, a parallel to the issue of premature mortality. Where mean SF-36 scores are reported, these are weighted means using the cross-sectional weights. Means are calculated and compared for Scotland and England based on different subgroups to reflect smoking characteristics, educational qualifications and employment status. Income and health are analysed by comparing the percentages of people with poor health in high- and low-income groups. The definition used for poor health is a score in the lowest 30% of the distribution. The income measure used is household equivalent income before housing costs. Low income is defined as below 60% of the median and high income as above this level.

Individual responses to the SF-36 questions are summed to provide the eight component scores and these are transformed to a scale of 0–100. Higher scores indicate better health and, where necessary, the original item scores are reversed to accord with this interpretation. A weighting system has been devised to convert the eight component scores into two summary scores, the physical component summary (PCS) and the mental component summary (MCS) (Ware et al, 1994). There can be some problems with the interpretation of these summary scores (Taft et al, 2001; Ware and Kosinski, 2001) and they are generally reported alongside the individual component scores rather than replacing them. This allows the whole health profile to be taken into account. However, the summary scores are used in isolation for the analysis of income and health because the distributions of the individual component scores are not amenable to division by percentiles.

Results

SF-36 measures

Comparisons of mean SF-36 scores for England and Scotland identify no significant differences (Figure 7.1). This finding is consistent with the similarities in self-reported health status found in other surveys. Most adult respondents in Scotland (age 16-74) rate their health as good or very good (77%) and only 6% report having bad or very bad health (Shaw et al, 2000, table 11.14). Comparable results for England are 76% good or very good health and 6% bad or very bad health. The similar question in the BHPS results in only 4.8% of the sample responding that they have poor health.

Figure 7.1: Comparison of mean SF-36 scores: Scotland and England

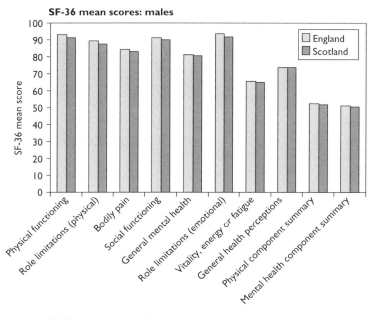

SF-36 mean scores: males

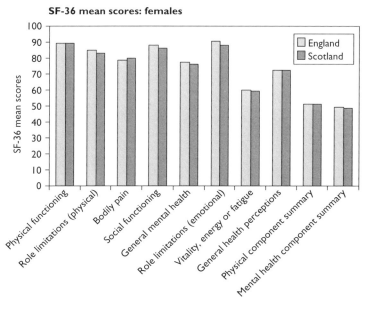

SF-36 mean scores: females

Smoking

Figure 7.2 compares the mean SF-36 scores for current smokers and those who have never smoked. The scores are lower for current smokers on all the components of SF-36 and the differences in mean scores are all significant. However, when it comes to comparing Scotland with England, mean scores for current smokers in Scotland are lower than England (significant for five out of eight of the components), whereas non-smokers in Scotland have the same or better scores for six out of eight of the components (although none of the differences are significant).

Note that the difference between Scotland and England for smokers on the MCS is significant. Although this summary score is intended to reflect mental health, it is more highly correlated with physical component scores (Taft et al, 2001). Thus, it appears that the effect of smoking on current health is greater in Scotland but those who have never smoked have similar levels of health[4]. Data from the Scottish Health Survey (Shaw et al, 2000) show that a higher proportion of cigarette smokers in Scotland than England smoke 20+ cigarettes daily: 46% compared with 36% (males); 34% compared with 27% (females). Average weekly consumption per smoker is higher in Scotland than England: 126 cigarettes compared with 106 (males); 107 compared with 91 (females).

Figure 7.2: Effect of smoking status on mean SF-36 scores: Scotland and England

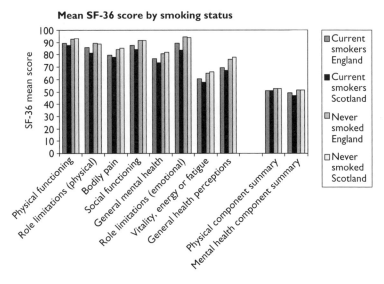

Income

The relationship between income and health was examined by comparing the proportion of people experiencing poor health according to whether their household equivalent income (before housing costs) was above 60% of the median (high income) or below 60% of the median (low income). Poor health was defined as being in the bottom 30% of the distribution of SF-36 summary component scores. Figures 7.3 and 7.4 present the results by country and gender for physical health and for mental health, respectively. There is a consistent finding that the percentage of people with poor health is higher in the low-income groups and these results are all statistically significant[5].

The proportions of each income group having poor health are mostly very similar for England and Scotland, although low income for males in England appears to have more impact on the proportion having poor physical health than in Scotland. There is also a bigger difference in the proportions with poor health for both health measures for females in Scotland compared with England.

Figure 7.3: Relationship between income and poor physical health

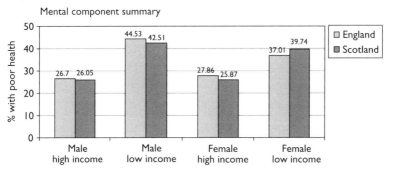

Figure 7.4: Relationship between income and poor mental health

Education

Figure 7.5 compares mean SF-36 scores for respondents having no educational qualifications and those having the highest qualifications. The differences are quite marked and are significant. By contrast, the comparison between England and Scotland within these groups gives results in differing directions and only one is statistically significant (better general mental health score for those with no qualifications in England compared with Scotland). Note, however, the significantly lower MCS for Scotland for those with no qualifications: there is a gradient in the results, showing a fairly consistent increase with level of qualification, although by far the largest difference is between those with no qualifications and those with O-levels or equivalent.

Employment status

Table 7.1 compares the SF-36 mean scores for different employment status. There is no significant difference in scores for employed and self-employed people. The unemployed have lower scores in all but two cases and the differences are significant on all components of SF-36 for Scotland and five out of eight components for England. Retired people mostly have worse health than the unemployed[6]. Few of the results are statistically significant. Unsurprisingly, those classed as long-term sick report the worst health scores and they are significantly

Figure 7.5: Self-reported health by level of education

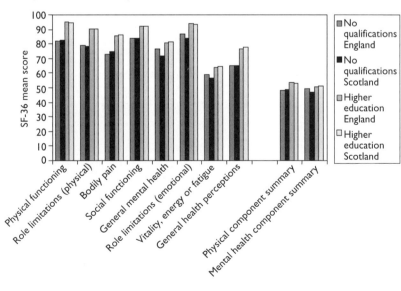

Table 7.1: SF-36 mean scores by employment status, Scotland and England

		Self-employed	Employed	Unemployed	Retired	Long-term sick
Physical functioning	Scotland	96.10 (94.58-97.61)	95.51 (94.89-96.12)	88.42 (85.43-91.40)	74.89 (70.46-79.32)	46.92 (41.39-52.45)
	England	95.09 (94.18-96.01)	94.93 (94.57-95.29)	92.20 (90.32-94.09)	76.61 (74.04-79.19)	44.23 (40.33-48.12)
Role limitations (physical)	Scotland	93.35 (90.26-96.44)	91.59 (90.25-92.92)	81.81 (75.20-88.42)	71.46 (64.90-78.02)	38.12 (30.52-45.71)
	England	90.84 (88.52-93.17)	91.20 (90.39-92.00)	92.41 (88.98-95.85)	73.24 (69.14-77.35)	40.17 (34.72-45.62)
Bodily pain	Scotland	87.40 (84.47-90.33)	86.32 (85.11-87.53)	77.65 (72.38-82.92)	72.87 (68.01-77.73)	42.48 (36.89-48.07)
	England	84.69 (82.80-86.58)	84.54 (83.84-85.24)	83.06 (79.77-86.34)	72.06 (69.18-74.95)	45.01 (41.10-48.92)
Social functioning	Scotland	92.13 (89.53-94.73)	92.63 (91.68-93.58)	82.95 (78.47-87.43)	85.02 (81.02-89.01)	48.63 (42.50-54.76)
	England	93.48 (92.12-94.84)	92.50 (91.97-93.02)	88.05 (84.94-91.16)	83.86 (81.23-86.49)	51.92 (47.83-56.00)
General mental health	Scotland	83.84 (81.81-85.87)	80.96 (80.12-81.80)	70.02 (66.31-73.74)	77.77 (74.55-80.98)	58.60 (54.13-63.06)
	England	83.21 (81.98-84.43)	81.09 (80.59-81.58)	72.37 (69.42-75.33)	79.27 (77.29-81.25)	61.89 (58.98-64.79)
Role limitations (emotional)	Scotland	94.13 (90.97-97.30)	95.58 (94.59-96.58)	80.54 (74.11-86.97)	85.03 (79.69-90.37)	53.31 (45.03-61.58)
	England	95.21 (93.40-97.03)	94.99 (94.39-95.59)	89.79 (85.81-93.77)	87.32 (84.23-90.40)	59.75 (53.81-65.70)
Vitality, energy or fatigue	Scotland	69.19 (65.98-72.41)	64.94 (63.91-65.96)	57.54 (53.79-61.29)	59.04 (54.89-63.19)	34.53 (30.49-38.56)
	England	66.16 (64.37-67.95)	64.54 (63.92-65.16)	64.57 (61.74-67.38)	60.48 (58.18-62.78)	36.92 (34.13-39.70)
General health perception	Scotland	79.97 (77.19-82.75)	77.92 (76.92-78.92)	65.83 (61.79-69.86)	64.59 (60.49-68.69)	32.85 (28.48-37.22)
	England	77.06 (75.42-78.71)	76.75 (76.18-77.31)	70.13 (67.12-73.14)	65.38 (62.93-67.83)	32.47 (29.71-35.24)

worse on all components. There is a marked tendency for Scotland to have better health scores among the self-employed and employed and worse health among the unemployed, retired and long-term sick but only two of the differences are significant.

Conclusion

Differences in self-reported health measures are not as great as the difference in age-standardised mortality rates between Scotland and England. In large part, this is explained by the very small numbers included in mortality data. The SF-36 data provided in the BHPS offer an opportunity to examine in some detail the relationships between validated measures of health status and aspects of lifestyle and life circumstances in Scotland and England.

Overall, it is found that health measures are similar for the population aged 18-65. However, further analysis provides some interesting insights. The effects on health of factors such as smoking, income, education and employment status, all of which have been well investigated with respect to mortality, are confirmed by the data analysed in this chapter. In general, the relationship between income and health appears to be highly significant. Income is related to both education and employment status and may also be capturing effects due to these factors. However, the issue of causality in these relationships requires further investigation.

The results also reveal that lifestyle and life circumstances may have a differential impact on health in Scotland and England. Thus, for instance, smoking has a greater negative effect on the health of those in Scotland who smoke compared to their English counterparts, possibly because in Scotland those who do smoke, smoke more. If, however, the unemployed in Scotland have worse health than their counterparts in England, other potential explanations need to be explored, such as the average duration of unemployment in the two countries. The tendency for positive life circumstances to produce better health measures in Scotland than in England, while negative life circumstances produce worse health measures, suggests that simple comparisons of average health states between the countries may mask significant but offsetting differences at either end of the distribution. In general, the findings suggest that the examination of health differences between Scotland and England should consider both the different frequency of health damaging or enhancing factors and the differential impact of those factors.

The analysis has been restricted by the availability of data and would benefit from further development. The potential usefulness of the component summary scores requires further examination and a method has been proposed for translating a subset of the items into a single utility-based score (Brazier et al, 2002). These developments might simplify the analysis of multi-factorial effects on health status. A larger sample size would be more likely to confirm the significance of differences identified and would also facilitate the analysis to establish multi-factorial effects.

Longitudinal analysis would allow for examination of changes in SF-36 scores and the importance of cumulative effects, such as persistent rather than transitory low income and duration of unemployment. The potential for longitudinal analysis will emerge as the extended Scottish sample continues to accumulate in future years, and this will also increase the sample size available. However, the utility of the panel for health research will also be enhanced if the inclusion of the SF-36 as one of the health measures is repeated. The relationship between health and lifestyle and life circumstances is complex. While other databases exist to explore certain parts of this relationship, the strength of the BHPS lies in its wide range of longitudinal data.

Notes

[1] Funding from the Chief Scientist Office, Scottish Executive Health Department is gratefully acknowledged. The views expressed are those of the authors and not the funding body.

[2] A search of electronic databases identified 22 references to published studies in this area, although in some cases there was more than one publication arising from the same study.

[3] One-hundred-and-one items were identified. Titles and abstracts were then examined to identify the subset of references relating to health (22 items). Some of the studies were concerned with issues such as methodology, use of health services and psychiatric illness. These are not discussed further here.

[4] Results for ex-smokers lie between the two extremes in all cases. Ex-smokers in Scotland have lower scores on six out of eight components, but none of the differences are significant.

[5] The analysis was also carried out with London excluded from the England sample, but this did not affect the results.

[6] There are five exceptions out of 16 results. Note that this category consists mostly of early retirers, given the age restriction.

References

Abbott, P., McDonald, M. and Sapsford, R. (1999) 'Women and health checks: making sense of differential uptake', *Critical Public Health*, vol 9, pp 233-50.

Benzeval, M. and Judge, K. (2001) 'Income and health: the time dimension', *Social Science and Medicine*, vol 52, pp 1371-90.

Benzeval, M., Judge, K., Johnson, P. and Taylor, J. (2000) 'Relationships between health, income and poverty over time: an analysis using BHPS and NCDS data', in J. Bradshaw and R. Sainsbury (eds) *Experiencing poverty*, Aldershot: Ashgate, pp 78-101.

Bergmann, M.M. and Scott, J. (2001) 'Young adolescents' wellbeing and health-risk behaviours: gender and socio-economic differences', *Journal of Adolescence*, vol 24, pp 183-97.

Brazier, J., Roberts, J. and Deverill, M. (2002) 'The estimation of a preference-based measure of health from the SF-36', *Journal of Health Economics*, vol 21, pp 271-92.

Brindlecombe, N., Dorling, D. and Shaw, M. (1999) 'Mortality and migration in Britain, first results from the British Household Panel Survey', *Social Science and Medicine*, vol 49, pp 981-8.

Brindlecombe, N., Dorling, D. and Shaw, M. (2000) 'Migration and geographical inequalities in health in Britain', *Social Science and Medicine*, vol 50, pp 861-78.

Chandola, T. (2000) 'Social class differences in mortality using the new UK National Statistics Socio-Economic Classification', *Social Science and Medicine*, vol 50, pp 641-9.

Clark, A. and Etilé, F. (2002) 'Do health changes affect smoking? Evidence from British Panel data', *Journal of Health Economics*, vol 21, pp 533-62.

Contoyannis, P. and Rice, N. (2001) 'The impact of health on wages: evidence from the British Household Panel Survey', *Empirical Economics*, vol 26, pp 599-622.

Graham, H. and Der, G. (1999a) 'Patterns and predictors of tobacco consumption among women', *Health Education Research*, vol 14, pp 611-18.

Graham, H. and Der, G. (1999b) 'Patterns and predictors of smoking cessation among British women', *Health Promotion International*, vol 14, no 3, pp 231-40.

Graham, H. and Der, G. (1999c) 'Influences on women's smoking status – the contribution of socioeconomic status in adolescence and adulthood', *European Journal of Public Health*, vol 9, pp 137-41.

Klein, T. and Unger, R. (2001) 'Income, health and mortality in West-Germany, Great Britain, and the USA', *Kolner Zeitschrift fur Soziologie und Sozialpsychologie*, vol 53, pp 96-111.

Nettleton, S. and Burrows, R. (1998) 'Mortgage debt, insecure home ownership and health: an exploratory analysis', *Sociology of Health and Illness*, vol 20, pp 731-53.

Scottish Executive (2000) *Our national health: A plan for action, a plan for change*, Edinburgh: The Stationery Office.

Shaw, A., McMunn, A. and Field, J. (eds) (2000) *The Scottish Health Survey 1998*, Edinburgh: The Stationery Office.

Taft, C., Karlsson, J. and Sullivan, M. (2001) 'Do SF-36 summary component scores accurately summarize subscale scores?', *Quality of Life Research*, vol 10, pp 395-404.

Theodossiou, I. (1998) 'The effects of low-pay and unemployment on psychological well-being: a logistic regression approach', *Journal of Health Economics*, vol 17, pp 85-104.

Ware, J.E. and Kosinski, M. (2001) 'Interpreting SF-36 summary health measures: a response', *Quality of Life Research*, vol 10, pp 405-13.

Ware, J.E., Kosinski, M. and Keller, S.D. (1994) *SF-36 physical and mental health summary scales – A user's manual*, Boston, MA: New England Medical Centre, The Health Institute.

EIGHT

Trends in absolute poverty

Vernon Gayle, Gregor Jack and Robert E. Wright

Introduction

Unlike in the US, there is no 'official' poverty line in the UK. Although the Scottish Executive acknowledges that there is a "poverty problem", it has not introduced a poverty line that could be used to direct their policies aimed at poverty reduction. The UK government does produce 'low income' statistics based on the so-called 'Households Below Average Income' (HBAI) approach (for example, DWP, 2003). However, the HBAI reports do not routinely include estimates broken down by region. In addition, there are well-known problems with the approach that it uses, which has led to a growing dissatisfaction with it among poverty researchers.

There is also no official poverty line in the European Union (EU). However, there has been a series of European poverty programmes aimed at comparing poverty across the member states. Much of this comparative research has been carried out using data from the European Community Household Panel study, of which the British Household Panel Survey (BHPS) is a part, and utilises a poverty line set at 60% of the median equivalised disposable household income. There is a growing view that the EU should have an official poverty line and that it should be set at this level. In several member states, this poverty line is de facto official.

The purpose of this chapter is to examine trends in absolute poverty in England and Scotland in the 1990s using data from nine waves of the BHPS. In the BHPS, disposable income is not directly collected. However, it is estimated on a regular basis from gross income and other information collected in the survey (see Bardasi et al, 2002). With these variables, it is not only possible to replicate the HBAI estimates but also to explore with much rigour a variety of other interpretations and measures of poverty.

The BHPS also allows one to extend the analysis of poverty to an exploration of what can be termed the 'dynamics of poverty'. Since the data is longitudinal in nature, and the same households and people are interviewed through time, it is possible to use the data to study movements into and out of poverty (see, for example, Cappellari and Jenkins, 2002). Since this shifts the focus away from the incidence of poverty at a given point in time towards changes in poverty over time (poverty transitions), it is also possible to comment on the duration of poverty (subject to a set of assumptions being made). This is a major development since any policy aimed at poverty reduction must not only take into consideration the incidence of poverty but also the length of time individuals have been poor and are expected to be poor. Finally, over the past decade, there has been a rapid expansion in the statistical techniques needed to analyse the dynamic nature of poverty (see Jenkins, 2000, for a comprehensive review of these methods).

One of the problems with using the BHPS to explore the dynamics of poverty in Scotland are the small Scottish sub-samples collected in the first eight waves. From a practical point of view, the number of Scottish individuals in these waves is too small to be used to examine movement into and out of poverty. However, this is no longer the case. Beginning with the 1999 wave, there has been a large increase in the size of the Scottish sub-sample (Laurie and Wright, 2000). At the time of writing, the disposable income variables mentioned above were only available for one of these enhanced waves (1999). Therefore, it is not possible at this point in time to study poverty transitions in Scotland with much confidence and hence comment on any differences in the duration of poverty between Scotland and England (although such work is planned for the future).

Identifying the poor

If we define economic well-being as the ratio of economic resources to need, then an individual is 'poor' if their available resources do not meet their needs at some minimum level. As with most empirical studies of poverty, we employ disposable equivalent household income as the empirical counterpart to economic well-being. The household's economic resources are assumed to be determined by its total weekly disposable income, which is equal to gross income from all sources minus National Insurance contributions, taxes and other mandatory deductions. This is the same concept of disposable household income used in most of the comparative EU studies mentioned earlier in this chapter.

The household's needs are assumed to be a function of the number and age of its members. It is also assumed that there is equal sharing of resources among household members. Disposable income is standardised for differences in household composition using equivalence scales. The particular scale used is the so-called 'modified OECD equivalence scale'. The weights are:

- first adult=1.0;
- second and subsequent 'adults' (age 14+)=0.5;
- children (age <14)=0.3.

It is again worth noting that these are the same scales used in much of EU comparative poverty research referred to earlier.

A household is poor if its disposable equivalent income falls below the poverty line. Of course, the key question is at what level should the poverty line be set? As already mentioned, EU comparative research is based on a poverty line set at 60% of the median equivalent income. In this chapter, we adopt the same standard. Finally, an individual is assumed to be poor if they reside in a 'poor household'. Therefore, we are not taking into account the possibility that a poor individual can reside in a 'non-poor' household. This is less than satisfactory given there is considerable research suggesting that resources are not always equally shared among all household members.

The problems associated with choosing a poverty line are heightened if one is interested in examining changes in poverty over time. The key choice the researcher has to make is whether or not the poverty line is allowed to change over time with the average living standard in the society. If poverty is viewed as an 'absolute' concept, the poverty line is defined to be independent of the average living standard in the society. In this case, the poverty line moves only with changes in the average price level (that is, it is only adjusted for inflation). On the other hand, if poverty is viewed as a 'relative' concept, the poverty line is defined in relation to the average standard of living in the society. In this case, the poverty line is adjusted for both inflation and the growth in average income.

Both concepts of poverty have their merits. The poverty estimates presented in this chapter are based on an absolute poverty line. The poverty line is set at 60% of the median equivalent income in 2000. This gives a poverty line of about £95 per equivalent person per week (in real 2000 £s). Clearly, if an individual were poor in 2000 based on this poverty line then an individual with the same real income in 1991 would also be poor. As Sen points out (1979, p 289), this is a desirable outcome since "there is an irreducible core of absolute deprivation in the notion of poverty". However, this outcome is not guaranteed when poverty estimates are based on a relative poverty line, since the poverty threshold changes over time. Furthermore, it seems that if one is trying to construct and evaluate policies aimed at reducing poverty then there should be a target set that does not move. Indeed, there is considerable debate and little agreement in the poverty literature about whether an absolute or relative poverty line should be used to evaluate changes in poverty over time (see Sen, 1979; Townsend, 1985; and more recently Brady, 2002, for a precise discussion of both sides of this debate).

Analysis

Figure 8.1 shows the changes in the rates of absolute poverty for Scotland and England in the period 1991-99. It shows the percentage of individuals living in poor households. Several points about this figure are worth making. First, the small Scottish sub-samples in the 1991-98 waves cause the estimates to fluctuate considerably and confirm that it would be risky to use these waves to examine movements into and out of poverty on a year-to-year basis. Second, it appears that even with these fluctuations, absolute poverty has declined in both nations. The data suggest that in 1991 the rate was 23.4% in both Scotland and England. By 1999, the rate had declined to 16.1% in Scotland and to 13.9% in England. Third, since the 2000 estimate is based on the enhanced Scottish sub-sample, it seems reasonable to

Figure 8.1: Absolute poverty rates (EU) (1991-99)

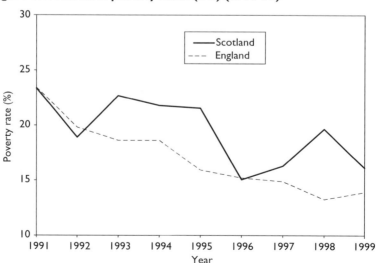

report that the difference of 2.2 percentage points is statistically significant (as is demonstrated later in this chapter). This suggests that, in 2000, absolute poverty was about 16% higher in Scotland. Fourth, we have also calculated absolute poverty rates based on the HBAI approach (not reported here). Although the rates of poverty differ slightly, the trends over time are very similar to those shown in Figure 8.1.

In order to explore the nature of the poverty difference between England and Scotland suggested by the raw data, a logit regression model is used. The dependent variable in this model is a dummy variable coded '1' if the individual is 'poor' and coded '0' if they are not. This model is fit using the pooled sample of 40,795 individuals so uses information for the whole of the 1991-2000 period. The independent variables included in the model to 'explain' differences in the probability of being poor follow closely the list suggested by Cappellari and Jenkins (2002):

- AGEHH = age of household head (measured in years);
- AGEHH2 = age of household head squared;
- FEMALE = household head is female;
- NOQUALS = household head has no qualifications beyond basic school leaving;
- WORK = household head is employed;
- ETHNIC = household head is a member of an ethnic minority;
- WORKERS = number of workers in household;
- HHSIZE = size of the household;
- HHSIZE2 = size of the household squared.

The model also includes a dummy variable, SCOT, coded '1' if the individual resides in Scotland and coded '0' if he/she resides in England and a linear time trend, *t*. This list is not meant to be exhaustive but such factors have been shown to be correlated with poverty and in our view do represent a reasonable starting point.

Standard regression techniques, such as the logit model, are not generally appropriate for the analysis of pooled data. The main reason being that the presence of repeated observations is likely to violate the key assumption that the observations are independent, which affects statistical inference. One way of dealing with this problem is to include in the specification an individual-specific error. More specifically, the model that we estimate is a 'logistic mixture model' and is fitted using the software package SABRE (Barry et al, 1998). The model is essentially a logit regression that includes an individual-specific normally distributed random error term. More generally, this estimator is a 'random effects' model where the key assumption is that the individual-specific errors are not correlated with the included variables. This model explicitly takes into account the dependence across individuals and should help control for unobserved factors that are persistent across individuals.

The estimates of the logit models are shown in Table 8.1. The table gives parameter values and their associated t-statistics. Column A reports a specification that only includes an intercept term and the dummy variable for Scotland/England. This specification is simply a convenient way of testing whether there is a difference in the poverty rate between Scotland and England. The parameter for the SCOT variable has a positive sign and is statistically significant at the 5% level (t=2.1). This

Table 8.1: Logit estimates of absolute poverty

Covariates? Heterogeneity control?	(A) No No	(B) No No	(C) Yes No	(D) Yes No	(E) Yes Yes
AGEHH	–	–	–0.066	–0.066	–0.073
			(1.7)	(12.7)	(7.0)
AGEHH2	–	–	0.0005	0.0004	0.0005
			(9.5)	(9.5)	(4.5)
FEMALE	–	–	0.054	0.055	0.012
			(1.5)	(1.5)	(0.1)
NOQUALS	–	–	0.458	0.458	0.602
			(12.1)	(12.1)	(7.2)
WORK	–	–	–1.118	–1.118	–1.649
			(14.4)	(14.4)	(15.1)
ETHNIC	–	–	0.450	0.493	0.387
			(2.5)	(2.5)	(1.3)
WORKERS	–	–	–0.966	–0.967	–1.329
			(18.7)	(18.7)	(18.5)
HHSIZE	–	–	–0.752	–0.752	–0.989
			(14.7)	(14.7)	(10.4)
HHSIZE2	–	–	0.080	0.080	0.111
			(10.4)	(10.4)	(7.8)
SCOT	0.100[a]	0.082	0.085	0.046	0.140
	(2.1)	(0.9)	(1.7)	(0.5)	(0.9)
t	–	–0.066	–	–0.067	–0.098
		(10.3)		(9.6)	(9.7)
SCOT × t	–	–0.016	–	0.009	0.007
		(1.0)		(0.5)	(0.3)
Intercept	–2.06	1.80	2.06	2.06	2.30
	(123.2)	(60.6)	(13.6)	(13.6)	(8.2)
θ[b]	–	–	–	–	2.018
					(41.8)

Notes: [a] Ratio of parameter to its standard error in parentheses.
[b] Standard deviation of the mixing distribution.

finding suggests that at this level of confidence, there appears to be a difference between Scotland and England. The magnitude suggests that the difference (which is an average for the period) was in the order of about 10%. It also provides further support for the speculative remarks made above relating to Figure 8.1.

Column B provides some information on how this difference has changed through time. This specification not only includes the SCOT variable but also the linear time trend, t, and an interaction between the SCOT variable and the time trend (SCOT x t). This specification allows one to tentatively answer three questions:

1. Was poverty in the 1990s higher in Scotland than England?
2. Did poverty decline in this period in both Scotland and in England?
3. Did poverty decline at a faster rate in Scotland than in England (or vice versa)?

Given that we have two variables involved in an interaction it is not strictly correct just to base statistical significance on any of the variables by their individual t-statistics. The appropriate test is a comparison of the likelihoods of the models with and without the interaction. This test suggests that the answer to the first two questions asked earlier is 'Yes'. However, it is not possible to conclude with any confidence that the rate of decline differed much between Scotland and England.

Column C extends the specification shown in Column A by including the set of control variables discussed earlier in the chapter. We will delay discussing the signs and magnitudes of these variables until later. The important point about this specification is that the poverty difference between Scotland and England is smaller (about 8-9%) when factors that may be determinants of poverty are included as controls. It is also worth noting that the SCOT variable is no longer statistically significant at the 5% level, although it is at the 10% level ($t=1.7$). Column D in a similar manner extends the specification shown in Column B. This specification confirms that poverty has declined in both Scotland and England but there is little difference in the overall rate and little difference in the rate of decline.

Column E is the most elaborate specification. It takes the specification shown in Column D and attempts to control for unobserved heterogeneity by applying the logistic mixture model described earlier in this chapter. The parameter 'θ' shown is highly statistically significant ($t=41.8$) suggesting that there is considerable heterogeneity across individuals not accounted for by the included control variables. However, with respect to the three key variables, SCOT, t and SCOT x *t*, the findings are very similar. Poverty has declined in both Scotland and England but there is little difference in the overall rate of poverty and little difference in the rate of decline.

A comparison of the parameters of the specifications that include control variables (Columns C to E) suggests that most of these variables are correlated with poverty in the expected direction. Most are statistically significant and there is some consistency across the different specifications. However, there are some differences – perhaps troubling differences – worth noting. There appears to be a U-shaped relationship between age of the household head (AGEHH and AGEHH2) and the probability of being poor. Likewise, there is a U-shaped relationship between household size (HHSIZE and HHSIZE2) and the probability of being poor. The probability of being poor is lower if the household head is employed (WORK) and declines as the number of workers in the household increases (WORKERS). It is also higher if the household head has no educational qualification beyond basic school leaving (NOQUALS).

Somewhat surprising there is no strong evidence suggesting that the probability of being poor is higher in households that are headed by women (FEMALE). In none of the specifications shown in Table 8.1 is this variable statistically significant at even the generous 10% level and this is especially true in the model that attempts to control for unobserved heterogeneity ($t=0.1$). A clear difference across the specifications emerges with respect to the ethnicity of the household head (ETHNIC). In the specifications that do not attempt to control for unobserved heterogeneity (Columns C and D), this variable is statistically significant ($t=2.5$ in both cases). The positive sign suggests the probability of being poor is higher if one resides in a household headed by a member of a minority ethnic group. However, this effect is no longer statistically significant in the model that attempts to control for unobserved heterogeneity (see Column E) – it is hard to identify the effect of such a time-invariant variable while also controlling for time-invariant individual residual heterogeneity. It is also likely that the relationship between ethnicity and poverty is not adequately captured by the inclusion of a simple dummy variable for all ethnic groups.

Conclusion

The purpose of this chapter was to examine trends in absolute poverty using data from nine waves of the BHPS. Given the relatively small Scottish sub-samples in the first nine waves, no attempt was made to model transitions into and out of poverty. Such analyses are feasible for waves nine and onwards given that the size of the Scottish sub-samples has been increased significantly. However, an estimation method was used that does take advantage of the panel nature of the data by attempting to control for persistent differences across individuals. The main conclusions that emerge from this very limited analysis is that based on a poverty line widely used in comparative EU poverty research, absolute poverty was higher in Scotland than in England in the 1990s. The analysis also suggests that absolute poverty declined in both nations in this period. Finally, once factors that are correlated with poverty (and may in fact be determinants of poverty) are controlled for the difference found in the raw data effectively disappears. This suggests that the observed difference may be simply one of composition, with Scotland having a large proportion of it population with characteristics that increase the probability of being poor. Future research with the BHPS will be able to shed considerable light on this hypothesis.

References

Bardasi, E., Jenkins, S.P. and Rigg, J.A. (2002) *British Household Panel Survey derived current and annual net household income variables, waves 1-9, 1991-2000*, Colchester: Institute for Social and Economic Research, University of Essex.

Barry, J., Francis, B., Davies, R.B. and Stott, D. (1998) *SABRE Software for the analysis of binary recurrent events – A user's guide*, Lancaster: Centre for Applied Statistics, University of Lancaster.

Brady, D. (2002) *Rethinking the sociological measurement of poverty*, Working Paper no 264, Luxembourg: Luxembourg Income Study, Differdange.

Cappellari, L. and Jenkins, S.P. (2002) 'Who stays poor? Who becomes poor? Evidence from the British Household Panel Survey', *Economic Journal*, vol 112, pp C60-C67.

DWP (Department for Work and Pensions) (2003) *Households below average income, 1994/95-2001/02*, London: DWP.

Jenkins, S.P. (2000) 'Modelling household income dynamics', *Journal of Population Economics*, vol 13, pp 529-67.

Laurie, H.M. and Wright, R.E. (2000) 'The Scottish Household Panel Survey', *Scottish Journal of Political Economy*, vol 47, pp 337-9.

Sen, A.K. (1979) 'Issues in the measurement of poverty', *Scandinavian Journal of Economics*, vol 81, pp 285-307.

Sen, A.K. (1983) 'Poor, relatively speaking', *Oxford Economics Papers*, vol 35, pp 153-69.

Townsend, P. (1985) 'A sociological approach to the measurement of poverty – a rejoinder to Professor Amartya Sen', *Oxford Economics Papers*, vol 35, pp 659-68.

NINE

Income inequality

David Bell and Gregor Jack

Introduction

Scotland has a highly unequal distribution of income both by international and historical standards. The UK as a whole experienced a substantial increase in inequality in the 1980s and 1990s and the experience in Scotland largely mirrored that trend. Nevertheless, there have been some significant differences in the evolution of income inequality between Scotland and the rest of the UK (RGB), particularly since the mid-1990s.

The British Household Panel Survey (BHPS) offers a unique insight into these changes, particularly due to its ability to follow income variations among the same group of individuals through time. Unlike the Family Resources Survey, Family Expenditure Survey and Scottish Household Survey, it is not restricted to regular snapshots of different groups of individuals. The potential policy benefits of using longitudinal data are now recognised by UK government. They are succinctly paraphrased by HM Treasury (1999):

> In the past, analysis of these factors has focused on static, snapshot pictures of where people are at a particular point in time. Snapshot data can lead people to focus on the symptoms of the problem rather than addressing the underlying processes that lead people to have or be denied opportunities. To understand why people's life chances differ, it is important to look for the events and experiences that create opportunity and those which create barriers, and to use this as a focus for policy action.

With only two waves of the boosted sample for Scotland currently available, and only one complete wave of income data, it is too early to construct dynamics models of *net* income for Scotland of the form that Cappellari and Jenkins (2002) have done for the UK as a whole.

We therefore supplement the BHPS data with data from another longitudinal survey: the New Earnings Survey (NES).

In the future, it may be possible to estimate transition models, which are able to predict levels of 'state dependence' in low-income states. That is, conditional on a household's observed and unobserved characteristics, the models estimate how much the probability of having a low income in one year is affected by the experience of low income in previous years. This is important for policy making since it focuses attention on the need to prevent individuals either becoming poor or returning to a state of poverty, rather than simply supporting them while they are poor. We return to this issue at the end of this chapter. Before this, however, we examine several issues relating to trends in inequality in Scotland and comparisons of the characteristics of inequality in Scotland with that in the RGB in relation to economic activity, age and educational attainment. We also consider whether the so-called 'tartan' tax would be an effective redistributive instrument, given current levels of inequality in Scotland. However, we begin by reviewing some of the key issues that have been highlighted in the extensive literature on inequality and that are relevant to the debate in Scotland.

Income inequality: a review of issues

Interest in income inequality usually stems from an interest in variation in living standards. Discussions of income inequality and poverty are closely linked. Where a *relative* definition of poverty is used, such as 60% of the median wage (this is the most commonly cited definition of poverty by the UK government), an income distribution with a relatively high mean but also high levels of inequality often implies higher levels of poverty than may be the case with a low average income that is more narrowly spread.

Income inequality has also been associated with variations in standards of health, levels of crime and social exclusion inter alia. If such linkages can be convincingly established, then the economic processes that underlie variations in income inequality may have profound, and often unforeseen, social consequences. Issues of disparities in living standards and health are not the only motivation for studying inequality, however. There is a growing literature on the relationship between economic inequality and economic development. For example, a number of arguments have been put forward to suggest that *greater inequality* is associated with *lower growth*, including:

- greater inequality implies a poorer median voter, higher marginal tax rates and disincentive effects on labour supply;
- inequality implies failure of the poor to realise their potential due to capital-market imperfections;
- greater inequality may impose greater social costs on society (for example the cost of dealing with increased crime), which inhibit a country's growth potential.

This literature has yet to produce conclusive results. Hence, we concentrate in this chapter on the most common motivation for the study of inequality: variation in living standards. This focus suggests that we should concentrate on:

- net income rather than gross income, since living standards are determined by take-home pay and benefits, rather than gross income;
- household income rather than individual income. Apparently poor individuals may have rich partners and hence data on individual income may be a misleading guide to living standards. On the other hand, concentrating on household income implicitly suggests that the distribution of income *within* households is relatively even, so that all members of the household are able to enjoy comparable living standards. This assumption may be incorrect (see, for example, Browning et al, 1994).

To compare households of different size, some adjustment must be made for the number of household members. This is usually done by 'equivalising' income. A value from an 'equivalence scale' is allocated to each household member to reflect his or her resource consumption within the household. Childless couples are taken as the baseline. In our empirical work, the contribution of additional household members is calculated using the McClements Scale, the most commonly used equivalence scale for the UK.

The final adjustment before calculating levels of inequality is to remove housing costs from net household income. This is common practice in official discussions of inequality in the UK. The argument is that variations in living standards should be measured after the deduction of housing costs because individuals have no choice over these and they vary substantially in different parts of the UK. The decision to deduct housing costs thus implicitly assumes that individuals have little choice about the housing costs that they face. This assumption is open to question, particularly for richer families. Where housing is often used as an alternative investment vehicle, the notion that housing costs are inescapable seems hardly compelling.

Nevertheless, we adopt the standard approach and exclude housing costs. Then, having selected a measure of income, the next stage is to select how to calibrate inequality. A succinct resume of the properties of the most frequently used inequality measures is given in Cowell (1995) and Litchfield (1999). These measures typically satisfy a number of axioms that are widely accepted as being useful attributes for inequality measures. They tend to differ in their sensitivity to income transfers across the earnings distribution, but are generally highly correlated when substantial shifts in the income distribution occur. In this chapter, we concentrate on two measures. The first of these is the 90:10 percentile ratio. Ordering income by size, this ratio measures how much richer someone nine tenths of the way up the income distribution is compared to someone only one tenth of the way up. It is a relatively crude but intuitive measure. More sophisticated is the generalised entropy (GE) measure, which is given by:

$$ GE = \frac{1}{\alpha^2 - \alpha} \left[\frac{1}{n} \sum_{i=1}^{n} \left(\frac{y_i}{\bar{y}} \right)^{\alpha} - 1 \right] $$

Here the y_i, $i = 1....n$ are the incomes of the n households in the sample. Mean income is given by $\bar{y}$. Increasing values of the parameter *a* reflect increasing sensitivity to transfers towards the upper end of the income distribution. The value of unity that we adopt gives equal weight to transfers wherever they occur in the distribution. This generalised entropy index has the further property that it is *decomposable*. This means that if the population is divided into a number of subgroups, this index can attribute the *total* rise in inequality to that occurring *between* the subgroups and that occurring *within* subgroups, thus giving additional insights into the composition of inequality.

Recent trends in inequality

Many countries experienced increases in inequality in the 1980s and 1990s. The increases have been particularly pronounced in the UK and US. Figure 9.1 shows inequality measured by the ratio of the 90th to the 10th income percentile from the Luxembourg Income Study for a variety of countries over a selection of recent years. The UK not only experienced one of the largest *increases* in inequality, it also ended the 1990s with one of the highest *levels* of inequality among developed countries.

Figure 9.1: Income inequality: Luxembourg Income Study

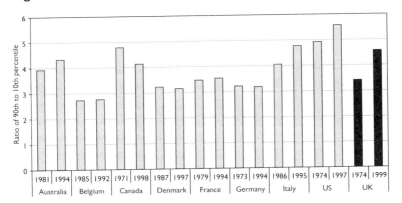

Concentrating on the most recent decades can be misleading. Jenkins (1999) cites five distinct movements in UK inequality since 1961:

- 1961-72, when inequality was fairly constant;
- 1972-78, when it fell;
- 1978-84, when inequality was rising;
- 1984-90, when it was rising faster still;
- 1990-96, when it was roughly constant.

Nevertheless, he argues (1999, p 4):

> The growth in UK income inequality during the 1980s was faster than for virtually all other western industrialised nations, and inequality actually fell for some nations over the period. At the beginning of the 1990s, the degree of income inequality in Britain was nearly the same as in the US. By contrast inequality in the Nordic countries was more like Britain's at the start of the 1960s.

Changes in inequality in the UK have been episodic. They have had no clear linkage to the state of the labour market; during different periods, unemployment and inequality moved together, while at other times they moved apart.

There is a substantial literature on the causes of increases in inequality in the US and UK. Technological change, trade, returns to education and skills and changes in labour market institutions have all been cited as direct or indirect causes of increases in inequality. There is some consensus that part of the increase has been due to relative shifts in demand and supply for skilled and unskilled workers. In relation to

growth in the number of households where no adult of working age was engaged in the labour market. Thus, while the number of mixed households was decreasing by 100,000, there was an overall increase of almost 130,000 working-age households in Scotland. This was focused on households where either *all* adults work or where *none* do. The polarisation of households into those that are work-rich and those that are work-poor widens the distribution of household income and will offset the impact of redistributive policies.

One noticeable feature of Figure 9.2 is the slower growth of inequality in Scotland than in the RGB during the mid-to-late 1990s. To understand what lies behind this development, we have conducted two more detailed analyses. First, to see if the slowdown in the growth of inequality in Scotland is located in the upper or lower part of the earnings distribution, we have plotted the ratio between 90th percentile earnings and median earnings as well as the ratio of the median to the 10th decile. The results are shown in Figure 9.3. It is first worth noting that since the early 1990s, the gap between the 10th decile and the median has been smaller in Scotland than in the RGB. And since 1997, the gap between top earners and the median in Scotland has also diminished relative to the RGB. Thus the decline in wage inequality in Scotland relative to the RGB during the 1990s appears to have been mainly driven by a compression of differentials among

Figure 9.3: Movements at the top and bottom of the income distribution: Scotland and the RGB (1975-2001): 50/10 and 90/50 percentile ratios

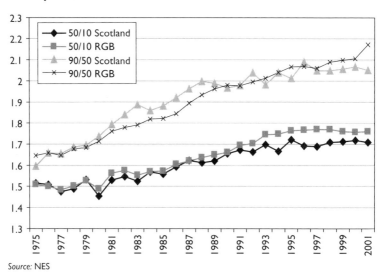

Source: NES

low earners and, from the mid-1990s, a relative narrowing of the gap between the centre and top of the earnings distribution.

Our other analysis involved the use of generalised entropy indices to decompose the recent behaviour of earnings inequality in Scotland. Using occupational data, these indices indicate how much of the increase in earnings inequality is attributable to increasing differentials *within* occupations and how much to increasing differentials *between* occupations. Results are shown in Figure 9.4. These indicate that the rise in inequality during the 1980s was driven both from within occupations and between occupations. However, since the early 1990s, there has been an interesting divergence between Scotland and the RGB. In contrast to the robust growth in the RGB, differentials within occupations in Scotland have *fallen* since 1987. Further, the increase in differentials between occupations has tailed off since 1994, while in the RGB they have continued their steady growth. It is unclear what circumstances in the Scottish labour market have led to these significant differences in the evolution of earnings inequality. Clearly this is an issue worthy of further research.

These earnings data provide us with some indication of trends in inequality in Scotland. We now focus on specific analyses of inequality using the BHPS.

Figure 9.4: Generalised entropy measures of within and between occupational inequality

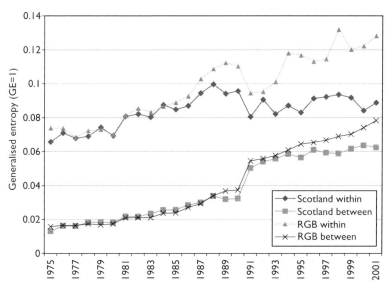

Inequality and economic activity

Table 9.1 shows the distribution of economic activity of the head of household in the lowest and highest income decile in the earliest and latest waves of the BHPS for Scotland and the UK as a whole. A number of features are apparent:

1. Both in Scotland and the UK as a whole, the bottom income decile is dominated by the unemployed and the retired. Consistently over 30% of households in the lowest income decile have a head of household who is retired. Other groups featuring prominently include those where the head of household is caring for someone in the family, is long-term sick, or is disabled.
2. The self-employed are also disproportionately represented in the lowest income decile. However, they also feature disproportionately in the highest income decile. In Scotland in 1999/2000, 14% of the heads of household in the top decile were self-employed. The disproportionate showing of the self-employed among the top and bottom deciles would partly explain a narrower overall distribution of income in Scotland, given that there are relatively fewer self-employed than in the UK as a whole. If Scots are more risk averse than other Britons, then the relatively wide distribution of self-employment income might partly explain why Scots are more reluctant to become self-employed.
3. A significant development between 1990/91 and 1999/00 is the increase in the proportion of retired households in the top income decile. In the first wave of the BHPS, when the Scottish sample was

Table 9.1: Economic activity of head of household by income decile (%)

	1991				1999/2000			
	UK		Scotland		UK		Scotland	
Decile	1st	10th	1st	10th	1st	10th	1st	10th
Self-employed	10.47	19.61	9.42	10.03	9.81	15.69	9.49	14.33
In paid employment	6.4	74.51	5.65	84.45	8.32	68.82	6.36	66.97
Unemployed	23.57	0.47	18.8	4.62	12.56	0.03	22.78	
Retired	31.24	4.96	35.08		42.38	13.8	32.74	15.57
Family care	20.37	0.19	14.76		11.66	0.26	9.68	0.96
Full-time student	1.61		5.28	0.91	7.04	0.48	8.8	2.18
Long-term sick/disabled	4.66	0.08	5.8		6.35		7.56	
Govt training scheme	0.73		5.2		0.71		0.53	
Something else	0.94	0.17			1.17		2.06	

relatively small, there was an insignificant number of retired households in the top 10% of household incomes. By 1999, 15.6% of retired households were in the top income decile. This suggests a widening gap between rich and poor retired households in Scotland. With an increasing older population who are substantial consumers of public services, and several non-means-tested policies aimed specifically at older people, the distribution of income among older people is definitely an issue worthy of further research.

Inequality and educational attainment

As mentioned earlier in this chapter, the trend increase in inequality in the UK and the US in recent decades has partly been driven by widening skill differentials. We are not able to analyse such trends with the BHPS, since reliable data for the early and mid-1990s is not available for Scotland. Nevertheless, we can compare educational differentials in the boosted sample between Scotland and the RGB. Figure 9.5 compares net weekly income after housing costs cross-referenced by the highest educational qualification of the head of household. Substantial differentials, particularly for degree-level qualifications, exist in both Scotland and the UK as a whole. They are

Figure 9.5: Mean weekly income by highest educational qualifications of head of household

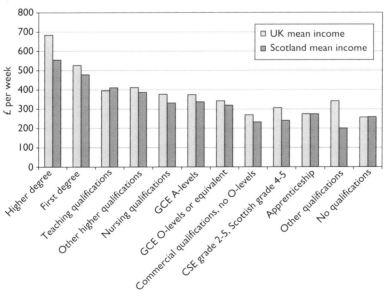

generally smaller in Scotland, with the exception of teaching qualifications, which may be misleading because of the requirement that teachers in Scotland be graduates. Given the greater supply of graduates in Scotland, it is not surprising that returns to teaching qualifications might be lower. However, lower-average earnings indicate weaker demand in the Scottish labour market. Not only are differentials *between* educational qualifications relatively smaller in Scotland, it is also true that differentials *within* these qualifications (measured using the generalised entropy [GE=1] indicator) are also lower. Given that occupations are often qualification specific, this result is in line with our earlier finding of narrower *within* occupation differentials in Scotland.

Inequality and age

An interesting feature of the UK BHPS is that the income shares of older people (those aged 55+) are *rising* compared to households where the head of household is aged less than 55. In Scotland, this trend is discernible but less clear-cut. Nevertheless, there is an upward movement in *gross* income shares of those aged 45+ in Scotland, which is shown in Figure 9.6. This may partly be the result of changing demographics, although the BHPS data also suggest that household incomes of older workers have been rising relative to younger workers since the early 1990s. This may be the result of increases in occupational

Figure 9.6: Gross income shares by age band of head of household: Scotland (1991-2000)

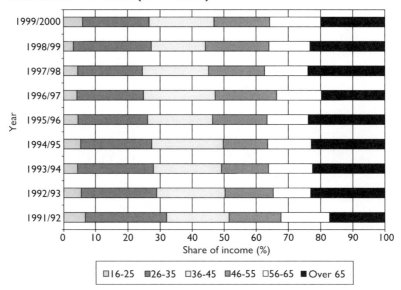

pension provision and improved state provision for older people, but it is difficult to reconcile this finding with the decline in labour market activity of older Scots, unless unearned income has been the principal source of the enhanced income of older people.

Inequality and the 'tartan' tax

Another way to think about inequality in Scotland is to consider how extensive would redistributive policies require to be in order to produce a more egalitarian income distribution. The Scottish Executive has one obvious fiscal instrument that it could use to effect redistribution: its power to vary the standard rate of income tax by up to three pence in the pound (3p/£) – the so-called 'tartan' tax. Suppose that the monies collected from a 3p increase were simply redistributed to poor Scottish households; that is, those whose household income is below 60% of the UK median net household income after housing costs. Would this redistribution be sufficient to increase the income of these poorer households above the poverty line?

We investigated this issue using the 1999/2000 BHPS. Poverty gaps were calculated for each household below the poverty line. These were summed and compared to the likely revenue that might be raised by applying the extra 3p tax (see Bell and Christie, 2002). The Treasury estimate of £690 million was very close to a simple estimate of likely revenue using BHPS data of £694 million. Both estimates assume no adverse supply consequences from raising the additional revenue.

This level of tax revenue would not make a huge impact on poverty in Scotland. In fact, it would only cover 44% of Scotland's aggregate 'poverty gap'. Simple redistribution of tartan tax revenue would not substantially close the poverty gap.

Simple dynamics of income inequality in Scotland

So far, we have not exploited the longitudinal aspects of the BHPS. It is these that offer the most exciting opportunities for investigating income inequality and poverty in Scotland. In particular, they provide an opportunity to understand the processes by which households either move up or down the income distribution.

So far, with two boosted Scottish waves, it is only possible to construct a single transition matrix. This shows the probabilities of moving between different deciles of gross equivalised income between the 1990 and 2000 waves of the BHPS. This is shown in Table 9.2. The results indicate substantial volatility in equivalised gross household incomes in the sense of high levels of transition between income deciles in Scotland. These will be driven by a variety of life events, including changing household composition, retirement, unemployment, sickness, disability as well as entry and withdrawal from the labour market.

Volatility is most pronounced in the middle of the income distribution and lowest in the highest income deciles (Figure 9.7). At the bottom of the income distribution there is also considerable movement, although 40% remain in the lowest income decile after one year, whereas the same can also be said of only 24% of the fourth income decile. There are also differences between Scotland and the RGB in that exit probabilities from income deciles in Scotland are

Table 9.2: Transition matrix for household income in Scotland (%)

	Year 2 decile									
Year 1 decile	**1**	**2**	**3**	**4**	**5**	**6**	**7**	**8**	**9**	**10**
1	**40.5**	19.3	11.9	9.6	3.4	3.4	3.6	4.7	1.5	2.4
2	22.4	**37.4**	12.9	10.5	5.2	3.9	2.1	3.0	1.4	1.2
3	12.8	22.7	**29.7**	20.2	5.9	6.2	0.7	0.5	1.0	0.3
4	7.7	5.1	24.3	**24.1**	16.5	11.3	5.1	3.9	0.5	1.5
5	4.6	8.5	11.5	18.1	**27.7**	14.5	7.4	4.0	0.3	3.4
6	5.9	2.3	6.1	6.9	18.8	**27.9**	19.7	7.7	3.3	1.2
7	0.6	2.5	5.1	5.2	11.9	14.4	**30.8**	22.4	5.9	1.1
8	1.7	2.2	0.0	1.8	2.1	5.1	21.8	**38.0**	22.4	4.9
9	1.5	1.1	2.3	4.2	4.7	4.5	4.8	10.0	**49.8**	17.2
10	0.0	0.0	0.4	1.5	5.7	0.8	3.9	2.9	16.9	**67.9**

Figure 9.7: Annual probability of exit by equivalised gross income decile

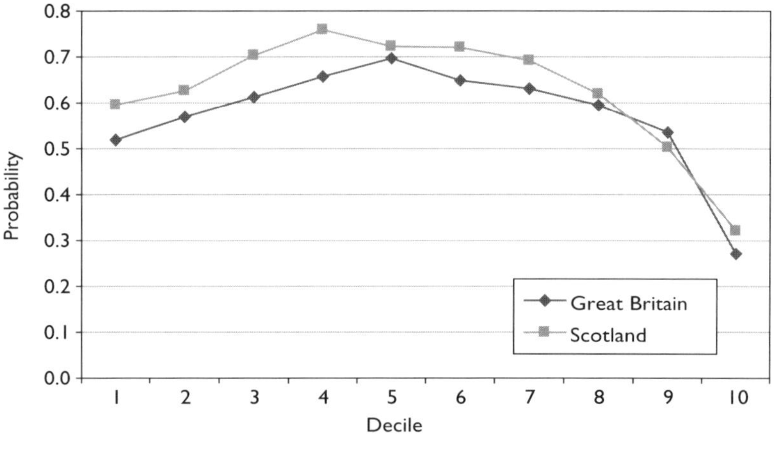

generally *higher* than in the RGB. This suggests that both low and high incomes are *relatively* more transient states in Scotland than in the RGB. With additional waves, it will be possible to carry out more detailed event analyses, but if this finding is still intact after taking account of standard control variables (along the lines of Cappellari and Jenkins, 2002), then it has important implications for how the Scottish Executive addresses the issue of poverty.

Conclusion

This chapter has considered the issue of differences in household income in Scotland. It has shown that the distribution of income in Scotland is relatively unequal by the standards of most developed countries. However, in recent years, the growth in earnings inequality has been attenuated, and in Scotland both the growth in *between* occupation earnings differentials and *within* occupation earnings differentials has slowed or been reversed. Considering recent trends in inequality by economic status, two interesting findings emerge. First, that there is increasing inequality among retired households: while 30% of these households can be found in the lowest income decile, a substantial 15% have income that places them in the top 10th of the income distribution. Second, the self-employed, who are a relatively small proportion of the Scottish workforce, also tend to be found at the extremes of the income distribution. This, in itself may be a reason why Scots appear relatively reluctant to enter self-employment.

Education explains significant differences in mean earnings. However, not only are differences in household income between the highest educational level of the head of household smaller in Scotland than in England, it is also true that variation *within* educational qualifications is more limited in Scotland. There are also substantial age differentials in household income. However, although economic activity among older Scots is declining, older people are taking an increasing share of total income. This is true even after taking account of the increase in cohort size among older people.

The tartan tax could be used as a simple redistributive fiscal instrument. However, even after discounting supply side-effects, it would only cover approximately 40% of Scotland's current aggregate 'poverty gap'. Its redistributive role is clearly limited.

Finally, data on income transitions suggest that Scots are less likely than their counterparts south of the border to remain in the same income decile from one year to the next. Although this is an extremely tentative finding, this could have important implications for a range of policies in which the Scottish Executive has an interest.

References

Bell, D. and Christie, A. (2002) 'A new fiscal settlement for Scotland?', *Scottish Affairs*, vol 41, pp 121-40.

Bell, D. and Jack, G. (2002) *Worklessness and polarisation in Scottish households*, Scotecon Discussion Paper, Stirling: University of Stirling.

Blanchflower, D. (1996) *The role and influence of trade unions in the OECD*, CEP Discussion Papers, no 0310, London: Centre for Economic Performance, London School of Economics and Political Science.

Blanchflower, D. and Slaughter, M. 1999) 'Causes and consequences of changing income inequality', in A. Fishlow and K. Parker (eds) *Growing apart: The causes and consequences of global wage inequality*, Council on Foreign Relations, pp 67-94.

Borjas, G., Freeman, R.B. and Katz, L.F. (1997) *How much do immigration and trade affect labor market outcome?*, Brookings Papers on Economic Activity, Vol 1, Washington, DC: Brookings Institution Press.

Browning, M., Bourguignon, F., Chiappori, P-A. and Lechene, V. (1994) 'Income and outcomes: a structural model of intrahousehold allocation', *Journal of Political Economy*, no 102, pp 1067-96.

Cappellari, L. and Jenkins, S. (2002) *Modelling low income transitions*, ISER Working Paper, 2002-8, Colchester: University of Essex.

Cowell, F.A. (1995) *Measuring inequality* (2nd edn), Hemel Hempstead: Harvester Wheatsheaf.

Ferreira F. (1999) *Inequality and economic performance: A brief overview to theories of growth and distribution*, June, World Bank (www.worldbank.org/poverty/inequal/index.htm).

HM Treasury (1999) *Tackling poverty and extending opportunity*, London: HM Treasury.

Jenkins, S.P. (1999) *Trends in the UK income distribution*, ISER Working Paper 1999-22, Colchester: Institute for Social and Economic Research, University of Essex.

Litchfield, J. (1999) *Inequality methods and tools*, London: STICERD, London School of Economics and Political Science.

Machin, S. (1997) 'Wage inequality', *Oxford Review of Economic Policy*, vol 12, no 1, pp 47-64.

TEN

The structure of gender differentials

Kostas G. Mavromaras and Ioannis Theodossiou

Introduction

The objective of this chapter is to investigate the differences in male–female labour market differentials between Scotland and the rest of the UK using the British Household Panel Survey (BHPS) dataset. The year 1999 is a particularly opportune one for the examination of the Scottish dimension since it is the first one for which the Scottish over-sampling component of the BHPS is available.

The BHPS data set with the Scottish over-sampling since 1999 has a major advantage over other published data sets regarding the study of male–female wage differentials, in that it allows the sufficiently detailed comparison of earnings and other important labour market indicators such as industry, occupation, educational attainment, and so on, between Scotland and the rest of the UK. This is because it contains a very rich set of variables along with a sufficiently large sample size for (over-sampled) Scotland. As its panel use will start becoming feasible in the next years, it is bound to develop into one of the major research tools in this area of study for Scotland.

The BHPS's extensive information should enable one to detect much more clearly the extent to which there may be regional differences in job segregation by gender and to measure the degree to which this depresses female relative to male pay and opportunities. The BHPS also provides good information on length of service, another variable that may affect male–female differentials. There is data on those who have been employed by the same firm along with the number of years spent with the firm. There is also detailed information on the make-up of pay, including overtime premium payments, which guarantees the high statistical accuracy of results using this data set.

This chapter sets out to study some of the main labour market indicators that may be related to male–female differentials. Before starting, the expectation was that few differences between Scotland

and England would be found, mainly due to the almost non-existent mobility barriers between Scotland and the rest of the UK. This expectation has been confirmed in part: indeed the position of females in Scotland is very similar to that of their counterparts in England. Nonetheless, several important points have emerged:

• there are significant participation differences between Scotland, England and Wales;
• there are differences in occupational segregation, but they are not all of the same direction;
• male–female earnings differentials in full-time employment in Scotland are shown to be among the highest in the UK (London being the lowest), with differential union coverage and public sector employment influencing male–female wage differences;
• multivariate decompositions of the wage gap and counterfactual analysis show differences between Scotland and England that the investigation of gross data conceals.

The chapter is structured as follows. The next section discusses differences in economic activity rates. The third section discusses occupational segregation; the fourth discusses earnings differentials; the fifth gender differences in job tenure and job experience. The sixth section presents earnings estimation results and discusses the components of the wage gap, and the seventh concludes the chapter. An appendix contains details on data selection.

Male–female differences in economic activity rates

Participation in the labour market is an important precursor to many other labour market outcomes of interest, such as pay, occupational segregation, unemployment and tenure. Hence, it forms the natural starting point for the investigation of male–female differences between Scotland and England. Table 10.1 presents participation rates for Scotland, London, rest of England and Wales. It reveals that London has the highest overall economic activity rate for both males and females. The RUK is roughly the same, with the rest of England coming first, followed by Scotland and then Wales, which has the lowest activity rates in the UK. Male–female splits show that full-time employment differences are at their smallest in London, with male full-time propensity only 19% higher than female (the difference being 22.1%, 22.2% and 27.5% for Scotland, Wales and Rest of England respectively).

Part-time employment is overwhelmingly female, with roughly one

Table 10.1: Participation rates by type of economic activity and region

Economic activity	Scotland			London			Rest of England			Wales		
	Fem	Males	M-F	Fem	Males	M-F	Fem	Males	M-F	Fem	Males	M-F
Employed full-time	0.3785	0.5995	*0.221*	0.4373	0.6269	*0.190*	0.3747	0.6495	*0.275*	0.3352	0.5571	*0.222*
Employed part-time	0.1858	0.0289	*-0.157*	0.1943	0.0444	*-0.150*	0.2218	0.0257	*-0.196*	0.1892	0.0250	*-0.164*
Self-employed	0.0374	0.1082	*0.071*	0.0707	0.1285	*0.058*	0.0451	0.1272	*0.081*	0.0451	0.1190	*0.074*
Unemployed	0.0371	0.0692	*0.032*	0.0308	0.0529	*0.022*	0.0261	0.0427	*0.017*	0.0394	0.0669	*0.027*
Out of the labour force	0.3612	0.1943	*-0.167*	0.2670	0.1473	*-0.120*	0.3323	0.1549	*-0.177*	0.3911	0.2320	*-0.159*
Participation rate (%)	63.88	80.57	16.69	73.3	85.27	11.97	66.77	84.51	17.74	60.89	76.80	15.91

Note: Out of all employed (14,612), 207 are excluded from Table 10.1 because the distinction between full time and part time was not recorded.

in five females in part-time employment. The highest male–female difference is found in the rest of England at 19.6%, the other three regions lying between 15% and 16.4%. Interestingly, male part-time employment in London is the highest in the sample at 4.4%, with Scotland following at 2.9% and the rest of England and Wales at 2.5%. The lowest male–female difference in the propensity for self-employment (at 5.8%) is found in London, along with the highest self-employment percentages (7.1 for females and 12.8 for males). Self-employment levels and male–female differences are very similar for the RUK.

Male unemployment is highest in Scotland at 6.9% and female unemployment is second highest in Scotland at 3.7% after Wales at 3.9%. Male–female unemployment rate differences are highest in Scotland with males being 3.2% more likely to be unemployed than females. Note that, for the purpose of the present comparisons, we are not using the conventional definition of unemployment rate as the inactive population is contained in the denominator. The remainder of the sample in the row marked Out of the labour force in Table 10.1 contains all those who were not actively engaged in the labour market for various reasons in the 1999 BHPS wave. This row contains students, early retirements, housewives, maternity leaves and other non-active categories. Females clearly top this category, with London again exhibiting the lowest non-activity rates for both males and females and the lowest male–female differential at 12%. Rest of England, Scotland and Wales follow in a descending order at 17.7%, 16.7% and 15.9% respectively.

In summary, all labour market participation categories follow a similar pattern in the UK, with London exhibiting signs of a more active labour market with high participation rates and low male–female participation rates differentials.

Segregation

Table 10.2 shows the female:male employment ratio by industry, in order to identify possible differences in over- or under-representation of females in specific industries. Females are found in a slightly higher proportion in distribution, hotels and catering, repairs and the 'other' category, in both Scotland and England to a similar degree. Females are employed in a higher proportion compared to men in banking and related services in Scotland but not in England. Traditionally male-dominated industries like metal goods, engineering and vehicle industries, other manufacturing industries, construction and transport

Table 10.2: Full-time employment distribution by industry (female:male ratios)

Industry, SIC	Scotland	England	UK
Metal goods, engineering and vehicle industries	0.31	0.29	0.29
Other manufacturing industries	0.56	0.59	0.57
Construction	0.12	0.18	0.16
Distribution, hotels and catering, repairs	1.89	1.45	1.60
Transport and communication	0.55	0.40	0.43
Banking, finance, insurance, business services and leasing	1.15	0.94	0.98
Other	1.54	1.71	1.64

and communications are similarly male dominated in Scotland as in England, with the sole exception of communications employing a higher female proportion in Scotland than in England. All in all, there appear to be few differences between Scotland and England in the representation of females by industry.

An alternative comparison can be made by looking at the male:female ratio across occupational classifications. Occupational differences may be a more potent means for spotting male–female differences in employment circumstances. Table 10.3 shows that the female:male ratio is higher in most occupations in Scotland than in England. It is only clerical and secretarial, personal and protective service occupations (both highly female-dominated occupations with ratios above two) that are more segregated in England, and craft and related occupations (a highly male-dominated occupation with a ratio of 0.14), where segregation is practically the same in England and Scotland.

All remaining occupations in Table 10.3 show lower segregation in Scotland. A possible explanation for the generally higher female presence in female-dominated occupations may be the much higher proportion of public sector employees in Scotland. As will be seen later in this chapter, a possible result of this may be the observed much

Table 10.3: Full-time employment distribution by occupation (female:male ratios)

Occupations, SOC	Scotland	England	UK
Managers and administrators	0.77	0.56	0.59
Professional occupations	1.43	1.06	1.14
Associate professional and technical occupations	1.51	1.20	1.37
Clerical and secretarial occupations	2.32	2.79	2.75
Craft and related occupations	0.13	0.14	0.13
Personal and protective service occupations	2.00	2.30	2.38
Sales occupations	3.41	2.18	2.61
Plant and machine operatives	0.42	0.25	0.28
Other occupations	1.52	1.23	1.28

smaller female pay advantage in England than the corresponding male advantage.

Earnings differentials

Male–female earnings differentials are one of the most extensively researched areas in labour economics. In the UK, striving for gender equality in pay has been an explicit political target since the 1970s through UK legislation, and from the 1980s through EU legislation. Despite all that has been done in most industrialised nations, the male–female pay gap has proved to be very hard to reduce. The UK forms no exception to the international picture. Table 10.4 shows the hourly rates adjusted for overtime for full-time employees by gender. A clear gap against females can be seen for both Scotland and the rest of the UK.

There are several explanations regarding the causes of the wage gap, some often observed and rarely contested, and some rarely observed and often contested. A usual and clear-cut candidate for the latter category, where data is hard to come by and opinions differ drastically, is the possibility of unobserved gender-related differences in preferences regarding employment itself, which may result in gender-related reservation wage differences. Two of the often observed origins of the wage gap are presented in Tables 10.5 and 10.6. Table 10.5 reports average earnings by collective agreement coverage. The breakdown shows that trades union coverage of the workplace reduces the wage gap by a substantial margin throughout the UK. Centralised bargaining for wages seems to improve female pay more than it improves male pay. This is hardly surprising as one of the features of centralised pay is that it has to abide by the law, which states explicitly that no distinction should be made between males and females. London has the lowest female:male wage gap (female:male pay ratio in union-covered firms is 0.95) and the highest impact of union coverage (the ratio increase resulting from union coverage is 0.95-0.77=0.18).

Table 10.4: Average hourly earnings of employees

	Scotland	London	Rest of England	Wales
Females	7.58	10.10	7.71	7.07
	(0.12)	(0.31)	(0.09)	(0.13)
Males	9.27	11.86	9.42	8.57
	(0.18)	(0.43)	(0.11)	(0.22)
F:M ratio	0.82	0.85	0.82	0.82

Notes: Full-time employees only. Standard deviations in parentheses. Cross section weights xrwtsw1 have been used. 1991 prices.

Table 10.5: Average hourly earnings by collective agreement coverage

	Union covered				Union not covered			
	Scotland	London	Rest of England	Wales	Scotland	London	Rest of England	Wales
Females	8.30	10.43	8.49	7.93	6.51	9.79	6.90	5.65
	(0.16)	(0.37)	(0.13)	(0.17)	(0.18)	(0.51)	(0.13)	(0.17)
Males	9.50	10.95	9.60	9.26	9.12	12.69	9.35	7.87
	(0.21)	(0.49)	(0.13)	(0.20)	(0.30)	(0.67)	(0.16)	(0.45)
F:M ratio	0.87	0.95	0.88	0.86	0.71	0.77	0.74	0.72

Notes: Full-time employees. Standard deviations in parentheses. Cross-section weights xrwtsw1 have been used. 1991 prices.

Table 10.6: Average hourly earnings by public/private sector employment

	Public sector				Private sector			
	Scotland	London	Rest of England	Wales	Scotland	London	Rest of England	Wales
Females	9.21	10.53	9.04	8.46	6.46	9.85	7.03	6.02
	(0.21)	(0.40)	(0.17)	(0.22)	(0.13)	(0.43)	(0.11)	(0.14)
Males	10.34	11.51	10.57	9.84	8.96	11.96	9.20	8.24
	(0.36)	(0.68)	(0.23)	(0.35)	(0.20)	(0.52)	(0.12)	(0.26)
F:M ratio	0.89	0.92	0.86	0.86	0.72	0.83	0.76	0.73

Notes: Full-time employees. Standard deviations in parentheses. Cross-section weights xrwtsw1 have been used. 1991 prices.

Table 10.6 reports differences in average earnings of full-time employees between the public and private sectors. With the sole exception of males in London, public sector pay is higher than private sector pay. The pay premium associated with public sector pay is at its highest for females in Scotland and Wales and at its lowest for males in London. In a similar way to union coverage, pay negotiations in the public sector have less of an opportunity to differentiate by gender. Hence, the female:male pay ratio is considerably higher in the public sector.

It should be noted that the lower male–female wage gap observed in the union-covered workplace and the public sector may also be due to differences in the composition of the labour force employed in these parts of the economy. If, for example, female (male) labour employed in the public sector is better (equally or worse) qualified than female (male) labour employed in the private sector, very naturally, we will observe a lower wage gap in the public sector. This effect should not be confused with differences in employment practices between the public and the private sectors. Such issues can be best addressed using multivariate analysis presented later in this chapter.

Male–female current job tenure and job experience differences

The BHPS includes data on the number of years with the present employer. Although this does not provide a measure of experience in general, it can be used as a good indication of job mobility and firm-specific human capital. Table 10.7 shows some clear differences between Scottish and English job tenure averages, which appear to be common for most industries. Namely, it can be seen that in Scotland the female to male tenure length ratio is lower in all main industries with the exception of other manufacturing industries. It is interesting that this difference does not arise from Scottish females having much shorter tenure than English females, but rather from Scottish males having much longer tenure than English males. Several possible explanations could be offered for this finding, related to different aspects of firm-specific human capital as well as different types of mobility. The findings in Table 10.7 suggest the possibilities that Scottish males (in relation to Scottish females) possess higher firm-specific human capital and/ or are geographically less mobile than their English counterparts.

Further investigation into the gender differences in labour market and other types of related mobility for Scotland and England should be both possible and worthwhile to carry out using this data set.

Wage gap decompositions

Conventional Mincer-type earnings equations were estimated for full-time employees. Given that participation in full-time employment varies systematically by gender, the standard Heckman bias correction was applied. Estimations were carried out for the 1999 sample only. (Detailed estimation results can be obtained from the authors.) Here we concern ourselves mainly with the interpretation of the wage gap decompositions. Table 10.8 presents the Oaxaca-Blinder decomposition of the male–female wage gap into two constituents: the explained part (often referred to as the productivity or characteristics gap) and the unexplained part (often referred to as the discrimination, market or coefficients gap).

Table 10.8 shows that the male–female wage gap is smaller in Scotland

Table 10.7: Average current job tenure in years by industry (female:male ratios)

	Scotland			England			UK		
	Male	Female	F:M	Male	Female	F:M	Male	Female	F:M
Metal goods, engineering and vehicle goods	6.41	3.71	0.58	5.28	5.07	0.96	5.33	5.00	0.94
Other manufacturing industries	7.42	6.45	0.87	6.45	4.91	0.76	6.78	5.12	0.76
Construction	5.92	4.08	0.69	4.66	4.25	0.91	4.77	3.92	0.82
Distribution, hotels and catering, repairs	4.5	4.17	0.93	4.33	4.3	0.99	4.42	4.26	0.96
Transport and communication	6.75	3.07	0.45	5.57	4.79	0.86	5.78	4.67	0.81
Banking, finance, insurance, business services amd leasing	4.96	4.11	0.83	3.53	3.67	1.04	3.65	3.85	1.0
Other services	7.07	6.13	0.87	5.19	5.33	1.03	5.52	5.41	0.98

(20%) than in England (25%). (Strictly speaking, these are not percentage points but log points. Since the two are roughly equivalent, we will refer to them as percentage points.) The difference in the wage gap is mainly attributable to the much higher male earnings in England. Female earnings are only slightly higher in England. A small part of the wage gap is explained by the estimations, 3.64% (18.2% of the total gap) in Scotland and 4.88% (19.3% of the gap) in England. The remaining gap, 16.8% in Scotland and 20.1% in England, is unexplained by the estimations. Thus, while the English wage gap is larger than the Scottish gap, the way it is split between explained and unexplained parts is roughly the same in the two countries. One suggestion could be that the wage-setting structure that underlies and generates the wage gap may be very similar in the two countries.

An important issue in this context is to see the degree to which male–female wage gap differences between Scotland and England are due to observed human capital differences. To this purpose, we carry out a counterfactual analysis where English employees are put in the Scottish labour market and Scottish employees are put in the English labour market. The objective of this exercise is to establish the degree to which differences in the Scottish and English wage gaps are due to differences in human capital between the two countries or due to differences in the way human capital is rewarded in the two countries. Table 10.9 shows that English males would lose 2% of their pay if they were rewarded by Scottish labour market standards. Scottish males would gain very little pay in the English labour market, just over 1%. Interestingly, Scottish females would get roughly the same pay in the English labour market, while English females would lose over 6% of their pay if they were rewarded by Scottish labour market standards.

Thus, of the four possible counterfactuals in this context, the one that shows substantial differences is where the human capital of English females is evaluated by the Scottish labour market much lower than by the English labour market. There are several possible explanations for this difference. First, Table 10.1 has shown female participation

Table 10.8: Wage gap decompositions

	Scotland	England
Male log-wage	1.8257	1.8916
Female log-wage	1.6261	1.6391
Male–female wage gap (log points)	0.1996	0.2525
Explained	0.0364	0.0488
Unexplained	0.1683	0.2015

Note: The table reports log wages and their differences. As differences in log points are very close to percentage differences, the chapter uses the convention of referring to log points as percentages.

Table 10.9: Counterfactual wages and wage gaps

	English employees		Scottish employees	
	In England (actual)	In Scotland (counterfactual)	In Scotland (actual)	In England (counterfactual)
Male wage	1.8916	1.8703	1.8257	1.8388
Female wage	1.6391	1.5760	1.6261	1.6219
Wage gap	0.2525	0.2970	0.1996	0.2169
Explained	0.0488	0.0643	0.0364	0.0261
Unexplained	0.2015	0.2327	0.1683	0.1908

Notes: Calculations are based on regression results. Counterfactuals are generated by combining the data from one country/gender with the coefficients from the other country for the same gender.

differences between Scotland and England, which may be responsible for a different female workforce composition. This could happen if the tighter English labour market offered higher pay and attracted more females from the lower end of the human capital distribution to enter the English labour market, while the Scottish labour market did not manage to attract their counterparts (in human capital terms) into employment. Higher overall female participation rates and lower unemployment rates of English females would support this possible explanation. But then, similar (but not as large) participation and larger unemployment rates differences for males do not seem to affect the English male counterfactual wage. Second, Tables 10.2 and 10.3 have shown occupational and sectoral differences between the two countries, which may well account for some of the differences in pay. To the degree that employment matches are self-selecting, one would expect that counterfactuals like the ones performed in Table 10.9 could result in drops in pay if industries and sectors are not evenly distributed in the two countries. The evidence presented here is not conclusive, but is valuable as it points towards a direction for further investigation, both in terms of Scotland–England differences in the participation process and the occupational/sectoral structure.

The last two rows of Table 10.9 present the actual and counterfactual decompositions of the wage gap. The proportion of the wage gap that is explained in the actual markets (19.32% and 18.23%: the ratio of explained over total wage gap for England and Scotland respectively) is different in the counterfactual labour markets (to 21.64% and 12.03% respectively). This is indirect evidence of structural economic diversity between Scotland and England accompanied by self-selecting labour market mobility between the two countries, in accordance with the predictions of human capital theory.

It is important to bear in mind some interpretation issues. First, the discrimination estimate cannot be attributed without any further ado to pure discrimination; it can and should be used as the upper boundary of discrimination estimates. As it contains the constant term, all gender-systematic unobservables are in it, where some may be and some may not be discriminatory. For example, employer unobserved attitudes towards gender might well be discriminatory. However, employee unobserved gender-related differences in preferences would not be discriminatory, provided that preferences are not constrained differently by gender (for example, in occupational possibilities). As this is a highly contested and emotive issue, the reader is provided with the numbers and only their rudimentary interpretation.

Second, this chapter does not take advantage of the panel nature of the BHPS, mainly because the Scottish panel is only two years old. Panel analysis would allow us to control for unobserved and systematic gender-related differences and incorporate dynamic selection bias corrections. As the panel grows this will become a worthwhile research possibility for the Scottish BHPS.

Conclusion

The objective of this chapter was to investigate differences in male–female labour market differentials between Scotland and the rest of the UK using the BHPS data set.

This investigation generated some interesting findings. In particular, it was found that the London area appears to enjoy the highest overall economic activity rate for both males and females. The rest of the UK exhibits a similar level of economic activity, although England scores better compared to Scotland and Wales. Regarding gender differences in full-time employment, the London area exhibits the smallest male–female gap.

Labour market participation follows a similar pattern for all regions examined in this study, although the London area appears to have a slightly more active labour market and lower male–female participation rates differentials.

Segregation by industry exhibits few differences between Scotland and England regarding the representation of females by industry. However, in terms of segregation by occupation, in most occupations the female to male ratio is higher in Scotland than in England. An interpretation of this finding could be that the proportion of female to male employees in the public sector is higher in Scotland.

Male–female earnings differentials reveal a clear gap against females for both Scotland and the rest of the UK as compared to the London area. It is also revealed that trades union coverage of the workplace reduces the wage gap by a substantial margin throughout the UK. Thus, centralised bargaining for wages seems to improve female pay more than it improves male pay. In a similar way to union coverage, pay negotiations in the public sector have less of an opportunity to differentiate by gender. This study, indeed, has found that the female to male pay ratio is considerably higher in the public sector.

Regarding the current job tenure female:male ratio by industry, this study reveals that in Scotland the female:male ratio is lower in all main industries. It was also found that this difference does not arise from Scottish females having much shorter tenure than English females, but rather from Scottish males having much longer tenure than English males.

Furthermore, the study has found that the gender wage gap in England is larger than the gender wage gap in Scotland, but the way that it is split between explained and unexplained parts is roughly the same in the two countries. One suggestion could be that the wage-setting structure, which underlies and generates the wage gap, may be very similar in the two countries. In addition, using counterfactual methodology, it is shown that the human capital of females in England is evaluated by the Scottish labour market much lower than by the English labour market. Several possible explanations for this difference were suggested.

References and further reading

Becker, G.S. (1962) 'Investment in human capital: a theoretical analysis', *Journal of Political Economy*, Supplement, vol 70, no 5, pp S9–S49.

Becker, G.S. (1971) *The economics of discrimination* (revised edn), Chicago, IL: University of Chicago Press.

Becker, G.S. (1976) *The economic approach to human behaviour*, Chicago, IL: University of Chicago Press.

Blinder, A.S. (1973) 'Wage discrimination: reduced form and structural estimates', *Journal of Human Resources*, vol 8, pp 436–55.

Heckman, J.J. (1979) 'Sample selection bias as a specification error', *Econometrica*, vol 47, pp 153–61.

Jacobsen, J.P. (1994) *The economics of gender*, Cambridge: Blackwell Publishers.

Neumark, D. (1988) 'Employers' discriminatory behavior and the estimation of wage discrimination', *Journal of Human Resources*, vol 23, pp 279–95.

Oaxaca, R.L. (1973) 'Male–female wage differentials in urban labor markets', *International Economic Review*, vol 9, pp 693–709.

Oaxaca, R.L. and Ransom, M.R. (1988) 'Searching for the effect of unionism on the wages of union and non-union workers', *Journal of Labor Research*, vol 9, pp 139-48.

Oaxaca, R.L. and Ransom, M. (1994) 'On discrimination and the decomposition of wage differentials', *Journal of Econometrics*, vol 61, pp 5-21.

Wellington, A.J. (1993) 'Changes in the male/female wage gap, 1976-85', *Journal of Human Resources*, vol 28, no 2, pp 383-411.

Appendix

Data selection for regression analysis

The sample was restricted in the following manner: only males aged 18-65 and females aged 18-60 were included. Observations that had a cross-sectional weight of zero were excluded. Observations that had a missing value for the education variable were excluded. Only observations with a valid regional code of either England or Scotland were included. This brought the size of the 1999 wave from 11,934 down to 9,335. The sample is described in Table A1.

Table A1: Sample composition for estimations

	England		Scotland		
	All	Employees	All	Employees	Total
Males	3,117	1,981	1,173	657	4,290
Females	3,589	2,008	1,456	767	5,045
Total	6,706	3,989	2,629	1,424	9,335

Note: Weighted averages rescaled to generate the original total size of the sample.

The regressed model is of the standard form where a binary choice variable (Paid employment = 1, and zero otherwise) is first estimated using a Probit. The Inverse Mills Ratio is retained and entered in the RHS of the second stage OLS estimation. White heteroscedasticity corrected standard errors were calculated. (Over-)Identification of the system was achieved through the use of exclusion restrictions. The variables that entered the first (but not the second) stage as determinants of participation but not earnings were marital status and number of children, as variables that are much more likely to influence the participation decision and would have little direct influence on the earnings capacity of the individual. Many variables entered the second, but not the first stage by necessity, as they are only observed for those persons who obtain employment, such as SOC and SIC codes and the size of the establishment. These variables also improve identification to a good degree. Results of the earnings regressions can be obtained from the authors.

Section 3:
Labour market issues

The distinctive patterns and evolution of earnings differentials in Scotland relative to England discussed in Chapters Nine and Ten of this book reflect the operation of the Scottish labour market, but in ways that were not clear. Furthermore, policies directed at encouraging economic growth and improving social equality are likely to affect the Scottish labour market, and in many cases they may be designed to do so, as Chapter Twelve illustrates. This section of the book explores differences in labour market structure, institutions and dynamic processes between Scotland and England.

In Chapter Eleven, Robert Elliot, Vania Gerova and Euan Phimister document the present distribution and level of pay in Scotland, London and the rest of England, the characteristics of the workforce in each area and the pay dynamics. They find that average pay and pay inequality are virtually the same in Scotland and the rest of England. However, they find some important differences in the composition of the labour force. Compared to England outside London, Scottish workers stay longer in jobs, are more likely to be covered by collective bargaining, are more likely to be employed in the public sector, are more likely to have a university degree, but also more likely to have no qualifications, and the Scottish gender pay gap is lower. In line with the results for income dynamics in Chapter Nine, this chapter finds that the Scottish labour market is characterised by a greater degree of earnings instability. Also, pay growth over the 1990s was slower in Scotland, which may be partly a reflection of the higher incidence of public sector and unionised employment in Scotland, sectors which exhibited slower pay growth than private sector and non-union employment.

The further education (FE) sector is regarded by the Scottish Executive as one of the principal policy instruments through which the efficiency and equity aims of both the Social Inclusion and Lifelong Learning agenda are to be delivered. If the expected economic and social benefits from participation in lifelong learning and the acquisition of appropriate skills are to be realised, there must be sufficient individual incentives to participate in FE and acquire new skills. Anne Gasteen, John Houston and Carolyn Davidson (Chapter Twelve) review the relevant policy initiatives and examine how education is rewarded in the labour market by focusing on the impact it has on earnings. They demonstrate how the panel dimension of the British Household Panel Survey (BHPS) can be used to gain greater insight into what is a difficult measurement problem. Although the evidence that they present is not clear-cut, it suggests that degree and FE qualifications may be remunerated at a higher level in Scotland than in the rest of the UK. These results are consistent with the analysis in Chapter Eleven that shows that earnings returns to university degree, teaching and nursing qualifications are currently higher in Scotland than England, in part because they rose more rapidly during the 1990s in Scotland than England. However, the analysis also finds that lower-level FE qualifications (that is, below degree level, HNC/D), while offering a higher return in Scotland than in the rest of the UK, offer a lower return than Scottish 'Highers' and a similar return to the lower-level school qualifications (such as GCSEs). These results suggest that there are personal incentives for people to take up the expansion of the Scottish FE sector, particularly degree-level FE.

Public policy concern over the situation of the low-paid worker has grown as earnings inequality in Britain has risen. The national minimum wage is a response to this concern. Social welfare is not, however, only derived through income; job conditions are also important. Rannia Leontaridi and Peter Sloane (Chapter Thirteen) analyse various measures of job satisfaction. It is often argued that job satisfaction increases with pay and that 'happier workers' are more productive workers. They find that the overall levels and trends in job satisfaction are very similar in Scotland and England. They also find that low-paid workers have higher reported levels of job satisfaction than higher-paid workers in both nations. Unlike the rest of Britain, Scottish women and men express similar levels of job satisfaction, and Scottish workers are less concerned about the level of earnings of their co-workers.

Owing to low Scottish fertility and the lack of net inward migration, population ageing is proceeding rapidly in Scotland, and success in reducing mortality to levels in the rest of Western Europe would accelerate this process. For instance, population projections suggest that one in four persons in Scotland will be aged 60-74 in 2026, compared with one in five in England. Nearly half the population of both countries will be aged 45-74. This highlights the need for older workers to make a full contribution to society, already recognised by policy makers. In Scotland, the consultation paper on 'Training for Work' for the long-term unemployed included a proposal that those aged 50+ would be offered early entry to the 'New Deal for the over 50s' programme. This programme provides support for skills development for those who wish to return to work, with the aim of increasing the employment rates of older workers.

Mark Taylor and John Rigg (Chapter Fourteen) study the labour market status of older men and women in England and Scotland, and changes in it. They find that Scottish men aged 51-69 are less likely to be in employment and more likely to be unemployed or otherwise inactive than English men of these ages. Scottish women of these ages are more likely to be retired and less likely to be in work than their English counterparts. They also find that both employment and retirement are less stable states in Scotland than in England. That is, although older workers are more likely to retire in Scotland, they are also more likely to subsequently re-enter work, which may indicate greater financial difficulties among retired men and women in this age group in Scotland. Pension coverage significantly affects whether men aged 51-69 leave employment: being a member of an occupational pension scheme significantly increases the chances of leaving employment, but membership of a personal pension scheme reduces these chances (relative to having no private pension). After controlling for these and other measurable influences on the chances of leaving employment, Scottish people aged 51-69 are more likely to leave (lose) their job, particularly women. Thus, it appears that the relationship that older people have with the labour market differs in several fundamental ways between Scotland and England, and further exploration of the reasons for these differences can make an important contribution to policy making by the Scottish Executive.

ELEVEN

Distribution and structure of pay

Robert Elliott, Vania Gerova and Euan Phimister

Introduction

In 1999-2000, the average level of pay and the dispersion of pay in Scotland was lower than in London but virtually identical to the rest of England. However, these similarities between Scotland and the rest of England mask substantial differences in wage dynamics between the two. The principal focus of this chapter is to report these features of the Scottish and English labour markets and to explore some of the labour market dynamics that help explain the picture that had emerged by the end of the 1990s.

The average level of pay in Scotland would be expected to differ from that in England. The industrial and occupational structure of employment and the skill composition of the workforce are different in the two countries. Different proportions of the working population are employed in the public sector and the incidence of trade unionism differs between Scotland and England. Once we control for all these differences in the characteristics of the workforce in the two countries and are able to compare like-with-like, are Scots, on average, less well paid than their counterparts in England? And even if we find that average levels of pay are the same in Scotland and England, there may still be differences between them in the distribution of pay. Is pay inequality greater or smaller in Scotland than in England?

The long boom of the 1990s saw pay levels grow steadily throughout the UK. Did this growth in pay mean that pay in Scotland became more similar to that in England or did pay levels diverge? Recognising that some people will be poorly paid in both countries, is it easier to escape low pay in Scotland than in England?

Even when pay is growing, not all individuals necessarily gain. Some experience pay reductions, others experience periods of unemployment and some even leave the labour force altogether. During the 1990s, the unemployment differential between Scotland and England grew[1]. The Scottish unemployment rate, measured on the International Labour

Organisation (ILO) definition and expressed as an index of the rate in the rest of England, was 106 on average during 1991and 1992. However, by 1999 and 2000 the index had grown to 133; the Scottish rate was now 33% higher than the rate in the rest of England[2]. Do the dynamic processes that characterise the labour markets in Scotland and England differ between the two countries?

These are the central questions we seek to answer in this chapter. It represents the first detailed study of the differences in labour market processes and the structure and inequality of pay between Scotland and England.

Why do pay levels differ spatially?

Economic theory informs us that in long-run equilibrium the differences in pay between areas can be attributed only to differences in the supply side of the labour market. The relevant differences are the productive characteristics of the workforce and the characteristics of the places in which they work, the working environment. These differences reveal themselves in differences in human capital, in the structure of non-pay pecuniary rewards and in the structure of other non-monetary rewards from work. This long-run equilibrium theory originates in the theory of net advantages, in its modern guise called the theory of equalising differences, which was first advanced by Adam Smith in 1776[3].

However, for the net advantages of jobs in different areas to be equalised, as proposed by the theory, labour must be mobile, labour markets must be integrated. Labour must move from areas where real pay levels are low and employment prospects poor to the more attractive areas. Researchers have pointed to persistent differences in area unemployment rates as evidence that, although the equalising force of migration operates, it works only slowly. One consequence of the resulting temporary disequilibria in area labour markets is that there are differences in the unemployment rates between areas, and these differences have themselves been advanced to explain differences in pay.

Empirical evidence of a stable negative relationship between the levels of local pay and unemployment has been advanced to support the existence of a wage curve (Blanchflower and Oswald, 1994a and b). Although the existence of the wage curve has been contested (see Card, 1995; Blanchard and Katz, 1997; Black and Fitzroy, 2000), few researchers now dispute that in some way unemployment affects pay.

Disequilibria in labour markets may also result from the behaviour of the institutions that set pay. Where trades unions have an important role in pay setting they may raise the mean level of pay above the market-clearing rate and these higher rates of pay may result in higher unemployment. Trades unions may also be concerned about equity and fair pay with the result that they narrow the distribution of pay (see Metcalf et al, 2001). If the power of trade unions differs between areas (see Blackaby and Manning, 1999), this will affect patterns of pay.

Empirical research that has sought to explain disparities in pay across the areas of the UK has therefore focused on differences in the following factors: industrial mix; the human capital mix of the workforce; institutional procedures for setting pay; and the level of unemployment. This research has produced support for many of the elements of the theory of net advantages. Differences between areas in the human capital of the workforce (Reilly, 1992), in the working environment, as proxied by the industrial mix (Shah and Walker, 1983), and in the attractiveness of the external environment in which they live and work (Blackaby and Murphy, 1995), have all been found to be important in explaining the pattern of area pay differences in the UK.

A recent article by Duranton and Monastiriotis (2002) has suggested that over the period 1982-97 there was a movement towards pay equalisation across the principal areas of the UK. They argue that the area returns to all key labour market characteristics, which they argue are education, experience and gender, converged during this period. However, in common with other researchers into area pay differences they do not focus upon or distinguish separately the Scottish experience. Is this same convergence evident between Scotland and England as it is for all the areas of the UK?

Data and methods

In the following analysis, we explore the extent of differences in the level and inequality of pay and in labour market dynamics between Scotland and England. We measure differences between Scotland and England in many, but not all, of the factors, detailed in the previous section, which we know explain differences in pay.

The data from the British Household Panel Survey (BHPS) have been checked against that from the Quarterly Labour Force Survey (QLFS)[4]. In order to do this, we took the fifth (that is, final) wave of six quarters in 1999 and 2000 and aggregated them to achieve a reasonable sample size. We then conducted the analysis as follows. First, we undertook descriptive analysis to identify any Scottish–English differences in the characteristics of the workforce and the level and distribution of their pay in 1999-2000. Second, in order to gain some insight into whether England and Scotland experienced similar changes in the 1990s, we compared the results for 1999-2000 to those for the first two waves of the BHPS, 1991-92. The smaller sample numbers for the early period mean that this comparative analysis is of a more tentative nature, but it raises a number of interesting questions that could be explored more comprehensively when further extended waves of the BHPS become available.

Earlier it was explained that differences in pay between Scotland and England might result from measured differences in the observed characteristics of the workforce in the two countries. We therefore estimated a number of simple regression models in order to explain pay levels in the two countries and we then decomposed the results to distinguish that part of any English–Scottish pay differences that can be explained by differences in the observed characteristics of the workforces in the two countries. These regression models also enabled us to distinguish the extent to which the returns to education, and other determinants of earnings differed between England and Scotland. Finally, we used the extended sample available for 1999-2000 to analyse the growth and dynamics of pay in the two countries.

The economies of Scotland and England are far from homogeneous. Recent empirical work has established that the pay structure and level of pay in London is very different from that in the rest of England and the UK (see Elliott et al, 1996; London Weighting, 2002). In particular the structure of employment, the skills and qualifications of the workforce and many other factors that influence pay are very different in London from the rest of the UK. Furthermore, as Table 11.2 in the following section reveals, in the case of London, the distributions of pay reported in the QLFS are rather different in the BHPS (although for the rest of England and Scotland the two surveys tell the same story). The more appropriate comparator for Scotland seems to be England, excluding London. In the following analysis, we shall therefore always distinguish between London and the rest of England.

Labour force status

Table 11.1 reports the labour market status of the total population of working age in the three areas as reported in the BHPS surveys for 1999-2000. The figures in brackets are for the same period and are taken from the QLFS. It can be seen that in general the two surveys produce a very similar picture, except that in both the rest of England

Table 11.1: Labour force status by area (1999-2000)

	Labour force (LF) status							
	Employed (of which low pay)		Self-employed		Unemployed		Out of LF	
UK territory	BHPS	QLFS	BHPS	QLFS	BHPS	QLFS	BHPS	QLFS
London	0.655 (0.167)	*0.631 (0.198)*	0.097	*0.094*	0.041	*0.046*	0.208	*0.229*
Rest of England	0.638 (0.354)	*0.652 (0.353)*	0.085	*0.078*	0.034	*0.036*	0.244	*0.233*
Scotland	0.599 (0.363)	*0.627 (0.376)*	0.071	*0.056*	0.052	*0.047*	0.278	*0.270*

Notes: BHPS – weighted results for 1999-2000.
QLFS – weighted results, six quarters in 1999 and 2000.
Low pay is defined as hourly earnings in the bottom third of earnings distribution.

and Scotland the QLFS suggests a slightly larger proportion of the labour force are employed and a slightly smaller proportion are self-employed[5].

Table 11.1 reveals substantial differences between Scotland and the other two areas. First, Scotland had a larger proportion of the working-age population out of the labour force during 1999-2000. In Scotland, the BHPS shows that 27.8% were out of the labour force, compared to 24.4% in the rest of England and 20.8% in London. This is in part because Scotland had a larger proportion in full-time education. We also see that Scotland had a smaller proportion self-employed than either the rest of England or London, at 7.1%, 8.5% and 9.7% respectively. Scotland had a rather larger proportion of this population unemployed than the rest of England and London at 5.2%.

In Table 11.1, the proportion of those employed who are in low-paid jobs is detailed[6]. The QLFS shows that in Scotland 36.3% of all employees, men and women, are in low-paid jobs. As expected, in London the proportion is far less: only 16.7% of the employees in London are in jobs earning less than one third of the average national pay.

Relative pay

Pay is lower in Scotland than in London but the same as in the rest of England. In Scotland in 1991-92, real average hourly pay was £7.57 in London compared to £5.94 in the rest of England and £6.12 in Scotland. By 1999-2000, real hourly pay, still in 1991 prices, was £6.62 in Scotland compared to £8.48 in London and £6.61 in the rest of England. Real hourly pay in London rose relative to that in Scotland between 1991-92 and 1999-2000: in Scotland it was 24% higher in

proportion of total employees in each area whose level of pay places them in the bottom quintile, and the proportion whose pay determines that they fall in the second, third, fourth and fifth quintiles of the overall pay distribution. From Table 11.3, it can be seen that, while 22.6% of employees in Scotland and 21.2% of employees in the rest of England fell in the bottom quintile, the proportion in London was only 9.5%. At the other end of the pay distribution, 32.8% of employees in London fell into the top quintile but only 18.5% of employees in the rest of England and 17.3% of those in Scotland fell into the same band. London has a much larger share of the high-paying jobs than does either Scotland or the rest of England.

Workforce characteristics

Differences in the levels of and growth in pay may simply reflect differences in the characteristics of the workforce in the two countries. The BHPS allows us to measure many of these characteristics. The first and most important of these – the human capital of the workforce – is captured by distinguishing five distinct levels of educational qualification. Another aspect of this is the employee's tenure in the current job, where this later serves as a proxy for skills that are specific to the current employer and that have been acquired while working. The BHPS also allows us to measure differences in the industrial and occupational composition of employment and in the size of the establishments in which people work[7]. Finally, we are able to capture the impact of trades unions on pay through a variable that records the presence of a trades union at the workplace that has recognised negotiating rights on behalf of the employee.

Table 11.4 records the key features of the workforce in Scotland, London and the rest of England in 1991-92 and in 1999-2000. First we consider the extent to which the characteristics of employees in the three areas differed at the end of the 1990s using the data from the extended Scottish sample. Second, using the data from 1991-92, we briefly consider how the characteristics of the sample appear to have changed over the 1990s and we test to see whether these changes are statistically significant.

The first notable difference between Scotland and England in 1999-2000 is the higher level of job tenure in Scotland. Employees stay longer in the same job in Scotland where average tenure was 5.9 years compared to 5.1 and 4.8 for the rest of England and London respectively. Second, although the share of public sector employment fell in all three areas during the 1990s, public sector employment still

Table 11.4: Means of variables

	London		Rest of England		Scotland	
	1999 -2000	1991 -92	1999 -2000	1991 -92	1999 -2000	1991 -92
Percentage male	48.1	49.7	52.2	52.2	50.7	49.4
Age	40.5	36.1	39.9	37.1	38.6	37.2
Tenure (years)	4.8	3.6	5.1	4.3	5.9	4.9
Public sector	31.0	33.1	24.7	26.3	32.3	34.4
Full-time	82.5	84.7	81.5	81.3	83.3	80.9
No qualifications	10.4	16.3	12.4	21.2	13.7	21.8
O-levels and equivalent	24.2	28.9	28.7	36.3	23.2	26.6
A-levels/highers and equivalent	8.3	11.7	12.8	12.1	17.2	17.2
Nursing and other	28.2	20.1	29.5	18.4	26.5	20.9
Degree, teaching qualification	28.9	23.0	16.6	12.0	19.4	13.5
Agriculture, forestry, fishing	0.1	0.0	1.0	1.3	1.4	1.1
Energy and water	1.0	1.8	1.5	2.4	2.5	2.3
Extraction industries	0.9	0.5	3.6	3.5	1.9	2.4
Metal goods, engineering	3.9	5.2	9.7	12.6	7.9	7.3
Other manufacturing	5.2	6.0	8.7	10.7	8.5	9.7
Construction	2.9	1.9	3.8	3.1	4.3	4.4
Distribution hotels	13.2	17.1	18.4	17.7	14.2	14.8
Transport and communications	5.7	7.0	7.2	6.0	7.6	8.0
Banking, finance, insurance	22.2	18.5	13.8	11.9	11.9	12.0
Other services	44.9	42.0	32.3	30.8	39.8	38.0
Managers	16.4	16.7	15.4	11.4	11.9	10.0
Professionals	12.9	9.9	9.6	9.9	10.6	8.4
Associated professionals	15.0	15.1	10.7	9.7	13.5	11.5
Clerical and secretarial	20.8	24.3	18.9	20.4	17.9	18.1
Crafts and related	6.0	8.1	10.1	12.3	11.0	11.3
Personal and protective	12.9	11.7	10.0	9.8	10.7	11.9
Sales	7.2	5.3	7.0	7.3	6.5	5.6
Plant and machinery	3.7	4.3	10.5	11.1	9.0	12.6
Other occupation	5.1	4.6	7.8	8.1	8.9	10.6
Trades union recognised at workplace	48.3	52.3	48.3	51.7	56.0	59.7
Workplace size 1-9	17.0	15.0	17.3	18.0	19.1	19.7
Workplace size 10-24	14.7	15.6	15.8	15.4	14.9	16.7
Workplace size 25-99	25.2	25.3	25.5	26.8	25.4	25.8
Workplace size 100 and over	43.1	44.1	41.4	39.8	40.6	37.8

Note: Weighted results.

accounted for a much larger share of employment in London and Scotland than in the rest of England.

One particularly striking difference between the three areas is the differences in the level of education of the workforce. As might be expected, a much higher proportion of those in London have a degree or equivalent qualification. However, there are also large differences between Scotland and the rest of England. For example, at end of the period, nearly 29.0% of the London workforce held a first degree or equivalent education, compared to nearly 17% in the rest of England and just over 19% in Scotland. A higher proportion of the workforce in Scotland also had no qualifications relative to England. The workforce in each of these three areas appears to have become more qualified during the 1990s. The proportions of the workforce holding a first degree or equivalent increased in each of the three areas by over four percentage points over the period, while, at the other end of the qualifications spectrum, the proportion with no qualifications fell by over six percentage points in all three areas.

There are also differences between London, the rest of England and Scotland in the industrial and occupational distribution of employment. In London, a much larger share of the workforce are in banking and finance and in other services than in either of the other two areas. The industrial distribution of employment in Scotland is indeed quite similar to that in the rest of England, save for a larger share of employment in distribution, hotels and catering and in metal goods and engineering than in the rest of England, and a smaller share in energy and water and in other services. In all three areas, there has been an increase in the share of employment in banking, finance and insurance and in other services. There is, however, no consistent pattern in the change in the distribution of employment in the three areas across the remaining industries.

Although trades union recognition fell during the 1990s, Table 11.4 shows that, at the end of the period, almost half of all employees in London and the rest of England still worked in establishments in which trades unions or staff associations are recognised for purposes of collective bargaining on behalf of the employees in the survey. In Scotland, the proportion was considerably higher: 56% of all employees worked in such establishments at the end of the 1990s.

By the end of the period, there were only small differences in the shares of the workforce to be found working in different sized establishments in London, the rest of England and Scotland. While there was a significant increase in the share of the workforce working in very small establishments in London during the period, this appears to be simply catching up with the rest of England and Scotland.

Explaining differences in pay structure

As seen earlier in this chapter, there are a number of significant differences in the composition of the workforce across the three samples and these may explain many of the observed differences in pay, the pay distribution and pay dynamics. In this section, we explore how much of the pay difference can be explained by the differing workforce characteristics.

In order to do this, we estimate a number of pay equations across the three samples of the following form:

$$\ln w_{it}^{k} = X_{it}^{k} \beta^{k} + e_{it}^{k}, \; i = 1,.., N; t = 1,.., T \tag{1}$$

where: k = Scotland (S), Rest of England (E) and London (L); w_{it}^{k} is the pay for an individual in a given period; X_{it}^{k} is the matrix of explanatory variables such as education level, tenure, occupation and industrial classification, and so on; β^{k} represents the returns to these variables; and e_{it}^{k} is the error term.

The panel nature of the data and the associated presence of repeated observations on individuals means the data cannot be assumed drawn as a simple random sample, which complicates estimation of the pay equations. One simple and robust approach to the estimation of equation (1) is to treat each individual in the data as a cluster, and then use survey-type estimators to estimate consistent variances by assuming independence across clusters but allowing within cluster correlations to take any form (Sarndal et al, 1991).

Once equation (1) has been estimated for each area, the proportion of the differences in pay between any two areas that is accounted for by differences in workforce characteristics may be found as follows. From the pay equations, the average log of hourly pay in any area, $\ln \bar{w}^{k}$, is explained by the average of measured characteristics, $\bar{X}^{k}$, for each area, and the estimated returns to these characteristics, β^{k}, in that area. For example, for Scotland:

$$\ln \bar{w}^{S} = \beta^{S} \bar{X}^{S}$$

It follows that the difference in the log of average hourly pay between Scotland and the rest of England can be written as follows:

$$\ln \bar{w}^{E} - \ln \bar{w}^{S} = \beta^{E} \bar{X}^{E} - \beta^{S} \bar{X}^{S}$$

If we take the rest of England coefficients, b^{k}, and multiply these by the Scottish characteristics, $-X^{S}$, we compute a hypothetical average level of pay, which shows us what Scots would have been paid had they received the same returns for their productive characteristics, and the same returns for the industries and occupations in which they work as received by employees in the rest of England. This hypothetical level of pay, $\ln \bar{w}_{H}$, in Scotland is:

$$\ln \overline{w}_H^S = \beta^E \, \overline{X}^S$$

Now, subtracting this hypothetical or estimated average level of pay in Scotland from the actual level of pay in England tells us how much of the difference in average pay between the rest of England and Scotland can be explained by the difference in the characteristics of the workforce in the two areas. As we have used exactly the same returns – that is, the rest of England returns – to compute the average levels of pay, this is the impact of the difference in the X's in the equation. This difference in pay is sometimes called the explained difference for it is accounted for purely by explicable differences – namely the differences in the composition of the workforce in the two countries. Thus:

Explained difference in average log of pay $= \ln \overline{w}^E - \ln \overline{w}_H^S$

It further follows that the remaining part of the difference between average hourly pay in the rest of England and Scotland must be accounted for by differences in the returns to these characteristics, differences in the b^ks. This remaining part of the difference is the unexplained part, that part which is due to differences in the pay structure (the structure of returns) between the rest of England and Scotland. This decomposition of the difference in pay into the explained and unexplained component was first proposed by Oaxaca (1973).

Before estimating equation (1) for each area, we considered the overall pay gaps under the hypothesis that the returns to the explanatory variables were equal across all areas[8]. That is, using the data for 1999 and 2000, we ran a single regression in which we pooled all the observations for the three areas but included dummy variables for each area. The coefficient on these dummies variables indicates the extent of the area pay gaps under the hypothesis of identical returns. The results indicate that the pay gaps between London and Scotland and between London and the rest of England are substantial (17.5% and 16.6% respectively) and statistically significant. In contrast, the gap between Scotland and the rest of England is small, 0.8% and insignificant.

The results of the estimation of equation (1) in each of the three areas for 1999 and 2000 are reported in Table 11.5. In addition, the equality between the estimated coefficients across the three areas was tested using a series of Wald tests. These reject (at less than 1% significance) the hypothesis that returns to all explanatory variables are equal. Hence, even where the overall pay gap is not significant there are still apparent differences in pay structure across the three areas.

A few individual coefficients are statistically significantly different across the areas. For example, there were no returns to the presence of unions recognised for purposes of collective bargaining in London, but in the rest of England and Scotland the percentage mark-up[9] was significantly larger, at 3.9% and 4.7% respectively. The gender pay gap was lowest in London and little different from Scotland, but in both these areas it was significantly lower than in the rest of England.

Interestingly, a substantial public sector pay premium only existed in Scotland. In Scotland the public sector mark-up was 7.3% and highly significant. In the rest of England, the mark-up was 4.2% but only barely significant at the 95% confidence level and in London there was no significant difference between pay in the two sectors. However, the differences in the underlying coefficients were not statistically significant at 10%.

The joint Wald tests on various subsets of variables provide the strongest evidence on the source of inter-area differences. They showed that overall the structure of returns to education in Scotland differs from that in both the rest of England and London. For each area, the Table 11.5 results show that the patterns of industry and occupational returns are highly significant. However, there is also strong evidence (at less than 1% significance), that this industrial and occupational pay structure is different in Scotland from that in the other two areas. Workplace size is also a significant determinant of pay in the three areas. Although the evidence that the structure of these returns differs between Scotland and the rest of England is rather weak (Wald test *p*-value 12%), there is more compelling evidence that the pattern of workplace size returns in Scotland is different to those in London.

How did the pay structure at the end of the 1990s differ from that at the start? Table 11.6 on page 172 provides the results of the equation (1) estimation for the three areas using the data from 1991 and 1992. Although the difference in the weighting and sampling over the two periods mean these results need to be treated with some caution, they do indicate a number of possible differences, which could be investigated further. First, the hypothesis test that the returns to all factors remained the same across the two periods is rejected in all three areas[10]. However, the results provide little evidence on the source of any changes. For example, from the estimated coefficients, the gender pay gap appears greater at the start of the 1990s than at the end, for example, in London it fell by 2.7 percentage points over the period, in the rest of England it fell by 4.8%, while in Scotland it fell by 8.3%.

Table 11.5: The determinants of hourly pay in London, the rest of England and Scotland (1999-2000)
Dependent variable: log of real hourly pay adjusted for overtime

Log pay	London		Rest of England		Scotland	
	Coefficient	t	Coefficient	t	Coefficient	t
Gender	0.1343	3.16	0.1895	12.20	0.1471	6.73
Age	0.0471	4.30	0.0589	15.29	0.0492	9.76
Age^2	-0.0005	3.80	-0.0007	13.89	-0.0005	8.35
Tenure	0.0174	2.37	0.0024	0.90	0.0093	2.69
Tenure^2	-0.0004	1.54	0.0000	0.32	-0.0002	1.71
O-levels and equivalent	0.1475	2.16	0.1232	5.98	0.0793	2.80
A-levels/highers and equivalent	0.0812	0.76	0.2021	8.08	0.1774	5.22
Nursing and other	0.2562	3.59	0.2357	10.85	0.2728	8.16
Degree, teaching qualification	0.3888	4.25	0.4233	15.01	0.5094	11.72
Agriculture, forestry, fishing	0.2308	2.55	-0.1028	2.25	-0.1325	1.84
Energy and water	0.2192	2.16	0.2164	5.37	0.2061	3.40
Extraction industries	0.1824	1.42	0.1550	4.57	0.2035	3.36
Metal goods, engineering	0.1923	1.94	0.1141	4.37	0.1980	4.26
Other manufacturing	0.1555	1.80	0.0117	0.39	-0.0161	0.33
Construction	0.1200	1.38	0.1050	3.65	0.0937	1.81
Distribution hotels	-0.0899	1.29	-0.1130	5.11	-0.1911	5.18
Transport and communications	0.1209	1.48	0.0194	0.61	0.0439	1.15
Banking, finance, insurance	0.1640	2.43	0.1498	5.96	0.1908	5.52
Professionals	-0.0584	0.83	-0.0015	0.05	-0.0773	1.74
Associated professionals	-0.1842	2.61	-0.1808	6.92	-0.1578	3.97

(continued)

Table 11.5: cont ...

Log pay	London		Rest of England		Scotland	
	Coefficient	t	Coefficient	t	Coefficient	t
Clerical and secretarial	-0.4221	6.29	-0.3832	16.21	-0.3835	10.11
Crafts and related	-0.5231	5.37	-0.4292	17.85	-0.3469	7.44
Personal and protective	-0.5520	7.77	-0.4777	17.33	-0.4257	9.72
Sales	-0.5505	6.00	-0.4129	12.73	-0.3087	5.73
Plant and machinery	-0.6954	6.57	-0.5578	21.55	-0.4681	10.91
Other occupation	-0.6057	7.43	-0.5283	19.16	-0.4799	11.10
Workplace size 10–24	0.1760	2.77	0.0521	2.60	0.0111	0.39
Workplace size 25–99	0.1584	2.64	0.1070	5.53	0.0755	2.79
Workplace size 100 and over	0.3359	5.59	0.1705	8.94	0.0948	3.42
Trades union recognised at workplace	-0.0718	1.64	0.0386	2.84	0.0462	2.07
Public sector	0.0601	1.09	0.0412	1.98	0.0704	2.52
Full–time	-0.0068	0.15	0.0685	3.61	0.0100	0.34
Constant	0.7369	2.83	0.3326	3.80	0.5212	4.84

Notes: Weighted results. Robust t–statistics.

London: Number of observations = 825; R–squared = 0.5033; Number of individuals = 503.

Scotland: Number of observations = 2,784; R–squared = 0.5076; Number of individuals = 1,689.

Rest of England: Number of observations = 6,975; R–squared = 0.5127; Number of individuals = 4,012.

Table 11.6: The determinants of hourly pay in London, the rest of England and Scotland (1991-92)
Dependent variable: log of real hourly pay adjusted for overtime

Log pay	London Coefficient	t	Rest of England Coefficient	t	Scotland Coefficient	t
Gender	0.1580	3.68	0.2290	13.83	0.2179	4.31
Age	0.0551	5.18	0.0573	14.65	0.0488	4.85
Age^2	-0.0006	4.67	-0.0006	12.75	-0.0006	4.57
Tenure	0.0000	0.00	0.0018	0.72	0.0072	1.22
Tenure^2	0.0000	0.24	0.0000	0.58	-0.0002	0.74
O-levels and equivalent	0.1275	2.07	0.1199	6.51	0.1430	2.67
A-levels/highers and equivalent	0.2290	3.18	0.2126	8.81	0.1740	2.63
Nursing and other	0.2935	3.84	0.2473	10.51	0.2642	3.77
Degree, teaching qualification	0.3864	5.39	0.3770	10.46	0.3593	3.66
Agriculture, forestry, fishing	-0.0780	0.59	-0.1561	1.94	-0.1517	0.62
Energy and water	0.3022	2.11	0.2432	5.46	0.3261	2.63
Extraction industries	0.5783	6.12	0.1178	3.08	0.0075	0.06
Metal goods, engineering	0.1153	1.36	0.0984	3.38	0.0706	0.83
Other manufacturing	0.1631	1.93	0.0116	0.38	-0.0383	0.46
Construction	-0.1010	1.11	0.0529	1.35	-0.0131	0.13
Distribution hotels	-0.0749	1.10	-0.0734	2.63	-0.2281	3.06
Transport and communications	0.1376	1.61	0.0548	1.42	0.0967	1.32
Banking, finance, insurance	0.1959	3.05	0.2169	7.55	0.0991	1.01
Professionals	-0.1139	1.52	-0.0569	1.67	-0.0926	0.72
Associated professionals	-0.2116	3.62	-0.1676	5.34	-0.2503	2.09

(continued)

Table 11.6: cont ...

Log pay	London Coefficient	t	Rest of England Coefficient	t	Scotland Coefficient	t
Clerical and secretarial	-0.3909	7.56	-0.3653	13.72	-0.4383	3.55
Crafts and related	-0.3864	5.57	-0.409	14.02	-0.5275	4.56
Personal and protective	-0.5696	8.37	-0.4914	14.77	-0.5931	4.81
Sales	-0.5430	4.09	-0.3829	10.92	-0.4585	3.37
Plant and machinery	-0.5376	6.10	-0.4929	16.45	-0.5478	4.88
Other occupation	-0.6756	8.50	-0.5661	16.46	-0.7720	5.49
Workplace size 10-24	0.1596	2.53	0.1808	7.91	0.0591	1.00
Workplace size 25-99	0.1873	3.04	0.2088	9.84	0.0963	1.63
Workplace size 100 and over	0.2267	3.71	0.2575	12.09	0.1135	2.11
Trades union recognised at workplace	0.0642	1.50	0.0624	4.22	0.0268	0.56
Public sector	0.0831	1.32	0.0821	3.46	0.1417	2.31
Full–time	0.0369	0.57	0.0366	1.67	-0.0644	0.95
Constant	0.5182	2.14	0.1793	2.04	0.7018	2.51

Notes: Weighted results. Robust t–statistics.

London: Number of observations = 632; R–squared = 0.5076; Number of individuals = 560.

Scotland: Number of observations = 580; R–squared = 0.5124; Number of individuals = 518.

Rest of England: Number of observations = 4,336; R–squared = 0.5270; Number of individuals = 3,842.

However, only for the rest of England do the results indicate that the change in the underlying coefficients is significantly different across the two periods (*p*-value 0.052). Returns to education also appear to have risen quite substantially in Scotland, in contrast to a rise of only a modest degree in the rest of England and no change in London. However, the test for the significance of this change reveals that we cannot reject the null hypothesis that there was no change in the returns to education in Scotland during the 1990s. Moreover, these findings appear to be in line with other research that has revealed that, over the period 1985-95, there was only a very modest increase in the returns to years of schooling in Britain (Trostel et al, 2002). Nonetheless, the much smaller coefficients on education in London may reveal that London offers greater opportunities for high earnings to those without formal educational qualifications than the rest of England or Scotland. Alternatively, as most organisations in London add a uniform flat rate addition to the pay of their employees regardless of the level of that pay, these compressed returns to education in London may reflect the impact of London Weighting.

Although the public sector pay premium in Scotland and the rest of England appears much higher at the start than at the end of the 1990s, these changes were not found to be statistically significant. Similarly, there is no evidence of a significant change in the trades-union mark-up in Scotland or the rest of England. However, the fall in London was statistically significant (*p*-value 0.018). Finally, in the rest of England, the pay premium associated with working in the larger establishments fell significantly, while in London and Scotland the hypothesis that there was no change could not be rejected.

Finally, in Table 11.7 we report the results of the pay decompositions described above. Consider first the differences in mean pay between Scotland and London at the end of the 1990s. The results indicate that 0.083 (33.72%) of the 0.247 difference in log pay is explained by differences in workforce characteristics in the two areas but that the 0.164 (66.28%) remains unexplained and is due to the difference in the structure in returns across the two areas. As expected, the decomposition provides less information on the very small pay gap between Scotland and the rest of England. The results indicate that if the Scottish sample were to obtain the returns equivalent to the rest of England they would in fact earn slightly less.

A similar exercise can be performed to explain the growth in pay in each area to distinguish the extent to which this is explained by changes in the characteristics of the workforce and changes in the returns to these characteristics. These results are also reported in Table 11.7. It

Table 11.7: Decomposition of differences in pay

		Difference in pay	Due to changes in:	
			Characteristics (explained)	Pay structure (unexplained)
Rest of England-Scotland				
1991-92	Actual	−0.0065	0.0047	−0.0113
	Percentage	100	−72.6	172.6
1999-2000	Actual	0.0054	−0.0041	0.0096
	Percentage	100	−76.1	176.1
London-Scotland				
1991-92	Actual	0.276	0.103	0.173
	Percentage	100	37.3	62.7
1999-2000	Actual	0.247	0.083	0.164
	Percentage	100	33.7	66.3
		Real wage growth 1991-92–1999-2000		
Rest of England				
	Actual	0.141	0.084	0.057
	Percentage	100	59.8	40.2
Scotland	Actual	0.129	0.099	0.029
	Percentage	100	77.1	22.9
London	Actual	0.101	0.084	0.017
	Percentage	100	83.2	16.8

Notes: Weighted results. The difference in pay decomposition results use the rest of England and London estimated wage coefficients. For the real wage growth results, the relevant estimates for 1999-2000 are used.

can be seen that the largest part of the growth in pay in each of the three areas is explained by changes in the characteristics of the workforce. In the rest of England this accounts for 60% of the growth in pay, while in Scotland and London it accounts for 77% and 83% of pay growth respectively. One likely explanation for this is, as seen in Table 11.4, the workforce has become more highly educated.

Pay dynamics

How stable is individual pay in the each of the three areas? Earlier we reported the proportions of employees who fell into different quintiles in the overall pay distribution. How frequently do employees change pay bands in Scotland and the other areas, and if they change bands how far up and down do they move? Table 11.8 reports the overall extent of pay mobility for both the last two years for which the extended Scottish sample is available and for the average over the entire period 1990-2000. These figures are calculated as follows. For each year, individuals are classified by their pay quintile in the current and next year. Hence, Table 11.8 reports the proportion of individuals who on average moved 0, 1, 2, or 3-4 quintiles between consecutive years. For example, in 2000 on average 61.2% of employees in Scotland were in the same pay quintile as they were in 1999, 15% had moved down one quintile, 2.8% had moved down two quintiles, 14.9% had moved up one quintile, 4.3% up two.

The results suggest that there is greater 'pay mobility' in Scotland than there is in either of the other two areas. In both the results for 1999-2000 and for the entire period from 1991 a smaller proportion of the employed population in Scotland remained in the same quintile between consecutive periods. Moreover, in Scotland a larger percentage than in either of the other two areas saw a decline in their relative pay. Evidently different rates of pay growth explain the changes in quintile rankings reported in Table 11.8. Over the period as a whole the average annual rate of real pay growth was 4% in London, 3.4% in the rest of England but only 3% in Scotland. By the end of the period pay growth was higher in Scotland but it still lagged behind the other two areas: it was 4.3% in London, 4.4% in the rest of England and 4.1% in Scotland. Thus, again, in Scotland between 1999 and 2000, 18.8% moved to a lower quintile, while the proportion was 16.2% in the rest of England and 13.7% in London.

What explains the lower pay growth in Scotland? There are a number of possible explanations. The period after 1992 to 2000 was one of substantial economic expansion and rates of pay in the private sector are likely to have grown more rapidly than those in the private sector during this period. The large share of public sector employment in Scotland might be one contributor to this slower growth. Again, Scotland has a higher incidence of unionism that reflects in turn the greater incidence of employment in the public and manufacturing

Table 11.8: Overall relative inter-quintile movements

| | UK area | | | | | |
| | London | | Rest of England | | Scotland | |
Quintiles	1999-2000	All waves	1999-2000	All waves	1999-2000	All waves
−3-4	0.000	0.007	0.010	0.006	0.010	0.005
−2	0.009	0.015	0.016	0.016	0.028	0.022
−1	0.128	0.122	0.136	0.133	0.150	0.143
0	0.665	0.668	0.646	0.655	0.612	0.639
1	0.149	0.158	0.155	0.161	0.149	0.155
2	0.042	0.022	0.031	0.024	0.043	0.029
3-4	0.007	0.008	0.006	0.006	0.009	0.006

Notes: Weighted results.
Sample comprises only those individuals who appeared in consecutive years.

sectors. The latter was also a sector that generally saw slower pay growth during much of the 1990s. We also noted earlier in this chapter that Scotland had a rather larger proportion of the labour force inactive and unemployed than in the other two areas. A spell of unemployment or time spent out of the labour force can cause human capital to decay and slow pay growth when a job is found. Thus, there are several different explanations for the slower pay growth we observe in Scotland and in future research it is important to attempt to distinguish between these.

Another way of illustrating the differences in the growth of pay experienced by employees in Scotland and England is given in Table 11.9. To construct this table, we pooled the observations of pay growth across all areas, specifically we calculated the change in the log of real pay in each of the years between 1991 and 2000 and pooled these observations. We then ranked the rates of pay growth and distinguished the quintiles within this ranking. The final stage was to distinguish the proportion of employees in each region who fell within each quintile. Thus, if employees in Scotland experienced slower pay growth than those in London we will find a greater proportion of employees in Scotland in the lower quintiles.

For the whole of the 1990s, the distribution of growth rates appears rather similar across all three areas. However, for the last two years, there do appear to be some differences, with a smaller proportion falling in the highest quintile in Scotland than in the other two areas. This does suggest differences in the dynamics of pay growth in the three areas. What Table 11.9 will not tell us, however, is whether pay *levels* are converging or diverging because it does not reveal whether the fastest rates of pay growth are experienced by those with the highest levels of pay or the lowest.

Table 11.9: Pay growth

	UK area					
	London		Rest of England		Scotland	
Quintiles	1999-2000	All waves	1999-2000	All waves	1999-2000	All waves
1	0.192	0.193	0.200	0.201	0.199	0.205
2	0.185	0.198	0.201	0.201	0.206	0.195
3	0.223	0.210	0.199	0.198	0.209	0.204
4	0.190	0.195	0.201	0.201	0.218	0.203
5	0.211	0.205	0.199	0.200	0.169	0.193

Note: Weighted results.

Conclusion

Comparisons of Scotland with the rest of England reveal some differences in the composition of the workforce. In Scotland, people stay in jobs longer, are more likely to be covered by collective bargaining and are more likely to be employed in the public sector. A higher proportion holds a degree but also a higher proportion has no qualifications at all. The industrial and occupational distribution of employment is also different in Scotland from that in England. London is shown to be very different from both the other areas in several respects.

The average level of real pay in Scotland in 1999-2000 was the same as in the rest of England. However, the analysis showed that if employees in Scotland received the same returns for their characteristics as employees in the rest of England then they would earn slightly less than employees in that area. Something was keeping rates of pay in Scotland rather higher than in the other parts of the UK studied here and the most likely explanation must be trades unions.

Pay inequality was virtually the same in Scotland as in the rest of England and in both areas was less unequally distributed than in London. Moreover, during the 1990s, pay inequality fell in all three areas, and it fell most sharply in London. This suggests that pay growth was greater among employees in the lower quintiles of the earnings distribution. However, although we looked for this effect, and discovered small differences in pay growth at different quintiles, a general effect was difficult to distinguish. We saw that overall pay growth was slower in Scotland, however, than in either London or the rest of England, suggesting that pay levels were diverging.

There was a greater degree of earnings mobility in Scotland than in either of the other two areas. Such mobility can be beneficial if it means a greater probability of escaping low pay. However, in fact, it emerged that Scottish employees had a greater probability of experiencing a decline in real pay than did employees in either of the other areas. We suggested a number of possible explanations for this: the higher incidence of employment in the public sector and/or in manufacturing; the greater unionisation of the Scottish workforce; and the consequences of unemployment and inactivity were all suggested as explanations. Clearly, this is an important area for further work and these differences in pay mobility should become more apparent, and explanations more researchable, as more waves of the dataset become available.

Notes

[1] *Employment Gazette* (1992) London, HMSO, p 156; *Labour Market Trends* (2000) 'Spotlight on the areas', November, London: The Stationery Office.

[2] The average rate over the two years 1991-92 was 9.3% in Scotland and 8.8% in England outside London. In 1999-2000, the Scottish rate averaged 7.3% while the rest of England rate averaged 5.5.% Note that the London rate at 10.5% was 119% of the rest of England rate in 1991-92 and although it had fallen to 7.3%, the differential had risen to 133% of the rest of England rate by 1999-2000.

[3] Smith (1776). For a review of this theory and a survey of empirical work, see Rosen (1986).

[4] We report in footnotes or in parenthesis in the early tables the results of identical analysis using the QLFS.

[5] In all of the tables reporting results from the BHPS, these are the weighted averages. The results for the last two waves use the cross-sectional respondent weights that include the extended Scottish sample. The results for the first two waves and for the analyses using all waves pool all person/year observations, other than the extended sample, and use the original cross-sectional respondent weights.

[6] Low pay is defined as receiving an overtime adjusted hourly rate of pay that falls within the bottom third of the earnings distribution.

[7] Once again we compared the results available from the BHPS with those from the QLFS. Such a comparison revealed a very similar industrial and occupational structure in the two datasets.

[8] It is usual to run separate pay equations for men and women because it is widely recognised that their wage structures are different. However, gender pay differences are the subject of more detailed investigation in a separate chapter in this book.

[9] The percentage mark-up is found by taking the exponent of the coefficient, subtracting 1 from the result and multiplying by 100; that is, [exp(coefficient)-1]x100.

[10] The p-values associated with these joint Wald tests were 0.06, <0.01, and 0.02 for London, rest of England and Scotland respectively.

References

Black, A.J. and Fitzroy, F.R. (2000) 'Earnings curves and pay curves', *Scottish Journal of Political Economy*, vol 47, pp 471-86.

Blackaby, D.H. and Manning, D.N. (1999) 'Industry characteristics and inter-area pay differences', *Scottish Journal of Political Economy*, vol 38, no 2, pp 142-61.

Blackaby, D.H. and Murphy, P.D. (1995) 'Earnings, unemployment and Britain's north–south divide: real or imaginary?', *Oxford Bulletin of Economics and Statistics*, vol 57, pp 487-512.

Blanchard, O. and Katz, L.F. (1997) 'What we know and what we do not know about the natural rate of unemployment', *Journal of Economic Perspectives*, vol 11, pp 51-72.

Blanchflower, D.G. and Oswald, A.J. (1994a) 'Estimating a wage curve for Britain: 1973-1990', *Economic Journal*, vol 104, pp 1025-43.

Blanchflower, D.G. and Oswald, A.J. (1994b) *The wage curve*, Cambridge, MA: MIT Press.

Card, D. (1995) 'The wage curve: a review', *Journal of Economic Literature*, vol 33, pp 785-99.

Duranton, G. and Monastiriotis, V. (2002) 'Mind the gaps: the evolution of areaal earnings inequality in the UK, 1982-1977', *Journal of Regional Science*, vol 42, no 2, pp 212-56.

Elliott, R.F., McDonald, D. and MacIver, R. (1996) *Local government finance: Review of the area cost adjustment*, Aberdeen: University of Aberdeen on behalf of the Department of the Environment.

London Weighting (2002) *London weighting: Report of the London Weighting Advisory Panel*, London: London Assembly, June.

Metcalf, D., Charlwood, A. and Hansen, S. (2001) 'Unions and the sword of justice', *National Institute Economic Review*, vol 176, April, pp 61-76.

Oaxaca, R. (1973) 'Male–female pay differentials in urban labour markets', *International Economic Review*, vol 9, pp 693-709.

Reilly, B. (1992) 'An analysis of local labour market pay differentials', *Regional Studies*, vol 26, no 3, pp 257-64.

Rosen, S. (1986) 'The theory of equalising differences', in O. Ashenfelter and R. Layard (eds) *Handbook of labor economics*, vol 1, Amsterdam: North Holland, pp 641-92.

Sarndal, C.-E., Swensson, B. and Wretman, J. (1991) *Model assisted survey sampling* (Springer Series in Statistics), Berlin: Springer-Verlag.

Shah, A. and Walker, M. (1983) 'The distribution of regional earnings in the UK', *Applied Economics*, vol 15, pp 507-19.

Smith, A. (1776) *An inquiry into the nature and causes of the wealth of nations*. Cannongate, UK.

Trostel, P., Walker, I. and Woolley, P. (2002) 'Estimates of the economic return to schooling for 28 countries', *Labour Economics*, vol 9, no 1, pp 1-16.

TWELVE

Earnings returns to further education

John Houston, Anne Gasteen and Carolyn Davidson[1]

Introduction: the policy environment

The Scottish Executive, in line with UK government policy, is committed to the expansion of further education (FE). The sector is regarded as one of the principal policy instruments through which the efficiency and equity aims of both the social inclusion and lifelong learning agendas may be delivered. The key contribution of the FE sector to these agendas is articulated in the Strategic Framework for Further Education (Scottish Office, 1999), which views FE colleges as offering the most popular and accessible route into lifelong learning. Accordingly, FE funding has been increased substantially in real terms. Between 1999 and 2002, the sector received an extra £214 million boosted by a further £26 million in January 2003 (www.sfefc.ac.uk/abfescot.htm). In its February 2001 letter of guidance to the Scottish Further Education Funding Council (SFEFC), the Scottish Executive placed particular emphasis on the link between colleges and skills and employability, and on "widening access to new learning opportunities for those from disadvantaged and under-represented groups" to promote social inclusion. It further stated that this was "all the more pressing because of the direct links between learning and earnings, both for individuals and for nations"[2]. The December 2002 letter continued this theme: prioritising skills.

The twin policy agendas of social inclusion and lifelong learning emphasise the need for individuals to *get qualified* and *stay qualified* by continually updating their skills. Social inclusion policy recognises that one of the main areas of 'exclusion' in UK society is the labour market where employment and wage prospects for unskilled and lower-skilled individuals have unequivocally worsened over the last 20 years (Robinson, 1994; Gasteen et al, 2000; Houston et al, 2001). The National Skills Task Force (DfEE, 2000) highlighted the existence of major adult skills gaps with a large proportion of the workforce having either no qualifications or qualifications below Level 2 (see Appendix to this chapter). It concluded that one of the main areas of skills deficiency in the UK lay in low-level basic skills, such as literacy and numeracy. Individuals lacking in these skills are those most at risk of being excluded from the labour market.

Lifelong learning is thus viewed as central to the promotion of social inclusion. Policy in this area aims to address the UK's 'low skill/low quality employment equilibrium' (Finegold and Soskice, 2000) to improve economic performance and enhance ability to compete in the global economy. Individuals are to be encouraged and enabled to both upgrade and continually update their skills in an attempt to produce 'flexibility of the workforce'. Lifelong learning policies emphasise the need to expand and improve training and education infrastructure in general but more particularly in FE. With a significant proportion of the working population unable to attach themselves to the labour market, the need to develop Scotland as a 'learning society' and increase the percentage of the workforce with Scottish Vocational Qualifications (SVQs) at Levels 2 and 3 has been emphasised (Scottish Office, 1998)[3]. (It is at these levels that Scotland is seen to be under-performing relative to other parts of the UK as well as internationally.)

The FE sector is expected to play a major role in implementing and achieving a policy agenda that sees participation in lifelong learning and the acquisition of appropriate skills as bringing both economic and social benefits to Scotland. The implication is that the individual must also derive benefits. These, however, are not so clearly articulated and, where they are, tend to be discussed in terms of employability rather than the probability of actually getting a job or enhancing of earnings. The FE sector provides a range of education and training opportunities to a diverse student population intent on gaining new or additional qualifications and skills (Houston et al, 2002). Many of them have no previous qualifications and it is not unreasonable to assume that their decision to participate is taken in the expectation of gaining employment and increasing their earnings capacity.

There has been little research into the returns to qualifications in the Scottish labour market, something that was explicitly referred to in the report of the Cubie Committee to the Scottish Executive (HMSO, 1999). Given the FE sector's central role in both Scottish lifelong learning and, thereby, social inclusion policies, it is essential to measure the returns to different types, levels and modes of education for individuals so that the allocation of resources between the various educational sectors may be evaluated.

The returns to education literature

Research, and debate, in the recent past has focused more on how best to estimate the returns to education rather than attempting to quantify the returns themselves. 'Returns' are taken to mean the marginal benefit of possessing a formal qualification (or not) on the individual's real wage rate, for example, taking account of a range of factors such as age and gender. There has been a tendency to concentrate on returns to university degrees because of data limitations (for example, Blundell et al, 2000) with the result that few studies have attempted to estimate returns to sub-degree qualifications. Recent UK literature generally acknowledges the heterogeneous nature of the returns to education and the need to distinguish between different types of qualifications. Without exception, this work confirms the supremacy of higher education (HE) qualifications in attracting the highest returns and the presence of differential gender effects across all qualifications. The relative merits of FE and school qualifications, however, prove to be inconclusive across studies with respect to their premia rankings.

Robinson (1997) compared the rewards to academic and vocational education. Labour Force Survey (LFS) data from 1993 to 1995 were used to examine the employment and earnings profiles of men and women, working full time, and with 20 years' work experience. Findings showed that there was a significant earnings premium for men and an even more pronounced earnings premium for women at all levels of qualification. Women working full time with a first degree earned 90% more than unqualified women, while for men the figure was 78%. The returns to vocational qualifications compared to academic qualifications, however, showed no evidence of parity. For men with first degrees, premiums were 24% higher than for those with notionally equivalent vocational qualifications at HNC and HND level. This pattern, of academic qualifications attracting significantly higher rates of return than vocational qualifications, was evident at every level of the qualifications framework (a finding that is generally reiterated in this study). Robinson (1997) concluded that academic qualifications improved access to more highly paid jobs, producing this lack of parity between FE and HE wage premia.

The LFS does not contain any intrinsic 'ability' variables and the key issue in the methodological debate concerns how a range of unobserved variables may influence educational choices. If these unobserved factors correlate with the education decision, then the estimate of returns to education would be significantly biased. The unobserved factors that are typically regarded as possible sources of bias are ability, family background and measurement error (unreported qualifications). Three main methods have been used to correct for these sources of bias. First, proxy methods, where some measure of ability is included in the estimate. Second, there are fixed effects studies that typically involve using data for twins or siblings. It is suggested that this will control for the influence of family background and ability because of the shared genes and upbringing, thus allowing for an improved measure of the effect of education. Differences between the wages within pairs of twins should only therefore reflect differences in education. Finally, the instrumental variables method has been used where an exogenous change, that influences choices in education but not earnings, allows this to be used as an instrument for education. An example of such might be a change in the school leaving age.

The National Child Development Study (NCDS) is a longitudinal, panel dataset that includes family background information and test scores in reading and mathematics at age seven and 11. Its panel feature allows unobserved, individual characteristics to be 'captured' independently of qualifications. Its data were used by Dearden (1999) to compare estimates from models that included reading and mathematics 'ability' variables with those obtained from conventional (ordinary least squares) methods. Differences were found but these were not statistically significant and Dearden concluded that the effects of measurement error and composition bias offset the effects of ability and family background bias. Other work (for example, Ashenfelter et al, 1999; Rummery et al, 1999) has also concluded that conventional methods combined with datasets that do not contain ability indicators, can be used reliably for estimating returns to education[4].

Intuitively, it must be preferable to use as complete a dataset as possible to estimate the returns to different levels of qualification. Datasets that contain ability variables and/or offer the possibility of controlling for unobserved characteristics of individuals (for example motivation) should therefore be regarded as superior. In more recent work using both the NCDS and the LFS, Dearden et al (2002) find once again that the omission of ability and family background controls results in upwardly biased estimates of returns to education. This was particularly pronounced in the case of vocational qualifications and suggests that they are more strongly correlated with ability. However, it is also reported that, while premia to academic qualifications do not differ significantly for *low* and *high* ability individuals, vocational qualifications premia are significantly higher for lower ability individuals. This would suggest that the NCDS reading and mathematics' test scores are not particularly good proxies for ability. Moreover, the NCDS is a single cohort panel, surveying only those individuals born between 3 and 9 March 1958. The *representative* British Household Panel Survey (BHPS) is used here, in preference, to examine the returns to HE, FE and school-level qualifications.

The data

As Laurie and Wright (2000) point out, it was felt necessary to increase the absolute size of the Scottish sub-sample from the 1,000 individuals surveyed from 1991 to 1998 by a factor of two-and-a-half. This was necessary, they argued, to permit quality databased applied research on the Scottish economy to be carried out. At the time of writing, only two boosted waves (1999-2000) were available for the analysis. While this gives a Scottish sub-sample of 5,000 observations on 2,800 individuals (80% observed in both waves: this includes those *not* of working age and those *not* reporting a wage), less than 1% of them reported increasing their qualification level. Fixed Effects models require a reasonable amount of variation in all variables included in the model, although Random Effects models less so. Accordingly, for the purposes of this chapter, Fixed Effects and Random Effects models were estimated using two different subsets of the BHPS as follows:

i) cohorts 1, 2 and 3 combined, observed at waves 3 (1993) and 10 (2000), the aim being to get a critical mass of Scottish observations *and* seven years during which a sufficient amount of qualifications upgrading might be observed;

ii) the Booster cohorts 9 and 10 observed at waves 9 and 10. While the prospects for the Fixed Effects model are poor for the reason mentioned above, the aim is to demonstrate the potential improvement in the quality of the models estimated using the larger booster datasets.

Individuals of working age (defined here as 16-59) only are included with age, gender, work experience, industry, hourly pay and, of course, qualifications extracted. This yielded 'Cohort 1/2/3' datasets of approximately 670 observations on 480 individuals for Scotland and 6,700 observations on 4,800 individuals for the Rest of the UK (RGB). The 'booster' datasets had approximately 2,200 observations on almost 1,500 individuals in Scotland.

With respect to qualifications, each individual is described by a set of *exclusive* dummies recording the highest level they held at that time. Five explicit levels of qualification are assumed for this analysis:

(1) Lower school ('O' grades/levels/standard grades);
(2) School leaving (highers, CSYS, A-levels);
(3) FE 'lower' qualifications (SNC, ONC, S/NVQ, modules and equivalents);
(4) FE 'degree-level' qualifications ((S)HNC/D);
(5) University/polytechnic (CNAA) undergraduate and postgraduate degrees.

Preliminary descriptive analysis

Figure 12.1 summarises the highest qualifications held in Scotland and the rest of Great Britain (RGB) in 1991, when the first wave of the BHPS was collected, and 2000.

In general, those residing in Scotland have tended to be 'better' formally qualified than those in the RGB. It is possible also to detect a general increase in the percentage of the population with at least a school-leaving qualification. Of particular note is the doubling from 15% to 30% of 'Scots' with at least a 'degree-level' FE qualification (the RGB equivalent is 12% to 20%).

Figure 12.2 plots the distribution of hourly pay rates in Scotland according to the 2000 BHPS wave (the results for the RGB are almost identical).

Given the almost identical match between the Scottish and RGB distributions, we might conclude that any differences in premia to

Figure 12.1: Analysis of highest qualification held: Scotland and RGB (1991 and 2000)

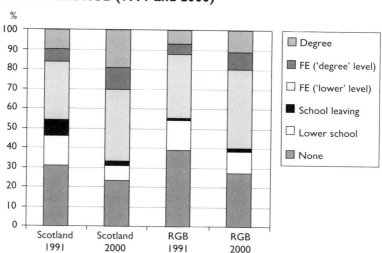

Figure 12.2: Distribution of hourly pay rates: Scotland (2000)

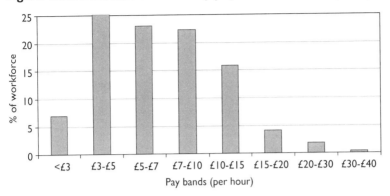

qualifications are not due to one region being more highly paid on average than the other.

Econometric model

It is conventional to model the hourly wage *rate (w)* as a function of variables that describe the individual earning that wage[5]. Such models normally include variables such as gender, age, work experience, industry and, of course, qualifications. The models used to estimate returns are all variants of this general model (this is normally referred to as a Mincer-style earnings equation):

$$ln(w_{it}) = \beta X_{it} + \rho Q_{it} + \lambda_t + v_{it}$$
where $v_{it} \equiv \alpha_i + u_{it}$.

In other words, the (log of) individual *i*'s wage rate at time *t* is a function of observed personal factors, such as their age, occupation and work experience (X_{it}) and qualifications held (Q_{it}) all at time *t*. λ_t is included to collectively model any general effects of time and time-based events (for example inflation, introduction of minimum wage legislation)[6]. As this is a panel-based model, α_i can be used as a proxy for those *unobserved* individual factors that may affect the wage rate (such as enthusiasm, 'natural' ability, and so on). This is combined with the normal disturbance term (u_{it}) to form the composite error term n_{it}.

One common problem with cross-sectional studies of the wage rate is the potential for significant bias affecting both ρ and β as a result of the correlation that can be expected to be present between α_i and Q and some elements of X. This correlation normally arises from the tendency for 'ability' to be translated (in part) into formal qualifications. In a cross-section this individual ability cannot be modelled. Instead, a common intercept (α) is assumed. As stated earlier, bias tends to *overstate* the estimates, exaggerating the returns to qualifications. Having repeated observations for the same individual implies that it is possible to estimate this unobserved individual ability and to filter it away from the general clutter surrounding the wage rate.

Results

Table 12.1 summarises the estimated returns to the assumed levels of qualifications (over and above lower school/no qualifications).

The Breusch-Pagan test indicates the existence of person-specific intercepts and the Hausman test indicates that the Random Effects models should be rejected in favour of Fixed Effects, indicating that, as might be expected, there is endogeneity between qualifications and the unobserved attributes of the individuals (and even, perhaps) the observed 'other' attributes. This is unfortunate, as the results from the Random Effects models are 'better' (than the Fixed Effects), insofar as they have smaller standard errors and indicate the typical 'pecking' order of returns to qualifications[7]. There is tentative evidence that HNC/D qualifications attract a greater wage premia than highers, although less than a full degree. Other FE qualifications attract a lower premia than both university degrees, HNC/Ds and highers, vying with 'O'/standard grades. This pecking order is consistent with that found in earlier work using LFS cross-sectional data for Scotland (Houston et al, 2002).

Considering the Fixed Effects models, despite trying to rally a reasonable number of observations by combining Cohorts 1/2/3 for both Scotland and the RGB in an effort to give individuals reasonable time to upgrade their qualifications, only the RGB model has any significant variables. This does perhaps confirm that absolute sample size is a factor in estimating models of this type. It is noticeable that the standard errors for the Fixed Effects model based on the Scottish Booster data are much smaller than the 'Cohort 1/2/3' model. This might be construed as evidence that, given enough time, the boosted Scottish data will eventually be both large enough and long enough to permit a good Fixed Effects model to be estimated.

It is interesting to note the comparison between the estimates derived from using the Scottish boosted data as a true panel against using it as a combined ('pooled') cross-section. While the (currently rejected) Random Effects model yields almost identical estimates, the (currently

Table 12.1: Returns to qualifications[a]

| | Scotland | | | | | RGB | |
| | Fixed Effects | | Random Effects | | Pooled | Fixed Effects | Random Effects |
	Cohorts 1/2/3	Booster cohorts	Cohorts 1/2/3	Booster cohorts	Booster cohorts	Cohorts 1/2/3	Cohorts 1/2/3
Degree	0.3471	0.3414	0.6515	0.7752	0.7939	0.3456	0.6879
	(0.5036)	(0.2345)	(0.0815)	(0.0398)	(0.0344)	(0.0888)	(0.0259)
HNC/D	0.4558	0.2818	0.3888	0.4316	0.4540	0.1865	0.4136
	(0.4652)	(0.1837)	(0.0761)	(0.0360)	(0.0315)	(0.0704)	(0.0218)
Other FE	–	0.1259	0.0565	0.2271	0.2349	0.0501	0.0799
		(0.3714)	(0.1533)	(0.0490)	(0.0444)	(0.1081)	(0.0352)
School leaving	0.4059	0.3314	0.2145	0.3445	0.3423	0.1084	0.2966
	(0.4639)	(0.1990)	(0.0770)	(0.0390)	(0.0339)	(0.0736)	(0.0242)
Lower school	0.3565	0.2681	0.0771	0.1936	0.1793	0.0671	0.2238
	(0.4254)	(0.1888)	(0.0766)	(0.0369)	(0.0320)	(0.0728)	(0.0221)
Male	–	–	0.2406	0.1558	0.1424	–	0.2514
			(0.0454)	(0.0219)	(0.0189)		(0.0139)
Year 2000	0.0829	0.0615	0.2376	0.0606	0.0598	0.0709	0.2402
	(0.5823)	(0.0212)	(0.0296)	(0.0109)	(0.0174)	(0.2716)	(0.0095)
Age	0.1050	0.0485	0.0792	0.0618	0.0589	0.1170	0.0829
	(0.0870)	(0.0442)	(0.0112)	(0.0059)	(0.0052)	(0.0394)	(0.0034)
Age^2	-0.0008	-0.0004	-0.0009	-0.0007	-0.0007	-0.0010	-0.0010
	(0.0003)	(0.0005)	(0.0002)	(0.0001)	(0.0001)	(0.0001)	(0.0000)

Note: [a] Models include dummy variables for each year.

(continued)

Table 12.1: continued ...

| | Scotland | | | | | RGB | |
| | Fixed Effects | | Random Effects | | Pooled | Fixed Effects | Random Effects |
	Cohorts 1/2/3	Booster cohorts	Cohorts 1/2/3	Booster cohorts	Booster cohorts	Cohorts 1/2/3	Cohorts 1/2/3
Tenure	0.0027	−0.0028	0.0069	0.0091	0.0123	0.0106	0.0114
	(0.0089)	(0.0055)	(0.0067)	(0.0037)	(0.0039)	(0.0036)	(0.0024)
Tenure^2	0.0001	0.0002	−0.0001	−0.0001	−0.0002	−0.0003	−0.0003
	(0.0004)	(0.0002)	(0.0003)	(0.0001)	(0.0002)	(0.0002)	(0.0001)
Constant	−10.1677	0.5077	−0.0944	0.2836	0.3721	0.0869	0.6010
	(20.7794)	(0.9892)	(0.2403)	(0.1186)	(0.1044)	(1.3751)	(0.4033)
N	667	2,222	667	2,222	2,222	6,721	
Wald (p)	—	—	484.38	1,283.48	—	—	4,592.93
			(0.0000)	(0.0000)			(0.0000)
Breusch_Pagan (p)	—	—	19.66	352.43	—	—	301.95
			(0.0000)	(0.0000)			(0.0000)
Hausman (p)	—	—	30.39	115.58	—	—	73.44
			(0.0237)	(0.0000)			(0.0000)
F (p)	11.07	4.79	—	—	91.41	91.50	—
	(0.0000)	(0.0000)			(0.0000)	(0.0000)	
R^2	—	—	—	—	44.09%	—	—

Note: [a] Models include dummy variables for each year.

insignificant) Fixed Effects estimates for post-school qualifications are considerably lower than the pooled estimates. This may be seen as further tentative evidence that cross-sectional studies tend to overestimate the true returns to these qualifications.

Conclusion

This chapter sought to examine the returns to Scottish FE given its pivotal role in Scottish Executive social inclusion and lifelong learning policies. The substantial increase in investment in the sector from 1999 onwards has been based on an assertion, that FE qualifications will increase individuals' employability and earnings, for which there is only a small amount of cross-sectional, LFS-based evidence to date. Recent UK literature suggests that the omission of unobserved ability and family background variables would tend to overstate the returns to qualifications. Therefore, representative BHPS data for Scotland were used to control for unobserved individual characteristics. The Random Effects models, while reproducing the pecking order of returns to qualifications found in previous cross-sectional work for Scotland, had to be rejected as a result of endogeneity between individuals' qualifications and their unobserved characteristics. The Fixed Effects models demonstrated that cross-sectional data will tend to overestimate returns but failed significance tests as a result of too small a sample ('Cohort 1/2/3') and a lack of change in the qualifications individuals hold (Booster). However, the smaller standard errors associated with the Fixed Effects booster model suggest that, in time, it will be possible to obtain significant estimates of the earnings returns to Scottish qualifications with this dataset. The features of the BHPS make it superior to other datasets used for this type of research and it is imperative to continue collecting the Scottish booster to properly inform critical, Scottish Executive education policy decisions.

Notes

[1] Material from the British Household Panel Survey (BHPS) is Crown Copyright. It has been made available by the Office for National Statistics (ONS) through the Data Archive and has been used by permission. Neither the ONS nor the Data Archive bear any responsibility for the analysis or interpretation of the data reported here. We would like to thank the Scottish Economic Policy Network (Scotecon) for providing financial support for this project.

---

[2] A letter of guidance is sent to SFEFC by the Scottish Executive each year as part of the funding round.

[3] Since the mid-1980s, 20% of Scottish (and UK) households of working age have been without work at any one time.

[4] It should be noted that sample selection bias remains a problem. Mincer (1974) assumed that the schooling decision was independent of earnings outcomes, an assumption known as exogenous selection. However, those from socially disadvantaged backgrounds are more likely to choose lower levels of education because of a higher aversion to incurring debt. Women have lower labour force participation rates so estimates will be biased as they are calculated solely on the characteristics of those in employment.

[5] The *rate* rather than the *total* wage is appropriate, as the latter involves the *hours worked*, which is a result of a complex decision process that would require to be modelled separately.

[6] Some researchers estimating wage equations based on data drawn from different time periods prefer to apply deflators to the observed wage rates. It is our view that this approach runs the risk of an inappropriate deflator being used, resulting in significantly biased results.

[7] All these models rank returns degree – higher FE – school leaving – lower FE/school intermediate. This ranking is typically found in other studies using cross-sectional data (for example, Gasteen et al, 2003).

References

Ashenfelter, O., Harmon, C. and Oosterbeck, H. (1999) 'A review of the schooling/earnings relativity with tests for publication bias', *Labour Economics*, vol 6, pp 453-70.

Blundell, R., Dearden, L., Goodman, A. and Reed, H. (2000) 'The returns to higher education in Britain: evidence from a British cohort', *The Economic Journal*, vol 110, pp F82-F99.

Dearden, L. (1999) *Qualifications and earnings in Britain: How reliable are conventional OLS estimates of the returns to education?*, Working Paper Series no W99/7, London: Institute of Fiscal Studies.

Dearden, L., McIntosh, S., Myck, M. and Vignoles, A. (2002) 'The returns to academic and vocational qualifications in Britain', *Bulletin of Economic Research*, vol 54, no 3, pp 249-274.

DfEE (Department for Education and Employment) (2000) *Skills for all: Proposals for a National Skills Agenda: Final Report of the National Skills Task Force*, London: The Stationery Office.

Finegold, D. and Soskice, D. (2000) 'The failure of training in Britain: analysis and prescription', in T. Jenkinson (ed) *Readings in Microeconomics* (2nd edn), Oxford: Oxford University Press.

Gasteen, A., Houston, J. and Asenova, D. (2000) 'UK monetary policy, earnings growth and labour market structure 1989-1998', *Economic Issues*, vol 5, no 2, September, pp 21-36.

Gasteen, A., Houston, J. and Davidson, C. (2003) *Scottish educational qualifications – The returns to educational routes*, Research Report for the Scottish Economic Policy Network (Scotecon), May (www.scotecon.net/menujs.html?index.html).

HMSO (1999) *Tuition fees and higher education in Scotland: Report of the Cubie Committee* (www.parliament.the-stationery-office.co.uk/pa/cm200001/cmselect/cmeduemp/205/20512.htm).

Houston, J., Gasteen A. and Asenova, D. (2001) 'Labour market flexibility in Scotland and the new Parliament's income tax varying powers', *Regional Studies*, vol 35, no 4, pp 321-8.

Houston, J., Gasteen, A. and Davidson, C. (2002) *Investigation of the private employment and earnings returns to further education in Scotland*, Research Report for the Scottish Economic Policy Network (Scotecon), April (www.scotecon.net/menujs.html?index.html).

Laurie, H.M. and Wright, R.E. (2000) 'The Scottish Household Panel Survey', *Scottish Journal of Political Economy*, vol 47, no 3, pp 337-9.

Mincer, J. (1974) *Schooling, experience and earnings*, New York, NY: National Bureau of Economic Research.

Robinson, P. (1994) *Is there an explanation for rising pay inequality in the UK?*, Discussion Paper no 206, London: Centre for Economic Performance, London School of Economics and Political Science.

Robinson, P. (1997) *The myth of parity of esteem: Earnings and qualifications*, Discussion Paper no 354, London: Centre for Economic Performance, London School of Economics and Political Science.

Rummery, S., Vella, F. and Verbeek, M. (1999) 'Estimating the returns to education for Australian youth via rank-order instrumental variables', *Labour Economics*, vol 6, pp 491-507.

Scottish Office (1998) *Opportunity Scotland*, Edinburgh: The Stationery Office.

Scottish Office (1999) *Opportunity for everyone: A strategic framework for FE*, Edinburgh: The Stationery Office.

Appendix: Classification of qualifications

Category	NVQ/SVQ level	Coded as qualification level number
'Degree level inc PGCE or professional member'	5	5
'Diploma in higher education'	4	5
'HNC, HND'	4	4
'ONC, OND'	3	3
'BTEC, BEC, TEC'	1-4	3
'SCOTVEC, SCOTEC, SCOTBEC'	1-4	3
'Teaching qualification (ex PGCE)'	4	4
'Nursing or other medical qualification'	4	4
'Other higher education qualification'	4	3
'A-level or equivalent'	3	2
'SCE highers'	3	2
'NVQ, SVQ'	1-5	3
'GNVQ, GSVQ'	1-3	3
'AS level'	3	2
'CSYS or equivalent'	3	2
'O-level or equivalent'	2	1
'SCE Standard/O Grade'	2	1
'GCSE'	2	1
'CSE'	1-2	1
'RSA'	1-4	3
'City & Guilds'	1-3	3
'YT certificate'	1	3
'Other professional, vocational, foreign qualifications'	–	4
'Don't know'	–	0

THIRTEEN

Low pay, higher pay and job satisfaction

Rannia M. Leontaridi and Peter J. Sloane

Introduction

Public policy concern over the situation of the low-paid worker has grown as earnings inequality in Britain has risen to unprecedented high levels, and this has been reflected in the introduction of a national minimum wage in April 1999, which was set initially at £3.60 per hour for adults, but subsequently raised to £4.10 per hour in October 2001 and £4.20 per hour in October 2002[1]. At the European level, too, there has been much interest in low pay issues, following the Lisbon summit of March 2000, with the European Union (EU) survey, *Employment in Europe 2001*, suggesting that:

> There is some evidence of the existence of a two-tier labour market where the first tier is made up of jobs subject to decent pay, relative job security and career prospects, involving generally good working conditions. The second tier comprises not only unemployment and discouraged workers, but also those employed in jobs of low quality, which have low pay, precarious employment relationships or lack of further education and career development prospects. (p 79)

Following on from this, four categories of jobs are distinguished:

- dead-end jobs which are short term, lacking in training and offering low pay (defined in the report as less than 75% of the country-specific median hourly wage);
- low-pay/low-productivity jobs with the same features as dead-end jobs but also with training and career prospects;
- jobs of reasonable quality, which offer decent pay and either relative job security or employer-provided training and career prospects;

• jobs of good quality, which have all the desirable characteristics listed earlier.

Implicitly in our analysis, we group together the first two categories as low paid and the last two as higher paid.

The report recognises that both objective and subjective criteria are involved in evaluating job quality, but seems to regard job satisfaction as a reasonable proxy, noting that 65% of workers report high levels of job satisfaction in jobs of good quality as opposed to only 30% in jobs of low intrinsic quality. This theme was continued in *Employment in Europe 2002*, which includes job satisfaction in its definition of quality of work and reports, on page 83, that in all member states self-reported job satisfaction is strongly positively correlated with wages, job status and job-related skills acquired through training. Yet the econometric results contained in Annex 3.1 of the report, on page 109, show a significant positive association between low skill and job satisfaction and a significant negative association between high skill and job satisfaction when controlling for the hourly wage, which casts doubt on the earlier claimed link between low pay and low job quality.

In this chapter, we make use of the British Household Panel Survey (BHPS) to examine the trend in job satisfaction over the period 1991–2000 and the Scottish booster to explain the determinants of job satisfaction, separately by gender and split according to whether or not the individual is low paid. We use a conventional below two thirds of the median measure for hourly earnings to identify the low paid and compare this to the remainder of the sample (higher paid). This division is made for Britain as a whole, rather than for Scotland on its own and this has the consequence of raising the level of average earnings for both groups separately, as in Scotland there is a transfer out of some of the lowest paid in the higher-paid category and a consequent transfer in of higher-paid individuals into the low-paid group[2]. We use job satisfaction measured on a seven-point scale to measure the quality of work. The BHPS has information not only on the overall level of job satisfaction as reported by individuals in employment, but also various facets of job satisfaction, such as satisfaction with pay and satisfaction with the nature of work itself, both of which are considered here.

While these measures of job satisfaction are subjective and we cannot be certain that a particular score given by one worker will correspond to that given by another, empirical research has shown that responses to questions on job satisfaction are strong predictors of individual behaviour over such dimensions as voluntary quits, absenteeism and productivity (see, for instance, Mangione and Quinn, 1975; Hamermesh, 1977; Freeman, 1978; Clegg, 1983). Thus, while it is the case that what two individuals perceive to be 'very satisfied' may not match each other, it can still be argued that satisfied workers are more likely to be productive and less likely to quit or be absent from work than those workers who report low levels of job satisfaction.

Figure 13.1 compares the responses in England with those in Scotland for overall job satisfaction. The similarities in responses between England and Scotland are striking.

More specifically, in each case the modal response is six on the seven-point scale and very few workers rank their job satisfaction in the lowest categories, while well over half report the highest levels of satisfaction. Similar figures for satisfaction with pay and satisfaction with work itself (not reported here) also have very similar profiles again in England and Scotland, although somewhat fewer individuals report the highest levels of pay satisfaction in each country and rather more the lowest levels, while rather more report the highest level of satisfaction with respect to satisfaction with work itself.

Changes in job satisfaction over time

When comparing changes in overall pay and work satisfaction over the period 1991-2000 using the BHPS, some care needs to be taken when analysing the Scottish figures because of the small sample size.

Figure 13.1: Overall job satisfaction: Scotland and England

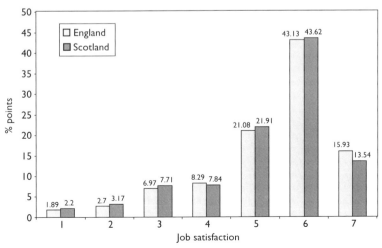

In 2000, there were only 322 Scots in employment in the sample, excluding 40 self-employed and those not in employment.

In terms of overall job satisfaction, Scotland appears similar to England with a tendency for satisfaction to decline over time, although at a slightly faster rate in England, which started with a higher level of overall satisfaction than Scotland (see Figure 13.2). In contrast, mean satisfaction with pay (not shown here) increased over the period in both countries, but at a slightly faster rate in England, which started from a level lower than Scotland, but satisfaction with pay is generally lower than overall job satisfaction. Finally, the level and trend in satisfaction with work (again not shown here) itself closely mirrors that for overall satisfaction, although having a slightly higher mean. According to labour market theory, workers expressing low levels of job satisfaction should move to jobs where job satisfaction is higher so we should not be surprised to observe the generally high levels of satisfaction that we do. Of more concern is the fact that job satisfaction is declining over time, which could reflect increases in the pressure of work or rising job insecurity.

Table 13.1 overleaf provides gender and low pay/higher pay splits for the three categories of job satisfaction, as well as providing some descriptive statistics using the Scottish booster aggregated over 1999 and 2000[3]. Figure 13.3 suggests that, in England, low-paid workers have higher levels of job satisfaction than higher-paid workers throughout the 1990s. In Scotland, the picture is more confused as

Figure 13.2: Mean overall job satisfaction by gender: Scotland and England

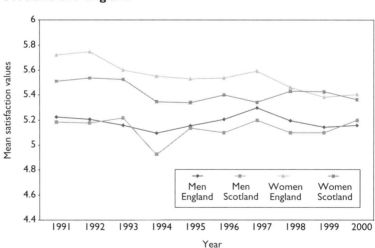

the two curves cross one another over time. We also observe in Table 13.1 the well-known result that women express themselves as more satisfied at work than men across the three separate measures of satisfaction (see Figure 13.2 for overall satisfaction), and this is the case for low-paid workers as well as higher-paid workers and for Scotland as well as the rest of the UK. For women, it is also the case that the lower paid have higher levels of overall job satisfaction and satisfaction with work itself than the higher paid, although in line with expectations the situation is reversed in relation to satisfaction with pay. For men, the means for overall job satisfaction and satisfaction with work are not very different between the lower and the higher paid in the rest of the UK, while in Scotland these means are higher for the higher paid. Thus, there are clear differences in the descriptive statistics for job satisfaction between men and women.

There are also some differences in the distributions of personal characteristics in Scotland relative to the rest of the UK that should be borne in mind in interpreting the regression results. First, lower-paid men in the rest of the UK are more likely to be in the younger age group, 18-25, relative to Scotland. Second, a higher percentage of the low paid in Scotland relative to the rest of the UK are married. Third, a greater proportion of Scottish employees rent a council house or flat than is the case in the rest of the UK, where employees are much more likely to have a mortgage or to have paid it off, and these differences are more marked for the low paid. Fourth, for both the

Figure 13.3: Mean overall job satisfaction: low pay/high pay: Scotland and England

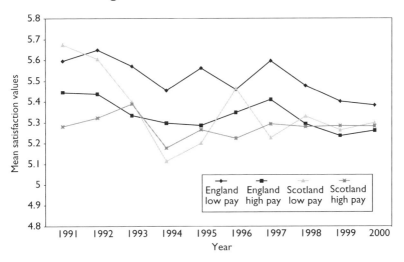

Table 13.1: Comparison of job satisfaction in Scotland and the rest of Great Britain

Characteristics	Scotland				Rest of GB			
	Higher paid		Low paid		Higher paid		Low paid	
	Women	Men	Women	Men	Women	Men	Women	Men
Overall job satisfaction	5.37	5.19	5.44	4.94	5.38	5.18	5.49	5.18
Job satisfaction with pay	4.98	4.87	4.62	3.98	5.04	4.85	4.72	4.23
Job satisfaction with work	5.43	5.31	5.53	5.18	5.40	5.34	5.53	5.36
Mean wage (£)	8.94	10.45	3.73	3.75	8.67	10.32	3.64	3.71
Mean of total hours (inc overtime)	32.58	42.25	29.87	47.93	32.57	42.55	28.09	46.28
Part-time work (%)	27.99	1.45	46.96	8.16	28.66	1.97	52.49	5.67
Trade union member (%)	65.38	54.61	32.36	30.61	58.14	48.89	27.17	27.66
Average time journey to work (minutes)	23.21	23.95	16.33	19.96	22.77	25.51	14.05	20.20

low and higher-paid, trades union membership is more substantial in Scotland than the rest of the UK. Fifth, incremental pay is more important in Scotland, perhaps reflecting the greater incidence of public sector employment. Finally, a higher proportion of the low paid are in small firms (employing one to 24 people) and a lower proportion in large firms (employing 500+) in the rest of the UK relative to Scotland.

Regression analysis of job satisfaction

We follow the established literature (see, for example, Clark and Oswald, 1996; Sloane and Williams, 2000) in estimating a model in which job satisfaction is treated as a measure of the individual's utility from work. This is a function not only of the individual's wage and hours of work as in the standard indifference curve approach to labour supply but also of his or her pay relative to the pay of others and of both individual and workplace characteristics. Thus we have

$$u = u(y, y^\star, h, i, j) \tag{1}$$

where u represents utility from work or job satisfaction, y is income, $y^\star$ is comparison pay derived from a separate dataset[4], h is hours of work and i and j are sets of individual and job-specific characteristics, respectively.

The regressions are estimated by ordered probit as linearisation of the seven-point rating scale, which would result if ordinary least squares regression had been used, fails to account for the ordinal nature of the dependent variable. That is, we cannot assume that the difference between, say, a '2' and a '3' rating is the same as the difference between a '4' and a '5' on the ranking scale. Ordered probit allows us to side step this problem. We pool the BHPS results for 1999 and 2000 in order to ensure that sample size is adequate when we split the sample according to both gender and low pay/higher pay.

Initially, we ran a regression for overall job satisfaction in Britain as a whole (not reported here). This confirmed the significance of both absolute and relative pay in determining overall job satisfaction. Overall job satisfaction was also significantly higher for women relative to men and for those who were married. It was U-shaped for tenure and declined the higher the level of educational attainment and the larger the size of firm. It was lower for those who were members of a trade union. All of this is consistent with earlier studies.

When the sample is split between Scotland and the rest of the UK some important differences emerge in the determinants of job satisfaction. Comparative pay and gender are insignificant in Scotland for all employees combined, and when the Scottish sample is split by gender, absolute pay is insignificant for women as well as comparative pay (Table 13.2). Results for the rest of the UK (not reported here) show that there are significant regional differences with overall job satisfaction being significantly higher in the north of England, the Midlands and Wales than elsewhere. Time taken to travel to work only negatively impacts on job satisfaction in Scotland. According to the figure, male and female job satisfaction seem to be converging in both Scotland and the rest of the UK, but the difference only remains significant in the latter in 1999-2000. Splitting the Scottish sample between the low paid (Table 13.3) and the higher paid (Table 13.4), we see that for lower-paid women absolute pay is negative and significant, a result that we had earlier found for Britain as a whole (Leontaridi and Sloane, 2002). It hardly seems appropriate to interpret this result as implying that one way to improve the well-being of low-paid women is to reduce their pay even further! What it does seem to suggest, however, is that women who have higher pay within this segment of the labour market have to sacrifice other non-pecuniary benefits such as flexible working hours or shorter journeys to work in order to achieve higher pay, some of which are not captured in our model. It should be noted that, in the higher-paid female regression, there is a significant positive relationship between absolute pay and overall job satisfaction in line with our prior expectations. Further, for all women there is a positive relationship between absolute pay and satisfaction with pay, although this relationship is insignificant for low-paid women[5]. Neither of the pay variables is significant in the

Table 13.2: Ordered probit regressions (overall job satisfaction): Scotland

Overall job satisfaction	All	Men	Women
Log gross hourly wage	0.106***	0.213**	0.047
Log comparative wage	−0.073	−0.180	−0.064
Log total hours	0.130	0.468**	0.044
Gender	−0.110		
Trade union member	−0.158*	−0.125***	−0.159**
Time travel to work	−0.003**	−0.002	−0.003***
Log likelihood	−3852.69	−1,843.22	−1,988.97
Number of observations	2630	1218	1412
LR χ^2	190.67	92.31	102.61
prob > χ^2	0.0000	0.0000	0.0000

Notes: *, **, *** denote 1%, 5% and 10% significance respectively.
**See Appendix to this chapter for list of other variables included in model.

Table 13.3: Ordered probit regressions (overall job satisfaction): low-paid Scotland

Overall job satisfaction	All	Men	Women
Log gross hourly wage	−0.198	0.143	−0.375***
Log comparative wage	−0.477***	0.734	−0.446
Log total hours	−0.026	−0.172	0.039
Gender	−0.014		
Trade union member	−0.108	0.216	−0.242***
Log likelihood	−908.53	−302.75	−584.52
Number of observations	601	195	406
LR χ^2	114.53	110.45	98.35
prob > χ^2	0.0000	0.0000	0.0000

Notes: *, **, *** denote 1%, 5% and 10% significance respectively.
**See Appendix to this chapter for list of other variables included in model.

Table 13.4: Ordered probit regressions (overall job satisfaction): higher-paid Scotland

Overall job satisfaction	All	Men	Women
Log gross hourly wage	0.204**	0.278**	0.202***
Log comparative wage	−0.035	−0.388	−0.063
Log total hours	0.280**	0.721*	0.111
Gender	−0.122		
Trade union member	−0.178*	−0.180**	−0.110
Time travel to work	−0.004**	−0.004***	−0.004***
Log likelihood	−2,896.01	−1,502.37	−1,368.31
Number of observations	2,029	1,023	1,006
LR χ^2	175.17	103.64	96.03
prob > χ^2	0.0000	0.0000	0.0000

Notes: *, **, *** denote 1%, 5% and 10% significance respectively.
**See Appendix to this chapter for list of other variables included in model.

satisfaction with work regressions for men or women, but the negative and significant sign reappears for low-paid women. This seems consistent with a situation in which low-paid women receive compensating non-pecuniary advantages from the type of work they do to offset the disadvantages of low pay.

Conclusion

In terms of levels of job satisfaction reported by workers and their trend over time, Scotland looks very similar to the rest of the UK. However, when we look at the determinants of job satisfaction, there are some important differences. For example, in Scotland there is no significant gender difference in the levels of overall job satisfaction, while, in the rest of the UK, women consistently report higher levels of job satisfaction than men. In Scotland, unlike the rest of the UK, comparison pay is insignificant, suggesting that Scottish workers are less concerned about the level of earnings of their co-workers.

What is most striking in these results is that low-paid workers have higher reported levels of job satisfaction than higher-paid workers both in Scotland (at least for women) and the rest of the UK. There is no evidence therefore that low-paid jobs are jobs of low quality as alleged by the EU. Indeed, for women in the low-paid sector, overall job satisfaction declines as pay increases. This is consistent first with men placing a higher premium on pay than women and second with low-paid women obtaining compensating benefits in terms of jobs conditions on which they place considerable value.

While in general reported job satisfaction is high, the trend over time is downward. While the reasons for this are a matter of conjecture this should be a matter of some policy concern, given the relationship, of job satisfaction to turnover, absence and productivity.

Notes

[1] We have not used these minima as our definition of low pay since we are concerned with changes over the 1990s as well as more recent evidence, but two thirds of the median, which we have used as our measure, roughly approximates to these figures.

[2] Earnings are measured in real terms to allow for comparisons over time, compared to a situation in which two thirds of the median in Scotland was the basis of comparison.

[3] We control for the possibility that job satisfaction will change over time by including a time dummy in the regressions.

[4] y^* is calculated using the results of the New Earnings Survey with mean gross hourly wage values over the population subgroups sorted by age, gender, industrial classification and year. These earnings data are then compared with the earnings data from the BHPS for the comparator group to derive the comparison pay variable.

[5] Men are significantly less satisfied with their pay than are women, despite the fact that their absolute level of pay is higher. This is consistent with men placing a higher premium on their level of pay than do women. Further, while for women the sign on hours of work is consistently negative, for men it is positive and significant. That is, men working longer hours are

more satisfied than those working shorter hours, suggestive of a relatively strong preference for income over leisure.

References

Clark, A.E. and Oswald, A.J. (1996) 'Satisfaction and comparison income', *Journal of Public Economics*, vol 69, pp 57-81.

Clegg, C.W. (1983) 'Psychology of employee lateness, absence and turnover; methodology, a critique and an empirical study', *Journal of Applied Psychology*, vol 68, pp 88-101.

European Commission (2001) *Employment in Europe 2001: Recent trends and prospects*, Employment and Social Affairs, Luxembourg: Office for Official Publications of the European Communities.

European Commission (2002) *Employment in Europe 2002: Recent trends and prospects*, Employment and Social Affairs, Luxembourg: Office for Official Publications of the European Communities.

Freeman, R.B. (1978) 'Job satisfaction as an economic variable', *American Economic Review*, vol 68, pp 135-41.

Hamermesh, D.S. (1997) 'Economic aspects of job satisfaction', in O.E. Ashenfelter and W.E. Oates (eds) *Essays in labor market analysis*, New York, NY: John Wiley, pp 53-72.

Leontaridi, R.M. and Sloane, P.J. (2002) 'Low pay, higher pay, earnings mobility and job satisfaction', Paper presented at Applied Econometrics Association Conference on the Econometrics of Wages, Brussels, 28-29 May.

Mangione, T.W. and Quinn, R.P. (1975) 'Job satisfaction, counter-productive behaviour and drug use at work', *Journal of Applied Psychology*, vol 60, pp 114-8.

Sloane, P.J. and Williams, H. (2000) 'Job satisfaction, comparison earnings and gender', *Labour*, vol 14, no 3, pp 473-502.

Appendix: Other variables included in ordered probit models

Current job tenure	Permanent contract
Current tenure^2	Incremental pay
Gender	Managerial tasks
Age	Part-time
Age^2	Time travel to work
University degree	Size 25-99
Vocational qualifications	Size 100-499
A-levels plus	Size 500 plus
O-levels plus	Manufacturing
Commercial or apprentice	Professional services
Married	Other services
Mortgage house	Professionals
Paid outright house	Managerial technical
Fair health	Skilled non-manual
Good health	Skilled manual
Excellent health	Year = 2000
Trade union member	

FOURTEEN

Labour market behaviour of older workers

John Rigg and Mark Taylor

Introduction and background

Over the past two decades, there have been considerable changes in the age distribution of the population within Britain. An ageing population, caused by an increase in life expectancy and a fall in fertility rates, may induce a variety of social and economic effects. Clearly, a large and growing proportion of older people has implications for the social security system. The retired constitute a significant and growing proportion of the population, and state retirement pensions account for some 40% of government social security expenditure (5% of GDP). The change in the age structure of workers may also alter the distribution of productivity and skills (Lam, 1989), influence the level of savings in the economy (Auerbach et al, 1989), and even affect the housing market (Ermisch and Jenkins, 1999).

Over this period, the British labour market has also gone through dramatic changes. These range from increased female labour force participation and growth in part-time work to the expansion of non-standard employment patterns (such as fixed-term contracts, flexitime, work sharing), and the diminishing importance of union membership and coverage. Of more direct relevance for older workers is the significant decline in the average retirement age (Tanner, 1998) and in economic activity (Taylor and Walker, 1996), and the proliferation of private and employer-provided pension schemes (Johnson and Stears, 1995). The ageing of the population and recent changes in the provision of pensions have highlighted the need for a better understanding of the labour market behaviour of older workers. In this chapter, we illustrate how British Household Panel Survey (BHPS) data can contribute to this understanding.

Policy makers have recognised the potential impacts of an ageing population and the need for older workers to make a full contribution to society. In April 2000, for example, the British government introduced the New Deal for the over 50s. This is a voluntary scheme available to people who are economically inactive or unemployed when they or their partner have been on benefits for more than six months. In Scotland, the consultation paper on 'Training for Work' for the long-term unemployed included a proposal that those aged 50+ would be offered early entry to the programme, which provides support for skills development for those who wish to return to work. These policies are aimed at increasing the employment rates of older workers in Britain, which have fallen in recent years. Tanner (1998), for example, documents the decline in employment rates among men aged 55-64 from 75% in 1978 to 40% in the 1990s.

Recent trends in Britain suggest that, among men, the transition into retirement is occurring on average at an earlier age (Tanner, 1998; Blundell and Johnson, 1999). There are two aspects to the retirement decision: the first concerns when (and how much) to reduce the amount of labour supplied to the market, and the second concerns when to start drawing on the pension rights accumulated during the working life. Many individuals may not face a retirement choice, but be forced into labour market withdrawal in older age through ill health or a lack of employment opportunities. Possible explanations for earlier withdrawal from the labour market include the growth in occupational and private pension schemes that have increased expected income on retirement (voluntary withdrawal), or shifts in relative demand for labour against older men, or against the skills embodied in older men, and age discrimination (involuntary withdrawal).

In this chapter, we compare the labour market behaviour of older workers in England and Scotland using data from the BHPS and the Scottish booster sample for 1999 and 2000. The analysis focuses on the employment status of men and women aged 51-69, and compares transition rates between labour market states in England and Scotland. We use multivariate analysis to examine the determinants of withdrawing from the labour market, and examine some differences between the two countries. Given differences in the occupational and industrial mix between Scotland and England, we may expect differences in the labour market behaviour of older workers between the two countries.

The ageing population

To illustrate the ageing of the British population and highlight the growing importance of older workers in the labour market, Table 14.1 presents the proportion of the adult (aged 18+) population aged 45-

Table 14.1: Proportion of adult (18+) population aged 45-74 and 60-74 (%)

	England		Scotland	
	Men	**Women**	**Men**	**Women**
Year 2000				
45-74	40.8	40.6	41.2	41.6
60-74	16.3	17.2	16.8	18.3
Year 2026[a]				
45-74	46.1	44.9	47.8	47.8
60-74	21.5	21.8	23.2	24.3

Note: [a] Projections.
Source: ONS

74 and 60-74 in England and Scotland. This shows that, as of 2000, 41% of adult men and women in England and Scotland were aged 45-74. This represents some 15.5 million people in England and 1.7 million people in Scotland. Of these, 40% were aged 60-74.

The second panel of Table 14.1 presents the current projections for the year 2026, and highlights the expected continuation in population ageing. In England the proportion of the male and female adult populations aged 45-74 are projected to increase by five percentage points (or 12%) to 45%. In Scotland, the projected increase is even larger at six percentage points (or 15%) to 48%. The proportion of the adult population in the upper half of this age range is also expected to increase by five percentage points (or 30%) among men and women in England, while in Scotland the projected increase is six percentage points (or 35%). Therefore, by the year 2026, one in five of the adult population in England will comprise 60- to 74-year-olds, compared with one in four of the population in Scotland. By the year 2026, almost one half of the adult population in England and Scotland will be aged 45-74, making it crucially important to understand their labour market behaviour.

Labour market choices of older workers

Our first step in investigating labour market choices and dynamics of older workers involves examining their current labour market status. Before examining the BHPS data, it is worthwhile briefly comparing some basic statistics with data from other sources to verify that the BHPS provides accurate descriptions of the labour market choices of older workers. To do this, we compare simple activity rates using the BHPS and the Labour Force Survey (LFS) among men aged 50-64 and women aged 50-59[1]. The results from doing so are presented in Table 14.2.

Data from the Scottish booster sample of the BHPS show that economic activity rates among men living in Scotland aged 50-64 were 66% in 1999 and 64% in 2000, while that from the larger LFS for spring 2000 suggest that 69% were economically active. For Britain as a whole, data from the BHPS suggest that about 72% of older men were active in the labour market, a figure almost identical to that from the LFS. For women, data from the Scottish booster sample of the BHPS suggest that 63% of 50- to 59-year-old women residing in Scotland in 1999 were either in work or actively searching for work, compared to 60% in 2000. This is very similar to the proportion in the LFS. Finally, data from the BHPS give economic activity rates of 66% and 69% among British women in 1999 and 2000, compared to the 66% suggested by the Spring 2000 LFS. These comparisons suggest that the BHPS and the Scottish booster sample provide comparable data to the LFS, verifying their use for further analyses.

Table 14.3 examines the labour market status of older men and women residing in England and Scotland in more detail using the BHPS. It shows the proportion of men and women aged 51-69 residing in England and Scotland who are in full-time work, part-time work, unemployed, retired or otherwise economically inactive. Full-time work is defined as working 30+ hours in the week prior to the date of interview, while part-time work is defined as working 1-29 hours in that week. Unemployment and retirement are self-defined: the respondents classify themselves as either being unemployed or in retirement. Other economic inactivity encompasses all other states – for example, looking after the family or home, education and/or training, and so on. Self-reported definitions of unemployment and retirement are not ideal since definitions may vary across individuals and potentially over time. However, more objective definitions are also problematical, particularly for retirement. Retirement may involve changes in consumption and saving, which are likely to depend on

Table 14.2: Economic activity rates among men aged 50-64 and women aged 50-59 (%)

Data source	Scotland		Britain	
	Men	Women	Men	Women
BHPS 1999	65.8	62.9	72.4	65.8
BHPS 2000	63.6	60.0	72.7	68.8
LFS Spring 2000	69.3	59.8	72.3	65.7

Note: BHPS data weighted using cross-sectional weights.

Table 14.3: Current labour market status of older men and women in Scotland and England: BHPS (column %)

Status	Men in England	Men in Scotland	Women in England	Women in Scotland
Full-time employed	45.4	39.2	19.9	15.7
Part-time employed	4.9	5.2	21.8	15.5
Unemployed	2.4	3.9	1.4	2.2
Retired	37.0	36.5	38.1	46.9
Other inactive	10.3	15.3	18.7	19.7
Unweighted *n*	1,727	631	2,110	787

Notes: Cross-sectional weights. Men and women aged 51-69 inclusive.

individuals' beliefs about their future labour market participation, which are difficult to unpack in a general-purpose survey. To maintain sufficient samples in each status, particularly for Scotland, we pool the data from 1999 and 2000 into one dataset.

This table shows that 50% of men in England aged 51-69 are in work, of which the vast majority is in full-time employment. Less than 3% of men in this group consider themselves to be unemployed, while 37% are retired and 10% are otherwise inactive. These proportions differ somewhat in Scotland, where 44% of men are in work (the majority in full-time work), 4% are unemployed and 37% are retired. This table suggests that older men in Scotland are less likely than those residing in England to be in work and are more likely to be unemployed or otherwise inactive.

The table also highlights important differences in the labour market status of women living in England and Scotland. About 42% of women living in England aged 51-69 are in work (one half of which are full-time workers), compared to under 32% of similarly aged women in Scotland. Older women in Scotland are more likely than in England to be retired or otherwise economically inactive. Therefore, employment rates among older workers in Scotland are lower than in England, while inactivity rates and, among women, the proportion in retirement, are higher in Scotland.

Labour market transitions

The analyses thus far in this chapter have not made use of the panel nature of the data, the fact that the same individuals are interviewed repeatedly over time. This aspect of the data allows us to examine movement between labour market states from one date of interview to the next, and so to identify which individuals for example retire between 1999 and 2000. Tables 14.4-5 present such labour-market transitions for older men and women living in England and Scotland. The figures in each cell show the percentage of transitions from the origin to destination states (row percentages). Ideally we would like to identify separately full- and part-time workers, employees and the self-employed, and the economically inactive from the unemployed. However, for the most part the sample sizes after just two waves of the Scottish booster sample make this difficult. This is clearly an avenue for further research as more years of data become available.

Table 14.4 shows that of older men in England who were in work at the time of the 1999 date of interview (either full-time, part-time or self-employed), 93% were also in work at the date of interview in 2000. A further 6% had retired, while fewer than 2% had left work to another non-retirement state (unemployment or economic inactivity). The next row, focusing on men living in Scotland, reveals that 88% remained in employment, 9% retired while 3% left work to another non-retirement state. This suggests that employment among older men is less stable in Scotland than in England, and that rates of retirement are higher in Scotland.

The next two rows examine persistence in and transitions from retirement among older men between 1999 and 2000. The first of these shows that in England 2% of retired men in 1999 had re-entered work in 2000, compared with 5% of similar men in Scotland. Retired men in Scotland also have higher transition rates into other non-work states than those in England. Retirement appears to be a more stable state in England than in Scotland, with 95% of retired men in 1999 also retired in 2000 compared with 90% in Scotland. Persistence in other non-work states is similar in the two countries: in England 69% remained in other non-work states compared with 71% in Scotland.

Table 14.4: Labour market transition rates among older men in Scotland and England: BHPS 1999-2000 (row %)

| Labour market state 1999 | Labour market state 2000 | | | |
	Employed	Retired	Other non-work	n
Employed				
England	92.5	5.7	1.7	554
Scotland	88.4	8.8	2.8	168
Retired				
England	1.9	94.5	3.6	249
Scotland	4.7	89.8	5.5	88
Other non-work				
England	7.2	23.5	69.3	123
Scotland	3.2	25.4	71.4	63

Notes: Longitudinal weights. Men aged 51-69 inclusive.

Table 14.5: Labour market transition rates among older women in Scotland and England: BHPS 1999-2000 (row %)

Labour market state 1999	Labour market state 2000			
	Employed	**Retired**	**Other non-work**	***n***
Employed				
England	86.6	9.1	4.3	469
Scotland	80.4	10.5	9.1	123
Retired				
England	1.7	90.2	8.0	330
Scotland	1.8	86.2	12.0	147
Other non-work				
England	4.3	22.1	73.6	206
Scotland	12.3	30.7	57.1	82

Notes: Longitudinal weights. Women aged 51-69 inclusive.

However, the transition rate from other non-work states into employment in England is twice that in Scotland: 7% compared with 3%.

Table 14.5 shows that transition rates out of employment are higher for women than men in both England and Scotland. In England, 87% of women aged 51-69 who were in work in 1999 were also in employment at the subsequent date of interview compared with 80% in Scotland. The transition rates from work into retirement are similar in each country with approximately 10% of the employed in 1999 being retired in 2000. However, the transition rate from work into other non-work is much higher in Scotland than in England: 9% compared with 4%. About 90% of retired women in England in 1999 remained in retirement in 2000, compared to 86% of retired women in Scotland – retirement is more stable among older women in England than in Scotland. Transition rates from retirement into employment, however, are similar: about 2% of the retired in 1999 were in work in 2000. Retired women in Scotland in 1999 were more likely to classify themselves in another non-working status in 2000 than those in England.

The final two rows of Table 14.5 examine persistence and transitions from other non-work states among older women. These show that women in other non-work states in Scotland in 1999 were three times more likely than those in England to have entered work in 2000 (12% compared with 4%). They were also more likely to have entered retirement (31% compared with 22%), although it is difficult to know how many of these transitions are genuine status changes and how many reflect measurement error. Some changes are likely to result from how women classify themselves rather than changes in actual labour market status. This is a potential avenue for further research. The consequence of these higher transition rates out of other non-work is that this state is less stable in Scotland than in England. Only 57% of older women in other non-work states in Scotland in 1999 were in the same state one year later, compared with 74% in England.

These transition tables suggest that retirement is the most stable labour market state among older men and women in Scotland, and that older workers are generally more mobile than their English counterparts. The exception is for older men in non-retirement, non-work states. In particular there appears to be less employment stability among older workers in Scotland, although most exits from work are into retirement. However, there is also less retirement stability. Therefore, although older workers are more likely to retire in Scotland than in England, they are also more likely to subsequently re-enter work, which may indicate greater financial difficulties among retired men and women in this age group in Scotland. Future work may be able to shed light on the causes of these transitions back into work.

These simple descriptive statistics do not take into account differences, for example, in education levels, age structures, occupational and industrial distributions of jobs, and acquired pension rights in the two countries, which are likely to effect labour market transitions. It is possible that differences in transition rates between labour market states are caused by differences in these other factors. To highlight the importance of panel data in addressing these issues, we examine one particular transition – that from work into non-work – in more detail in the following section, allowing for differences across individuals and across countries[2].

The determinants of leaving work

To examine what determines when older men and women leave work and to investigate whether the observed differences in transition rates between England and Scotland, highlighted in the previous section of this chapter, persist when controlling for other important socio-demographic and job-related characteristics, we estimate a simple limited dependent variable model. Such models are common in the economics and sociology literature (see Greene, 2000, for more details). In this analysis, the dependent variable takes the value 1 if an individual who is employed in 1999 is no longer in work in 2000, and takes the value zero if an individual who is employed in 1999 is again in employment at the time of the 2000 interview. Due to the binary nature of the dependent variable, we estimate this model using logistic regression.

Tables 14.4 and 14.5 revealed that in England, 7% of men and 13% of women employed in 1999 are no longer employed in 2000, while in Scotland the relative proportions were 12% and 20% respectively. We include as explanatory variables in the model a range of individual, household, employer and job characteristics that may influence an individual's decision to leave work, as well as information on the workers' pension rights (see Disney, 1996; Barrientos, 1998, for detailed accounts of the different pension schemes available in Britain). The latter are included allowing for different incentives to retire and expectations of retirement income. Previous research has shown that the labour market behaviour of men with an occupational pension is systematically different from that of men without one (Tanner, 1998). There is evidence that the transition rate to labour market inactivity for older people is different for workers covered by private pension schemes and those not covered (Disney et al, 1994; Blundell and Johnson, 1999). Disney (2002) finds significant relationships between the pension arrangements selected by a worker and their subsequent job mobility.

We also include a dummy variable that takes the value 1 if an individual resides in Scotland and zero if (s)he resides in England to examine whether country of residence is an important determinant of leaving work. The results from the estimation procedure are reproduced in Table 14.6. (Note that the models have been estimated separately for men and women, given the different retirement ages, possible work motivations and job markets in which men and women operate.) For ease of interpretation, the estimates reported are odds ratios rather than regression coefficients, so that estimates greater than 1 indicate a positive association with leaving work while numbers less than one indicate a negative association.

These multivariate results indicate that men and women residing in Scotland have more labour market mobility than in England. A man in Scotland is 37% more likely than an otherwise similar man living in England to leave work between 1999 and 2000, although this is not statistically significant from zero at conventional levels. Among women, the relative increase in the probability of leaving work associated with living in Scotland is 78%, and this is statistically significant at the 10% level. These results confirm the higher exit rates from employment in Scotland.

A number of other characteristics affect the probabilities of leaving work in England and Scotland. Not surprisingly, age is a major

Table 14.6: Determinants of leaving work: BHPS 1999-2000

Variable	Men	Women
Resides in Scotland	1.370	1.778*
Demographics		
Aged 51-59	Reference category	
Aged 60-64	2.020*	3.248***
Aged 65-69	12.546***	6.911***
Widow	1.304	1.282
Educated to degree standard or above	0.120**	0.512
Educated to A-level standard or equivalent	1.152	0.905
Educated to O-level standard or equivalent	0.905	0.972
Educated to below O-level standard	Reference category	
Satisfied with current health	0.619	1.127
Employer/job characteristics		
Job tenure (months)	1.002**	1.001
Non-permanent job	4.200***	2.068
Employer size <25 workers	1.477	1.849**
Employed in energy industry	3.955**	
Log hourly wage	1.117	0.818**
Pension		
No occupational or personal private pension	Reference category	
Member of occupational pension scheme	1.901*	0.732
Contributes to personal private pension	0.443*	1.618
Log likelihood	−159	−194
Chi^2	79	53
Prob > chi^2	0.0000	0.0000
Pseudo R^2	0.2075	0.1226
Mean of the dependent variable	0.092	0.133
Number of observations	652	566

Notes: Logit results. Dependent variable = 1 if employed individual in 1999 is not in work in 2000, and 0 if employed individual in 1999 remains in employment in 2000. Men and women aged 51-69 inclusive. Reported numbers are odds ratios rather than coefficients. ***, **, * indicate statistical significance at 1%, 5% and 10% levels.

determinant of who leaves work for both men and women. Men aged 65+ are almost 13 times more likely to leave work than those aged under 60, while women aged between 60 and 64 are three times more likely and those aged 64+ seven times more likely to leave work than those aged under 60. Therefore institutional arrangements regarding the retirement age are an important factor in determining when older individuals leave employment. For men, there is some evidence suggesting that the highly qualified are less likely to leave work, all else being equal. This is consistent with economic theory, suggesting that men who have invested more in their education at an earlier age remain in work longer to enjoy the returns to this education.

A number of job and employer characteristics emerge as significant determinants of leaving work among older men and women. Among men, the probability of leaving work increases with job tenure, the elapsed duration in the job. The size of the effect is such that each additional month in the job increases the exit rate from employment by 0.2%. Having a non-permanent employment contract (that is, being employed on a temporary, fixed-term, or seasonal contract) increases the exit rate from employment by a factor of four for men and a factor of two for women, although the latter is not well determined. Such forms of employment are less stable than permanent jobs, and it is possible that workers who are approaching retirement are more likely to accept such employment contracts given their limited future career. There is also evidence that women employed in small establishments (those employing under 25 workers) have higher probabilities of leaving employment. Small firms may offer less secure employment. Men employed in the energy industry also have higher employment exit rates, by a factor of four. The hourly wage received has little impact on the exit rate from employment for older men, but a negative relationship emerges for women. Women earning higher hourly wages are less likely to leave work, which may reflect the opportunity cost of leaving the job or the inherently more stable nature of higher-paying employment.

The final group of variables examines the role of pension coverage and rights. It is interesting to note that pension scheme membership has little significant impact on the probability of leaving work for women. Occupational pensions have two potential incentive effects on the time of labour market withdrawal (Tanner, 1998). The higher levels of post-retirement income they provide create a disincentive to carry on working. However, by continuing to work, individuals can increase their pension income by adding to their total contributions and/or increasing their final salary. For men the estimates are consistent with the former argument and are statistically significant from zero at the 10% level. Similar arguments hold for individuals who contribute to a personal private pension scheme. Men who contribute to such a pension have lower exit rates from employment than those with no employer or private pension provision, again at the 10% level of statistical significance. This may reflect an increased incentive to remain in employment and continue to invest in the private pension plan.

To illustrate more clearly how these characteristics influence the probability of leaving work, we estimate some predicted probabilities shown in Table 14.7. In particular we estimate the predicted probability of leaving work for a given man or woman and then investigate how this changes as we change the individual's pension provisions and age. For both men and women, the base individual is married, has no qualifications, is satisfied with their health, is in non-permanent

Table 14.7: Predicted probability of leaving work

Characteristics	Men		Women	
	England	Scotland	England	Scotland
No occupational or private pension				
Aged 51-59	0.09	0.12	0.12	0.19
Aged 60-64	0.17	0.22	0.30	0.43
Aged 65-69	0.56	0.64	0.48	0.62
Occupational pension plan member				
Aged 51-59	0.16	0.21	0.09	0.15
Aged 60-64	0.28	0.35	0.24	0.36
Aged 65-69	0.71	0.77	0.40	0.54
Contributes to personal private pension				
Aged 51-59	0.04	0.06	0.17	0.27
Aged 60-64	0.08	0.11	0.41	0.55
Aged 65-69	0.36	0.44	0.59	0.72

Notes: Base individual is married, has no qualifications, is satisfied with their health, in non-permanent employment, been employed in their current job for 6 years (sample median) and has a wage of £7 per hour (sample median). Authors calculations based on results presented in Table 14.6.

employment, has been employed in their current job for six years (the sample median) and has a gross wage of £7.00 per hour (the sample median).

A man aged 51-59 with such characteristics who makes no contributions to an occupational or private pension plan living in England has a 9% probability of leaving work in the next year, while a similar man living in Scotland has a 12% chance. The probabilities for similar women are higher: 12% if living in England and, 19% if living in Scotland. These probabilities increase with age, to 50% or more for men and women aged 65-69 with these characteristics. Being employed by a company that offers an occupational pension scheme increases the probability of leaving work among men of all age groups in England and Scotland. A man aged 51-59 with the given characteristics who lives in England and contributes to an occupational pension scheme has a 16% probability of leaving work, compared to 21% for a similar man living in Scotland. These probabilities increase to above 70% for men aged 65-69. Among women, membership of an occupational pension scheme marginally reduces the probability of leaving work.

The negative impact of contributing to a personal private pension is clearly evident among men in England and Scotland. Among such men aged 51-59, the probability of leaving work is about 5%, and about 10% among men aged 60-64. Further, raising the age to above the male statutory retirement age increases the probability of leaving work to 36% in England and 44% in Scotland. Women that contribute to a personal private pension have higher probabilities than women with no alternative pension arrangements and women who are members of an occupational pension scheme to leave work. Among such women aged 51-59, the predicted probability of leaving work is 17% in England and 27% in Scotland. These probabilities increase with age to 59% and 72% among women aged 65-69. Therefore, these predicted probabilities highlight differences in the likelihood of leaving work between men and women, between residents of England and Scotland and between individuals with different pension arrangements. They generally reflect the higher levels of labour market mobility among older men and women in Scotland documented earlier in this chapter. However, it is clear that age remains the most important determinant of when an individual leaves work.

Summary and conclusion

Given the large proportion of government expenditure accounted for by retirement pensions, the employment patterns of ageing members of the labour force have public expenditure implications. In this chapter, we have examined the labour market status of older men and women in England and Scotland. This analysis has highlighted important differences between the two countries. Men and women aged 51-69 living in Scotland are more likely than their counterparts in England to be retired or otherwise economically inactive and less likely to be in work. A comparison of labour market transition rates highlights greater mobility between states in Scotland with employment and retirement in particular being less stable states than in England. Preliminary analysis of the determinants of leaving work suggests important differences between individuals in England and Scotland and also between men and women. These differences largely remain even when controlling for a range of individual, household and job-related characteristics. Despite early retirement becoming more common and mortality rates falling, age remains the most important predictor of when men and women leave employment in England and Scotland. This finding is significant for the reform of pension policies and the reduction of public expenditure. The future structure of the labour market will be affected by overall changes in the age distribution of the population.

Notes

[1] Economic activity rates are defined as the number of individuals in work or actively searching for work divided by the total number in that age group.

[2] Attempts to model retirement behaviour explicitly were complicated by small sample sizes. This and the analysis of other labour market flows in Scotland are potential avenues for further research when more years of data become available.

References

Auerbach, A.J., Kotlikoff, L.J., Hagemann, R.P. and Nicoletti, G. (1989) 'The economic dynamics of an ageing population: the case of four OECD countries', *OECD Economic Studies*, vol 12, pp 97-130.

Barrientos, A. (1998) 'Supplementary pension coverage in Britain', *Fiscal Studies*, vol 19, no 4, pp 429-46.

Blundell, R. and Johnson, P. (1999) 'Pensions and retirement in the UK', in J. Gruber and D.A. Wise (eds) *International social security comparisons*, Chicago, IL: University of Chicago Press.

Disney, R. (1996) 'Occupational pension schemes: prospects and reforms in the UK', *Fiscal Studies*, vol 16, no 3, pp 19-39.

Disney, R. (2002) *Choice of pension scheme and job mobility in Britain*, Working Paper WP02/09, London: Institute for Fiscal Studies.

Disney, R., Meghir, C. and Whitehouse, E. (1994) 'Retirement behaviour in Britain', *Fiscal Studies*, vol 15, pp 24-43.

Ermisch, J.F. and Jenkins, S.P. (1999) 'Retirement and housing adjustment in later life: evidence from the British Household Panel Survey', *Labour Economics*, vol 6, no 2, pp 311-33.

Greene, W. (2000) *Econometric analysis* (4th edn), New Jersey, NJ: Prentice Hall.

Johnson, P. and Stears, G. (1995) 'Pensioner income inequality', *Fiscal Studies*, vol 16, no 4, pp 69-93.

Lam, D. (1989) 'Population growth, age structure and age specific productivity: does a uniform age structure minimise lifetime wages?', *Journal of Population Economics*, vol 2, pp 189-210.

Tanner, S. (1998) 'The dynamics of male retirement behaviour', *Fiscal Studies*, vol, 19, no 2, pp 175-96.

Taylor, P. and Walker, A. (1996) 'Intergenerational relations in the labour market: the attitudes of employers and older workers', in A. Walker (eds) *The new generational contract*, London: UCL Press, pp 159-86.

Section 4:
Social and political behaviour

'Scottish answers to Scottish questions' is probably the over-riding rationale for the Scottish Parliament. John Curtice (Chapter Fifteen) argues that if Scottish voters' concern is primarily instrumental (improving the quality of decision making in areas directly affecting Scotland), then people would vote according to the policy priorities they wish the Scottish Parliament to pursue. However, if they see the Scottish Parliament largely in symbolic terms, then we might expect them to vote according to their national identity. John Curtice examines whether the relative importance of policy preferences and national identify differ between the first Scottish General Election (in 1999) and the first Westminster Election held since devolution (in 2001). Individuals who feel 'Scottish rather than British' were found to be more likely to vote for the Scottish National Party in the Scottish Election than in the UK General Election. He concludes that the Scottish Parliament is indeed regarded as an expression of the country's national identity and is not simply valued for the difference it might make to public policy. This suggests that public support for the Scottish Parliament will survive occasional policy disappointment, but also that the Labour Party will not improve its position in the Scottish Parliament simply by improving the operation of the Scottish Executive. To achieve this goal, he argues that it needs to show that it is delivering a 'distinctly Scottish government' too.

The Scottish Executive has limited powers in the field of economic policy making. It and Scottish Enterprise have attempted to harness national identity in pursuit of a Scotland exhibiting more 'enterprise', in which greater emphasis is placed on creating wealth than questions of spending or distribution. Alex Christie, Nicola McEwen and James Mitchell (Chapter Sixteen) argue that such 'symbolic politics' has taken a central place in devolved economic policy making in Scotland. Their analysis indicates that social class remains important in any attempt to understand both national identity and attitudes towards work, employment and enterprise. They conclude that, while both national and class identity were important in bringing about a Scottish Parliament, these identities are less likely to be successful in creating an 'enterprise culture' in Scotland. An enterprise culture must somehow be attached to the existing identities and the beliefs and attitudes they embody if symbolic politics is to be successful in the economic sphere.

A society's religiosity is likely to affect the policies it adopts, their implementation and their success. There is general agreement that religion has become less important in British society, but less agreement concerning what is responsible for this decline. Nicole Bourque, Vernon Gayle and Robert Wright (Chapter Seventeen) find that Scots are more likely to attend church than their English counterparts. However, in the 1990s, church attendance plummeted in both nations. Even after controlling for factors that are correlated with the probability of attending church on a regular basis, a large difference still remains. They conclude that Scotland is simply a more church-going nation than England.

The 'Active Community Initiative', launched in 1999, has been strongly supported by the Scottish Executive, which views voluntary activity as a key component in promoting and developing active citizenship and in addressing issues of social exclusion. This initiative aims to encourage people to volunteer and to involve themselves in community action, in part by identifying and removing barriers to involvement. To do the latter, it is necessary to identify the composition of the existing volunteer group. Jeanette and Patricia Findlay (Chapter Eighteen) make considerable progress in this regard, using the British Household Panel Survey (BHPS). On the positive side, voluntary activity in Scotland is equally shared between the sexes and no significant age differences emerged. On the negative side, in both Scotland and England, an important influence on voluntary activity is religious belief, yet the previous chapter has shown that participation in organised religion continues to decline, although it remains higher in Scotland. In both countries, those people without qualifications are largely excluded from voluntary activities, and there appear to be lower levels of voluntary participation among unemployed people in Scotland than in England. Thus, there remain considerable challenges to encouraging voluntary activity, but these differ in some cases between countries.

FIFTEEN

What makes Scotland want something different?

John Curtice

Introduction

When Scotland voted in favour of having its own parliament in the September 1997 referendum, it created an institution with two important attributes. First, in the areas over which it had responsibility at least, the Scottish Parliament would be able to determine public policy for Scotland irrespective of what might be happening in the rest of the UK. Scotland could now do things differently from England if it wanted to. Second, irrespective of whatever decisions it might make, the new parliament could be considered a symbolic recognition of Scotland's nationhood and an acknowledgement that its citizens' sense of nationhood was no longer adequately encompassed by the multi-national 'state' nationalism of Britishness. Indeed, these two attributes were neatly brought together in the devolutionists' rallying cry, 'Scottish answers to Scottish questions'.

This dichotomy has been reflected in differing academic interpretations of why Scotland voted in favour of devolution. One interpretation has emphasised the importance of the instrumental arguments that were put forward in favour of devolution – that having a Scottish Parliament would improve the quality of decision making and thus the state of Scotland's economy, its hospitals and its schools (Surridge et al, 1998; Surridge and McCrone, 1999). It is argued that what most distinguished those who voted in favour of the parliament in September 1997 from those who did not was not whether they adhered to a Scottish rather than a British national identity, but rather whether they believed the new parliament would make a tangible improvement to Scotland's public services, its economy and its political process.

Others, in contrast, have preferred to give greater prominence to the argument that support for the Scottish Parliament was an expression of national identity (Curtice, 1999). While not denying that the perceived instrumental benefits of a Scottish Parliament played some role in persuading voters to back the new parliament, it is argued that there was also a clear and important relationship between national identity and willingness to vote 'Yes' in the referendum. In other words, support for the Scottish Parliament was indeed an expressive rather than just an instrumental act. Further support for this argument might be thought to have come from the fact that while expectations of the parliament have clearly fallen since 1997, support for the principle of a devolved parliament has not (Curtice, 2001a).

Looking at what appeared to influence voters in the 1997 referendum is, however, only one way in which we might ascertain what it is that Scots want from their parliament. The other is to look at how they vote in elections to that body. We might anticipate that the priorities that voters have for the parliament might be reflected in how they decide to vote in elections to the parliament. If their concerns are primarily instrumental we would expect them to vote primarily according to the policy priorities that they would like the parliament to pursue. If, on the other hand, they see the body largely in symbolic terms then we might expect them to vote according to their national identity.

Of course, there is potentially one important problem with such an exercise. Policy priorities and national identity are potential influences upon the electorate at any election. Demonstrating that one or other or both mattered in the 1999 Scottish Election does not in itself tell us whether this is simply the way that people always vote or whether the pattern is particular to a Scottish election. If we are to argue that voting behaviour in a Scottish Parliament election provides us with clues about how Scots view the parliament then we have to be able to demonstrate that that behaviour is different in a Scottish election than it is in a Westminster contest.

This is the principal task that is attempted in this chapter. Our aim is to examine whether the relative importance of policy preferences and national identity differs in a Scottish election from what happens in a Westminster election. In particular, we examine whether national identity had a greater influence on the way that people voted in the first Scottish Election, held in 1999, than it did in the first UK General Election to be held since devolution, which took place in June 2001. If this is indeed the case, then we have evidence to support the claim that a significant number of Scots do regard the parliament as an expression of their nationhood.

All of this argument is of course predicated on two key assumptions. The first is that Scots have a different set of policy priorities than do people in England. After all, creating a Scottish parliament would seem unlikely to improve Scotland's economy or its public services in the eyes of Scots voters unless it pursued policies that were different from those being adopted at Westminster. And it is only likely to be under pressure to do that if indeed Scots voters have different policy priorities than do voters in England, priorities that are then reflected in the way that they vote. The second key assumption is that Scots do indeed have a relatively low level of adherence to Britishness and as a result do have a distinctive sense of national identity that they might want to express. So, in the first half of this chapter, we look at the policy priorities and national identity of the Scottish electorate and how far they are different from those of people in England. Then in the second half we look at their role in voting behaviour in the 1999 Scottish and 2001 UK General Election.

Data

Our data come from the 1999-2001 waves of the British and Scottish Household Panel Surveys (BHPS/SHPS). Between them, they contain measures of each of our main concepts. Members of the panels in Scotland were asked about their national identity in 1999 while a set of questions that measure voters' preferences on the main ideological division in Britain, that is how much equality there should be in society and what action government should take to promote it, were asked of respondents on both sides of the border in the 2000 wave. Meanwhile, the 1999 wave also asked respondents in Scotland how they voted in the first Scottish Parliament Election held earlier that year, while the 2001 wave asked how they voted in that year's UK General Election. Although the questions were asked in different years, because they were asked of the same respondents in each year we can analyse the association in both 1999 and 2001 between vote and both national identity and voters' policy priorities.

Of course, not all of the respondents who were successfully contacted in 1999 were also contacted in 2000 or 2001. The results in the second half of the chapter are therefore weighted by the 1999-2000 panel weights or 1999-2001 weights as appropriate. In the first part of this chapter where we are simply looking at the data collected in one particular wave, the data have been weighted by the appropriate cross-sectional weights for that year[1].

Policy priorities

As we have indicated, the 2000 wave of the British and Scottish surveys included a set of six items that tap voters' attitudes towards the need for equality and the role that the government should play in achieving it. These items, full details of which are to be found in Table 15.1, are similar to the set of items that Evans and Heath (1995; see also Curtice, 1996a) have shown form a reliable and valid Likert scale of socialist/ laissez-faire attitudes that discriminates well between Conservative and Labour voters[2]. These items are thus a useful indicator of the principal ideological or value division in British politics and of the policy priorities that are associated with such values. So, if Scots do indeed have different policy priorities from England, priorities that were less likely to be pursued by a UK government than a Scottish one, then Scots ought to give rather different answers to these questions than do people in England.

Scotland has not returned a majority of Conservative MPs since 1959. Yet success south of the border gave them a majority in Westminster between 1970 and 1974, and then between 1979 and 1997. Not surprisingly, therefore, it is not uncommon for it to be claimed that Scots are more left-wing than people in England. And previous research has given some support at least to that view (Curtice, 1988, 1996b; Brown et al, 1998, 1999; Paterson et al, 2001; Paterson, 2002).

So also do our data. As can be most easily seen from the final column of Table 15.1, people living in Scotland are on balance less likely to support a pro-laissez-faire statement and more likely to back a pro-socialist one than are their counterparts in England. The one exception is the laissez-faire statement, 'Ordinary people get their fair share of the nation's wealth', where on balance opinion is the same in Scotland as it is in England. However, at the same time the gap should not be exaggerated. Most of the differences are relatively small. Perhaps just as importantly, on only one item (private enterprise) is it the case that the balance of opinion is in one direction in England and in the other in Scotland – and then only just. In truth both England and Scotland could be described as having a predominantly social democratic if not socialist political culture. It is simply the case that that culture is a little stronger in Scotland than it is in England.

Table 15.1: Socialist/laissez-faire values in Scotland and England

Laissez-faire statements		Strongly agree (%)	Agree (%)	Neither agree/ disagree (%)	Disagree (%)	Strongly disagree (%)	Agree- disagree (%)
Ordinary people get their fair share of the nation's wealth	England	1	15	22	51	11	+46
	Scotland	1	18	17	51	14	+46
Private enterprise is the best way to solve Britain's economic problems	England	4	26	43	25	3	−2
	Scotland	3	19	37	35	6	+19
There is one law for the rich and one for the poor	England	16	50	18	15	2	+49
	Scotland	22	51	13	14	1	+58
Major public services and industries ought to be in state ownership	England	6	29	33	29	4	+4
	Scotland	7	32	31	27	3	+9
It is the government's responsibility to provide a job for everyone who wants one	England	7	40	18	31	4	+12
	Scotland	9	45	15	27	4	+23
Strong trade unions are needed to protect the working conditions and wages of employees	England	11	47	22	18	3	+37
	Scotland	17	50	17	14	2	+52

Source: BHPS wave 10/SHPS wave 2

Notes: Those saying don't know and interviews with proxy respondents are excluded. The minimum weighted *n* in England is 7,112 and in Scotland is 3,161.

National identity

If the political culture of Scotland is more similar to that of England than might commonly be imagined, the same can hardly be said of its sense of national identity. That national identity is measured in our panel by asking the so-called Moreno question, which asks respondents what mixture of two possible national identities – in this case Scottish and British – best describes themselves (Moreno, 1988). They may say that only one of these identities applies to them, both equally, or one more than the other (Table 15.2). And, as can be seen, only one in eight people in our Scottish panel said that a sense of Britishness mattered more to them than any notion of being Scottish. In contrast, almost two in three gave priority to being Scottish rather than British.

For most people in Scotland then, their distinctive Scottishness appears to matter more than the Britishness that would seem capable of providing a sense of identity that was shared in common with people in England. Of course, Britishness could only be a source of common identity if it was also adhered to in England. In fact, BHPS respondents living in England were not asked the Moreno question about whether they felt English or British. However, it was asked in the 1999 British Social Attitudes survey and, as we can see in Table 15.2, three in five people in England say they feel British at least as much as they do English (Curtice and Heath, 2000). But that survey's sister survey in Scotland, the Scottish Social Attitudes survey, confirms that the picture in Scotland is indeed very different.

So it would appear then that national identity in Scotland is far more distinctive than are the policy priorities of the Scottish electorate. By this simple criterion at least, it would seem more likely that the demand for a Scottish parliament was a reflection of a wish for a symbolic expression of national identity rather than a need to find a

Table 15.2: Moreno national identity in Scotland and England

	Scotland		England
	SHPS (%)	SSA (%)	BSA (%)
Scottish/English, not British	29	32	17
More Scottish/English than British	35	35	15
Equally Scottish/English and British	22	22	37
More British than Scottish/English	5	3	11
British, not Scottish/English	8	4	12
Other answers	4	3	3
(n)	(3,263)	(1,482)	(2,718)

Source: SHPS wave I/Scottish Social Attitudes 1999/British Social Attitudes 1999

means of implementing a distinctive set of policy priorities. However, of course our analysis so far does nothing to prove that case. We now turn to the particular means of assessing the validity of that argument being used in this chapter, that is by looking at whether the balance of influences on voters in a Scottish Parliament election are rather different from what they are in a UK general election.

Some preliminaries

There is in fact one simple reason why we might think that voters were influenced by different considerations in Scottish Parliament Elections than they are in UK general elections. The outcome of the 1999 Election was very different from both the 1997 and the 2001 General Elections. Despite the fact that the constituency part of the Holyrood contest was run using the same first-past-the-post method of election as is used in UK General Elections, Labour's share of the vote was markedly lower in 1999 than it was in 1997 and 2001, while that of the Scottish National Party (SNP) was higher (see Table 15.3). Of course, this might simply reflect the possibility that voters regarded the Scottish Election as an opportunity to protest against the performance of the UK Labour administration (Reif and Schmitt, 1980). However, previous research has demonstrated that that was not the case. Instead, voters voted differently in the 1999 Scottish Election from the way that they said they would have voted in a UK general election held at the same time, with fewer voters indicating a preference for Labour in the Scottish Election while more backed the SNP (Curtice, 2001b; Paterson et al, 2001)[3].

Prima facie, at least, this of course is precisely the pattern that one would expect if national identity had more influence on the way that people voted in a Scottish election than it did in a UK general election.

Table 15.3: Scottish election results (1997-2001)

	1997 (%)	1999 (%)	2001 (%)
Labour	45.6	38.8	43.9
SNP	22.1	28.7	20.1
Conservative	17.5	15.6	15.6
Liberal Democrat	13.0	14.2	16.4
Scottish Socialist Party[a]	0.3	1.0	3.1
Others	1.5	1.7	0.9
Turnout	71.3	58.2	58.1

Notes: [a]Scottish Socialist Alliance in 1997.
1999 result is for the constituency part of the Scottish Parliament election.
Source: Curtice (2002)

UK General Election. Meanwhile we see the very opposite pattern among those who say they are 'Scottish, not British'. Among this group of our panellists turnout was only a little higher in 2001 than it was in 1999, and in contrast to the position in the 1999 Scottish Election, was lower than in any other group.

So, it appears then that national identity did make a difference to who voted in the 1999 and 2001 Elections. Those who felt predominantly Scottish were relatively more likely to vote in the 1999 Scottish Election than they were in the 2001 UK Election for the Westminster Parliament. So we have some evidence to support the view that the Scottish Parliament is seen as an embodiment of and perhaps a means of promoting a distinctive Scottish identity.

However, looking at turnout does not enable us to say much about changes in the importance of national identity compared with policy preferences. This is because there is no reason to believe that the relationship between policy preferences and turnout should be different in a Scottish election from a UK contest. Both those who favour a pro-socialist position and those who adopt a pro-laissez-faire one have just as much or as little reason to vote in a Scottish election as in a Westminster one. So to compare the relative influence of national identity and policy preferences in the two kinds of election we need ultimately to look at their relationship with vote.

Comparing influences

If policy preferences have a greater influence on the way that people vote in a UK general election than they do in a Scottish election, then what we should find is that the difference between the way that those who take a pro-socialist position vote and the way that those who take a pro-laissez-faire position do should be greater in a UK general election than it is in a Scottish contest. And as Labour is the traditional champion of socialist values in Scotland, we might expect this to be particularly the case so far as voting for that party is concerned.

Table 15.6 examines whether or not this is the case, using the same two of our six indicators of socialist/laissez-faire values that we used in Table 15.4. And we see much the pattern that we might expect. Labour's support rose more between 1999 and 2001 among those of a pro-socialist viewpoint than it did among those of a pro-laissez-faire one. As a result the gap between the two groups in their propensity to vote Labour was markedly higher on the second occasion.

Consider, for example, the first of the two items in the table. Among those who agreed with the pro-laissez-faire viewpoint, "Private

Table 15.6: Socialist/laissez-faire values and party support (1999-2001)

	% Labour			% SNP			
	1999	2001	Change	1999	2001	Change	(Min *n*)
a) Private enterprise is the best way to solve Britain's economic problems							
Agree	32	38	+6	26	17	−9	(372)
Neither	38	51	+13	34	23	−11	(502)
Disagree	40	57	+17	36	22	−14	(628)
b) It is the government's responsibility to provide a job for everyone who wants one							
Agree	42	57	+15	35	24	−11	(832)
Neither	33	43	+10	34	22	−12	(253)
Disagree	32	41	+9	27	17	−10	(491)

Notes: Agree includes:'strongly agree' and 'agree'; Disagree includes:'strongly disagree' and 'disagree'.
1999 vote is constituency vote.
Source: SHPS waves 1-3

enterprise is the best way to solve Britain's economic problems", Labour's support rose by six points between 1999 and 2001. But among those who disagreed with the proposition, the increase in Labour support was no less than 17 points. As a result what in 1999 was a relatively modest gap of eight points between the two groups in their level of support for Labour had by 2001 more than doubled to 19 points.

At the same time, and as we might expect given the change in the character of Labour's vote, we can also see that on one of our measures at least the SNP's vote seemed to fall rather more in 2001 among those of a more socialist persuasion than it did among those backing a pro-laissez-faire view. It seems that the SNP's ability to eat into what might be considered to be Labour's traditional support was somewhat lower in the UK General Election than in the Scottish contest two years earlier.

So it appears then that policy preferences did have less of an influence on the way that people voted in the 1999 Scottish Parliament Election than on how they voted in the 2001 UK General Election. In particular, voters of a more socialist persuasion were less likely to vote Labour in 1999 than in the 2001 Election, and instead were rather more willing to vote SNP. But did the SNP's vote also have a more nationalist tinge in 1999 than it did in 2001?

Table 15.7 suggests that indeed it might well have done. In 1999 over a half of those voters who said they were 'Scottish, not British', backed the SNP. In 2001 only a third did so. Among no other category, not even those who said they were 'more Scottish than British' (a third of whom backed the SNP in 1999), was the drop on anything like a similar scale. In contrast, Labour's support, which varies little by national identity, increased more or less evenly across most categories of national identity.

There is, however, an obvious problem with this analysis. Because so few of those who said that their identity was wholly or mostly British backed the SNP in 1999, it was impossible that SNP support could fall on the scale that it did among those who were wholly Scottish. It may be that once we allow for this we find that national identity was just as important to the chances of someone voting SNP in 2001 as it was in 1999. We can get around this difficulty by fitting a logistic model to the data in Table 15.7. At the same time we can also use this strategy to check the conclusions we have drawn from Table 15.6.

We proceed as follows. At each of the two elections we model, first, the probability that someone votes Labour versus their not doing so, and then follow this with an equivalent analysis of voting SNP versus not doing so. National identity is introduced into each model, and by doing so as a categorical variable we do not assume that the relationship between vote and national identity is a linear one. Then all six of the measures of socialist/laissez-faire values in Table 15.1 are included as a block (of interval-level variables). Our interest here is not in the relationship between any one of these items and vote, but rather their collective contribution to our ability to model vote choice. This can most easily be seen by looking at the model chi-square (χ^2) for this block of variables as whole, and so it is this statistic that is reported in Table 15.8 for our national identity variable and for our block of socialist/laissez-faire values. The larger the chi-square the greater the contribution our variables make to our ability to predict vote choice. Doing this helps to assuage our fears about the interpretation of Table 15.7. The model chi-square for the impact of national identity on voting SNP versus not doing so is lower in 2001 than it was in 1999, indicating that even after we allow for the low level of SNP

Table 15.7: National identity and party choice (1999-2001)

	% Labour			% SNP			
	1999	2001	Change	1999	2001	Change	(Min *n*)
Scottish, not British	33	46	+13	51	33	−18	(492)
More Scottish than British	40	51	+11	35	26	−9	(639)
Equally British and Scottish	41	55	+14	17	9	−8	(415)
More British than Scottish	24	36	+12	9	3	−6	(96)
British, not Scottish	38	45	+9	8	4	−4	(89)

Source: SHPS waves 1 and 3

Table 15.8: The changing influence of values and identity

	Model chi-square from logistic regression of			
	Lab v. not Lab		SNP v. not SNP	
	1999	2001	1999	2001
National identity	17.3	20.3	218.5	184.0
Values	116.7	227.1	37.2	24.1

Source: SHPS waves 1-3

support among wholly or mostly British identifiers in 1999, the fall among those who felt 'Scottish, not British' was rather greater than we would have anticipated if, after allowing for the fall in SNP support as a whole, national identity made as much difference to the chances of someone voting SNP in 2001 as it did in 1999. At the same time we secure confirmation that being of a more socialist persuasion made a much greater difference to the chances of someone voting Labour in 2001 than it did in 1999, while national identity remained as relatively unimportant as ever.

Conclusion

This chapter has cast further light on the reason why the outcome of the 1999 Scottish Election was so different from that of either the 1997 or 2001 General Elections. National identity appears to have mattered more in the 1999 Election than it does in a Westminster election. Those who felt Scottish rather than British apparently felt they had more reason to vote SNP in a Scottish than in a Westminster election if they did go to the polls, while at the same time they were also more likely to think it was worth voting in the first place. Meanwhile, those of a more pro-socialist persuasion apparently felt there was more reason to vote Labour in 2001 than they did in 1999.

What influences how people vote gives us clues about what they expect the institution for which they are voting to achieve. The relative importance of national identity in how people voted in 1999 as compared with 2001 suggests that the Scottish Parliament is indeed regarded as an expression of the country's national identity and is not simply valued for the difference it might make to public policy. So the good news for the Scottish Parliament is that public support for its existence should be capable of withstanding the occasional policy disappointment. However, the bad news for the dominant party in that parliament, Labour, is that it cannot hope to improve its position in Scottish Elections simply by delivering better government. Rather it needs to demonstrate that it can provide distinctly Scottish government too.

Notes

[1] Data for Scotland are reported using the weights supplied when analysing Scottish respondents separately. Data for England are reported using the set weights that produce a weighted sample size for the whole sample similar to the unweighted sample size for the BHPS prior to the expansion of the sample in Scotland and Wales; we do not use those weights that produce a weighted sample size similar to the unweighted sample size of the expanded panel. Use of the latter would appear to give a misleading impression of the size of the sample in England.

[2] The set of BHPS items is exactly the same as the balanced socialist/laissez-faire scale developed in Evans and Heath (1995) except that the direction of the trade unions item is worded in a pro-socialist rather than a pro-laissez-faire direction.

[3] At the same time the 2001 Scottish Social Attitudes survey indicates that Labour's share of the vote would have been six points lower and the SNP's 10 points higher, if a Scottish Parliament election were being held on the occasion of that year's UK General Election.

[4] It may also be the case that repeated participation in the panel in 1999 and 2000 may have stimulated panellists who did not vote in 1999 to do so in 2001.

References

Brown, A., McCrone, D. and Paterson, L. (1998) *Politics and society in Scotland* (2nd edn), London: Macmillan.

Brown, A., McCrone, D., Paterson, L. and Surridge, P. (1999) *The Scottish electorate: The 1997 General Election and beyond*, London: Macmillan.

Curtice, J. (1988) 'One nation?', in R. Jowell, S. Witherspoon and L. Brook (eds) *British social attitudes: The fifth report*, Aldershot: Gower.

Curtice, J. (1996a) 'Why methodology matters', in B. Taylor and K. Thomson (eds) *Understanding change in social attitudes*, Aldershot: Dartmouth.

Curtice, J. (1996b) 'One nation again?', in R. Jowell, J. Curtice, A. Park, L. Brook and K. Thomson (eds) *British social attitudes: The thirteenth report*, Aldershot: Gower.

Curtice, J. (1999) 'Is Scotland a nation and Wales not?: why the two referendum results were so different', in B. Taylor and K. Thomson (eds) *Scotland and Wales: Nations again?*, Cardiff: University of Wales Press.

Curtice, J. (2001a) 'Hopes dashed and fears assuaged', in A. Trench (ed) *The state of the nations: The second year of devolution in the United Kingdom*, Thorverton: Imprint Academic.

Curtice, J. (2001b) 'Is devolution succouring nationalism?', *Contemporary Wales*, vol 14, pp 80-103.

Curtice, J. (2002) 'Did devolution make a difference? The first post-devolution UK election in Scotland', *British Elections and Parties Review*, vol 12, pp 64-79.

Curtice, J. and Heath, A. (2000) 'Is the English lion about to roar? National identity after devolution', in R. Jowell, J. Curtice, A. Park, K. Thomson, L. Jarvis, C. Bromley and N. Stratford (eds) *British social attitudes: The seventeenth report: Focusing on diversity*, London: Sage Publications.

Curtice, J. and Seyd, B. (2001) 'Is devolution strengthening or weakening the UK?', in A. Park, J. Curtice, K. Thomson, L. Jarvis and C. Bromley (eds) *British social attitudes: The eighteenth report: Public policy, social ties*, London: Sage Publications.

Evans, G. and Heath, A. (1995) 'The measurement of left-right and libertarian-authoritarian values: a comparison of balanced and unbalanced scale', *Quality and Quantity*, vol 29, pp 191-206.

Moreno, L. (1988) 'Scotland and Catalonia: the path to home rule', in D. McCrone and A. Brown (eds) *The Scottish government yearbook*, Edinburgh: Unit for the Study of Government in Scotland.

Paterson, L. (2002) 'Ideology and public policy', in J. Curtice, D. McCrone, A. Park and L. Paterson (eds) *New Scotland, new society?*, Edinburgh: Polygon.

Paterson, L., Brown, A., Curtice, J., Hinds, K., McCrone, D., Park, A., Sproston, K. and Surridge, P. (2001) *New Scotland, new politics?*, Edinburgh: Polygon.

Reif, K. and Schmitt, H. (1980) 'Nine national second-order elections', in K. Reif (ed) *Ten European elections: Campaigns and results of the 1979/81 first direct elections to the European Parliament*, Aldershot: Gower.

Surridge, P. and McCrone, D. (1999) 'The 1997 Scottish referendum vote', in B. Taylor and K. Thomson (eds) *Scotland and Wales: Nations again?*, Cardiff: University of Wales Press.

Surridge, P., Paterson, L., Brown, A. and McCrone, D. (1998) 'The Scottish electorate and the Scottish Parliament', *Scottish Affairs*, Special Issue on Constitutional Change, pp 38-60.

SIXTEEN

Smart, successful Scotland? National identity, class, employment and enterprise

Alex Christie, Nicola McEwen and James Mitchell

Introduction

Identities are fluid. Each individual will have multiple identities, and these may change over time depending on context. The relevance of one identity over another is also subject to change. There has been considerable interest for many years in Scottish national identity, especially its political dimension. However, just as national identity is only one identity, politics is only one dimension to this identity. Less well explored is its relationship to the economy. Students of politics have explored the role of elites in identity formation, articulation and mobilisation. This chapter is concerned with the formation, articulation and potential mobilisation of national identity, especially Scottish identity, with reference to the economy. In particular, it explores national identity alongside class (which in its subjective form is effectively an identity) against attitudes towards work, employment and enterprise.

The Scottish Executive and Scottish Enterprise have attempted to harness national identity in pursuit of a 'smart, successful Scotland', a Scotland that is more enterprising in which greater emphasis is placed on creating wealth than questions of spending or distribution. With limited powers in the field of economic policy making, symbolic politics has taken a central place in devolved economic policy making. That is not to demean the efforts of this approach. First, policy makers are constrained by the tools available to them and, second, symbolic politics cannot be lightly dismissed. The long-term effects of symbolic policy making can be considerable. After considering the nature of national identity in Scotland, we will explore some of the ways in which the Executive has been attempting to give a symbolic push towards the promotion of an 'enterprise culture' among Scots. The final section of the chapter utilises the wealth of data from the British

Household Panel Survey (BHPS) to statistically examine this relationship between national identity, class, employment and enterprise.

National identity in Scotland

As individuals, we are defined by an array of distinctive identities that say something about us and about the groups to whom we feel we belong. These identities may reflect characteristics such as age, ethnicity, class and community. Like other identities, national identity contributes to defining who we are and helps to situate us in the context of our relations with those around us. In Benedict Anderson's celebrated definition, the national community is an 'imagined community'. We will never know, meet or even hear of most of our compatriots, but we imagine that we share with them a common bond that unites us (Anderson, 1991, p 6).

In countries like the UK, which are made up of several national communities, the people may identify with more than one nation. They may feel a dual sense of national identity – a sense of belonging to two nations at the same time – without contradiction. As Scotland has evolved within the Union, many Scots have expressed a feeling of being simultaneously Scottish and British. In the 1970s, the academic and Labour MP John P. Mackintosh remarked upon the dual national identity of the majority of Scots. While observing that a sense of Scottishness existed alongside an identification with and loyalty to Britain, he described (1974, pp 409-10) their Scottish identity as representing "an 'opt-out' solution which allows each person to imagine the kind alternative to the disappointment of being British which he or she wants".

This 'disappointment' in being British to which Mackintosh referred may be reflected in the predominance of Scottish national identity today. The BHPS indicates the relative strength of Scottish and British identity in Scotland. As Table 16.1 indicates, some two thirds of respondents to the survey defined themselves as at least more Scottish

Table 16.1: National identity in Scotland (%)

		Total
Scottish, not British	29.94	(987)
More Scottish than British	36.13	(1,160)
Equally Scottish and British	23.12	(692)
More British than Scottish	4.98	(153)
British, not Scottish	5.82	(175)

Source: BHPS, wave 9

than British, with just under 30% seeing themselves as exclusively Scottish. By contrast, only 10.8% defined themselves as at least more British than Scottish. Clearly, the 'imagined community' to which most Scots feel they belong is Scotland rather than Britain.

Theorists of nationalism have frequently suggested that the intellectual and professional classes provide the primary social base for nationalist movements (Nairn, 1977; Gellner, 1983; Hroch, 1985; Smith, 1998; Guibernau, 1999). As Nairn suggested (1977, pp 339-40), however, this elite depends upon and is actively engaged in the development of an inter-class community with a strong sense of its own identity for the realisation of their material objectives.

The social basis of nationalism in Scotland is rather different. In the last 20 years, in particular, Scottish nationalism and national identity have been characterised more by an association with the working class rather than the middle class. Whether measured as an objective socioeconomic category, or as a group with whom individuals subjectively identify, the middle class in Scotland are disproportionately to be found among those who see themselves as British. British identifiers, in other words, are more middle class. By contrast, those who hold a strong Scottish identity are more likely to be, and perceive themselves to be, working class (Bennie et al, 1997, pp 136-8). It is class as an identity that has proved most important in understanding political behaviour (Bennie et al, 1997, pp 101-5). However, we can also see a relationship between occupational class and national identity in the BHPS.

Table 16.2 explores this relationship between national identity and occupational class, as measured by respondents' employment category, and confirms the predominance of a Scottish identity within the working class. As noted earlier in this chapter, two thirds of Scots

Table 16.2: Social class and national identity in Scotland (%)

	Scottish not British	More Scottish than British	Equally Scottish and British	More British than Scottish	British not Scottish	Total
Professional occupations	10.35	41.93	27.48	7.13	13.12	(122)
Managerial and technical	24.04	36.89	25.02	5.54	8.51	(738)
Skilled non-manual	30.67	35.21	23.41	6.03	4.69	(720)
Skilled manual	33.66	35.66	22.58	4.39	3.70	(590)
Partly skilled	32.51	38.61	18.89	4.02	5.97	(496)
Unskilled	42.99	31.00	22.14	1.84	2.02	(241)
Armed forces	36.73	0.00	32.46	30.81	0.00	(3)
Total	(908)	(1,070)	(632)	(140)	(160)	

Source: BHPS, wave 9

considered themselves to be primarily Scottish. Among unskilled workers, this rose to 74% while among partly skilled and skilled manual workers, it was 71% and 69% respectively. Among professionals and managers, the proportion defining themselves as primarily Scottish fell to 52% and 61% respectively. By contrast, whereas less than 4% of unskilled workers and 10% of semi-skilled workers considered themselves to be primarily British, this rose to 14% and 20% among managers and professionals. It should be underlined, however, that even among the professional class, a Scottish identity is considerably more prominent than a British identity.

The 2001 Census provided insight into the changing nature and composition of Scotland. In particular, it indicated that 13% of the population were born outside of Scotland, including 8% born in England, an increase of 2% and 1% respectively since the 1991 Census (General Registrar Office for Scotland, 2003). National identity need not be an attribute of birth. Indeed, in line with civic conceptions of national identity, the political elite within Scotland has promoted an inclusive territorial identity, rather than an exclusive ethnic identity. Nationhood in the civic nation is reflected in a community of laws and institutions that give expression to common political aspirations and values. In determining who constitutes 'the people', a civic national identity is inclusive and, at least in theory, open to all who reside within its boundaries, regardless of their origins or place of birth.

Exploring the national identity of those born outside Scotland is usually constrained in other surveys by the small number of respondents within this category. However, the BHPS, with 15,625 respondents, is considerably larger and may allow us to draw significance from the associations it suggests.

Although the number of Scottish residents born in Wales is too small to draw any conclusions, the BHPS surveyed 269 resident Scots who were born in England. Unsurprisingly, more English-born respondents were willing to define themselves as British rather than

Table 16.3: Identity by place of birth of those resident in Scotland

	Scottish not British	More Scottish than British	Equally Scottish and British	More British than Scottish	British not Scottish	Total
England	11.09	15.20	21.22	19.00	33.50	(269)
Wales	17.50	82.49	0	0	0	(7)
Scotland	32.51	38.29	22.88	3.55	2.76	(2,700)
Total	(948)	(1093)	(638)	(143)	(154)	

Source: BHPS, wave 9

Scottish, or more British than Scottish. However, the data also suggest that the inclusive identity promoted by elites has some resonance among 'new Scots': 11% of English-born Scots defined themselves as Scottish and not British, while a further 15% considered themselves as more Scottish than British. Just under half of all English-born respondents considered themselves at least as Scottish as British.

There is little indication that the establishment of the Scottish Parliament has led to a recovery in feelings of Britishness in Scotland. Voters living in Scotland define themselves overwhelmingly as primarily Scottish rather than British. We have identified some differences with respect to social class and birthplace, but the predominance of Scottish identity among most Scots is clearly evident.

Thus far, we have been considering national identity as an individual identity, but what it means to belong to one nation or another requires consideration of the collective dimension of national identity. Here, there are some indications that the collective dimension of Scottish national identity is in the process of change.

Reinventing Scottish national identity: a smart, successful Scotland?

As well as helping define who we are as individuals, national identity also attempts to resolve who we are as a people and what it is that unites the members of one national community while distinguishing it from others. Breuilly insisted that to be meaningful, identification with a nation had to be accompanied by a shared understanding of what the nation represents; that is, an understanding of what it means to be Scottish, English or British. Discussing French national identity, Breuilly (1993, p 6) argued that "it is the shared meanings and their political organisation that constitute a form of nationalism rather than the purely subjective choices of individual Frenchmen".

Such shared meanings of who and what the nation represents are not given, but are contested and shaped in discourse and debate. As Yack (1999, p 107) put it, paraphrasing Renan (1882), "the nation may be a daily plebiscite but the subject of that plebiscite is what we will do with the mix of competing symbols and stories that make up our cultural inheritance". The collective dimension of national identity may thus be enhanced by a political discourse that develops and promotes the shared understandings of what it means to be Scottish, English or British. However, the nature of a particular national identity, its 'shared meanings' or characteristics, is not spatially or temporally fixed. It is, as Gellner (1983, pp 6, 56) observed, "a contingency, not a universal necessity".

For much of the 20th century, for most Scots, *being* Scottish complemented *being* British. The compatibility between the dominant conceptions of Scottishness and Britishness helped to sustain a sense of dual national identity in Scotland. During the Thatcher years, however, for a growing number of Scots the collective conceptions of Scottish and British national identity diverged. Britishness was reconstructed around the values of individualism, self-reliance, and enterprise (Hall, 1983, p 29), with a central place given to the "myth of British greatness" (Mitchell, 1990, pp 128-9). The Conservatives promoted a conception of Scottish national identity that was compatible with this new Britishness, and in tune with Thatcherite values. Addressing the Scottish Conservative conference in 1988, Mrs Thatcher insisted that "Tory values are in tune with everything that is finest in the Scottish character.... The values of hard work, self-reliance, thrift, enterprise – the relishing of challenges, the seizing of opportunities" (speech reproduced in Harris, 1997, pp 295-307; Henderson and McEwen, 2005: forthcoming). This appeal to and promotion of a particular conception of Scottish identity was combined with a rigorous defence of Thatcherite 'free market medicine', considered necessary to overcome the 'dependency culture' that post-war social democracy was deemed to have fostered in Scotland (Mitchell, 1990, pp 113-15).

However, this was not the prevailing view of Scottish national identity in the 1980s, and it had little resonance within the Scottish electorate. Against the backdrop of an unpopular Conservative government, a distinctive conception of Scottishness was nurtured and articulated within the discourse of the home rule movement. *Being* Scottish was considered to reflect a belief in social justice and egalitarianism, and was associated with support for some form of home rule, opposition to the Conservative government, and a defence of the social democratic welfare state (Mitchell and Bennie, 1996; McEwen, 2002). The idea that Scots are a compassionate and egalitarian people, championing social justice, has been a powerful myth in Scotland's story of itself. While the parties involved in the home rule movement all held different ideas of what home rule should entail, they shared in the articulation of a discourse that substantiated Scottish national identity and gave home rule its ideological justification.

The idea that Scots espoused social democratic values may have been more suited to the pre-1997 context in which opposition parties and much of civil society could generate a consensus against the Conservative government. Although social democracy was the prevailing ideology of the home rule movement, it is less prominent in the devolution era. Moreover, ideas of social justice are less central to the Scottish 'narrative', the collective conception of what it is to be Scottish – Scotland's story of itself.

Shared meanings of who and what the nation represents are not given, but are contested and shaped in discourse and debate. The social justice 'narrative' is now being challenged by a pro-business, pro-enterprise 'narrative', focused less upon the values of community and egalitarianism and more upon economic development and enterprise. In many keynote speeches and policy documents, social justice and public service delivery are now subordinate to the pursuit of skills development, innovation and support for business. The Executive no longer promotes an egalitarian Scotland but a 'smart, successful Scotland'. Fostering entrepreneurialism is at the heart of this strategy, which is supported by the principal opposition parties. In 2001, for example, the Executive introduced a schools programme, jointly funded by the private sector, to teach 'lessons in enterprise' to school children (McEwen, 2003). In the course of the 2003 Scottish Election campaign, the parties were each keen to embrace the enterprise culture, and instil a 'spirit of enterprise' among Scots.

In part, this is a response to the lobbying efforts of the business community. Largely hostile to devolution before the Parliament's establishment, the business community has since adopted the view that its interests should be given greater priority (Mitchell et al, 2003, pp 124-7). These attempts to attach an enterprise dimension to Scottish national identity also reflect concerns with Scotland's relative economic under-performance. Economic growth is slower than south of the border, levels of business investment in research and development are considerably lower than comparator countries like Ireland, Finland and Denmark, and the business birth rate is substantially lower than the UK average (Hood and Paterson, 2002; Star, 2002). This degree of under-performance is deemed to reflect a lack of entrepreneurialism, rooted in a general lack of self-confidence and prevailing cultural assumptions that mitigate against ambition and success. In a recent book, for example, Carol Craig (2003, pp 196-222) blamed Scotland's economic problems on its "dependency culture" and a corresponding lack of ambition and fear of failure that she found to be prevalent among the Scottish people and integral to the collectivist conception of Scottish identity.

As an effort to reinvent Scottish national identity, this discourse is intriguing in two respects. First, it is evident within both the Labour Party and the Scottish National Party. In each case, it operates alongside

Table 16.6: National identity by size of workplace

	1-2	3-9	10-24	25-49	50-99	100-199	200-499	500-999	1,000+	Don't know less than 25	Don't know more than 25	Total
Scottish, not British	25.12	29.87	34.23	31.65	23.83	31.38	24.98	24.03	24.62	33.14	37.64	(486)
More Scottish than British	32.37	42.95	39.37	38.91	39.05	42.10	40.49	46.24	41.15	66.86	34.66	(665)
Equally Scottish and British	27.11	15.46	16.05	20.23	24.86	18.05	24.83	27.01	23.51	0.00	20.95	(324)
More British than Scottish	6.62	4.65	4.18	3.68	3.74	5.55	2.66	0.46	5.20	0.00	1.64	(66)
British, not Scottish	8.79	7.07	6.16	5.53	8.52	2.92	7.03	2.26	5.53	0.00	5.11	(92)
Total	(69)	(262)	(248)	(194)	(185)	(158)	(181)	(108)	(183)	(2)	(43)	(1,633)

Source: BHPS, wave 9

prioritise Scottishness, but almost a third of those who were neither a manager nor a supervisor felt no British identity.

Breaking down economic status by the size of the workplace highlights some interesting results. As Table 16.6 indicates, while a majority of respondents in all sizes of workplace prioritise Scottishness, prioritisation of Britishness appears slightly higher in smaller workplaces.

Great emphasis has recently been placed on self-employment and business creation within Scotland, with the enterprise networks focusing much attention on the Business Birth-rate Strategy. The BHPS permits a link to be made between identity and the self-employed and further allows for the self-employed to be broken down to those who may be defined as sole-traders and those who have employees. There are also questions asked to all those in employment as to whether they would like to start their own business and whether they would expect to start a business within the next year. Taken together these questions can perhaps allow an examination of entrepreneurial intent.

Table 16.7 details the breakdown of identity according to whether the respondent is an employee or is self-employed. Again the majority of both employees and the self-employed prioritised Scottishness. However, although the difference is small the self-employed prioritise Britishness more and Scottishness less at each identity. The sample size for those who are self-employed and hire employees, what may be crudely termed as the entrepreneurs, is too small (51) to allow reasonable conclusions to be drawn other than to say that again the majority continue to prioritise Scottishness.

The entrepreneurialism of those within Scotland can be further explored in relation to national identity. Respondents who were in employment were asked whether they would like to start their own business and whether they expected to start their own business within the next year. Here, we are focusing on those individuals who could

Table 16.7: National identity of employees and the self-employed (%)

	Employee	Self-employed	Total
Scottish, not British	28.60	27.11	(544)
More Scottish than British	40.52	35.60	(730)
Equally Scottish and British	20.82	25.20	(370)
More British than Scottish	4.02	5.16	(76)
British, not Scottish	6.05	6.94	(106)
Total	(1,635)	(191)	(1,826)

Source: BHPS, wave 9

switch from being an employee to being self-employed, and therefore those who face a more substantial opportunity cost than those individuals out of work for whatever reason. Table 16.8 shows the results.

There is little difference between identities on either measure once small sample size is accounted for although, perhaps surprisingly, those prioritising Britishness more than Scottishness were slightly less keen to express a desire to start their own business. There is little difference between identity groups when asked if they *expect* to start their own business. What is of more significance is the low absolute level of desire to start a business – around 7% of the sample, while only around a third of those who would like to start a business expect to do so within the next year. Business starts have been low historically in Scotland and this is now a key indicator within the 'smart, successful Scotland' programme. However, it would appear from these results that national identity is not an important factor in determining an individual's willingness to start up their own business. The desire to start a business is low *regardless* of national identity. Moreover, some factor, or combination of factors, works to dissuade those who would like to start up a business from believing that they will do so.

The survey also asks those who do not have a job, but are about to start one or have looked for a job, or would like a job, what they consider the most important aspect of a job and the most important reason for working. Table 16.9 shows the results of the most important aspect of a job, broken down by national identity.

Some immediate differences are noticeable. Those prioritising Britishness are far more likely to see the use of initiative and the actual hours worked as the most important aspects of a job than those prioritising Scottishness, but less likely to view job security and promotion prospects as the most important. Job security and total pay

Table 16.8: Desire and expectation to start a business by identity (%)

	Scottish not British	More Scottish than British	Equally Scottish and British	More British than Scottish	British not Scottish	Total
Would like to start their own business	13.68	12.45	12.18	9.58	12.05	(233)
Expect to start their own business	4.12	3.88	3.26	7.22	4.86	(69)

Source: BHPS, wave 9

Table 16.9: The most important aspect of a job by national identity (%)

	Scottish not British	More Scottish than British	Equally Scottish and British	More British than Scottish	British not Scottish	Total
Promotion prospects	4.27	3.82	2.52	3.96	0.82	(77)
Total pay	27.15	23.09	23.16	32.69	19.75	(490)
Good relations with manager	8.72	5.98	7.74	3.09	7.55	(161)
Job security	28.71	25.21	22.53	17.21	12.34	(519)
Using initiative	8.07	8.86	10.71	15.59	21.29	(200)
Actual work	18.23	28.70	27.53	26.03	35.26	(538)
Hours worked	3.01	3.41	4.51	0.81	2.98	(77)
Something else	1.85	0.93	1.30	0.63	0.00	(27)
Total	(635)	(821)	(423)	(90)	(120)	(2,089)

Source: BHPS, wave 9

are the most important aspects of employment for those prioritising Scottishness.

Similarly, Table 16.10 indicates the most important reason for working broken down by national identity. It is hardly surprising that the main reason for working for all identity groups is for essential foodstuffs – we work to live – but this is more important to those prioritising Scottishness. Enjoyment of working and the development of a career are, however, more important to those prioritising Britishness than to those prioritising Scottishness.

It must be remembered that in both cases above these questions are addressed to those who are not in employment when the question was asked, but are about to start a job, have been looking for a job or would like a job. Given that Britishness is very much rooted in social

Table 16.10: Principal reason for working by national identity (%)

	Scottish not British	More Scottish than British	Equally Scottish and British	More British than Scottish	British not Scottish	Total
Working is normal	4.64	4.38	4.95	1.74	3.98	81
Essential foods etc	57.05	52.84	46.83	43.78	43.46	1090
Money for extras	9.25	7.96	9.55	10.92	5.98	185
Earn money for self	12.63	10.58	9.69	6.03	10.99	238
People's company	1.32	2.22	2.33	1.60	4.95	47
Enjoy working	9.62	12.88	14.66	24.50	18.31	270
Follow my career	4.92	7.59	9.53	8.26	12.34	154
Other reasons	0.57	1.55	2.46	3.17	0.00	26
Total	635	823	423	90	120	2,091

Source: BHPS, wave 9

Conclusion

Class remains important in any attempt to understand both national identity and attitudes towards work, employment and enterprise. However, while it might be tempting to subsume any understanding of and prescription for an 'enterprise culture' within perceptions of class or national identity, the experience of the 1980s and 1990s shows how the interaction of these identities, combined with skilful political leadership, can affect political behaviour. Class and national identity existed prior to their combined mobilisation: they were not created anew. This national/class identity was mobilised with efficiency to undermine and defeat Conservative politicians in Scotland and, in turn, to bring about the Scottish Parliament.

This is not to argue that economic behaviour can simply be replicated in a different form in the years ahead to bring about an enterprise culture. However, there are grounds for believing that, at the very least, the attitudes embedded in the identities discussed will be resistant to change in the short or even medium term. Turning Scots into British in the hope that this will make them enterprising seems implausible. Besides, the data presented here offer little to suggest that those who identify themselves as British are any more enterprising than those who define themselves as Scottish. Likewise, attempting to convert Scottish identifiers into opponents of social democracy seems unlikely given the relationship that exists between class and national identity. The most likely hope probably lies not in challenging predominant class and national identities but by somehow attaching an enterprise culture to these existing identities and to the beliefs and attitudes they embody. In this respect, the smart, successful Scotland strategy starts off in the right direction. However, symbolic politics will require an appeal to a wider section of the public than this strategy has hitherto sought to reach. What is more, change, if it comes, is likely to be slow.

References

Anderson, B. (1991) *Imagined communities*, London: Verso.

Bennie, L., Brand, J. and Mitchell, J. (1997) *How Scotland votes*, Manchester: Manchester University Press.

Breuilly, J. (1993) *Nationalism and the state* (2nd edn), Manchester: Manchester University Press.

Craig, C. (2003) *The Scots' crisis of confidence*, Edinburgh: Big Thinking.

Gellner, E. (1983) *Nations and nationalism*, Cambridge: Blackwell.

General Register Office for Scotland (2001) *Scotland's Census*, Edinburgh.

Guibernau, M. (1999) *Nations without states*, Cambridge: Polity Press.

Hall, S. (1983) 'Introduction: who needs identity?', in S. Hall and P. du Gay (eds) *Questions of cultural identity*, London: Sage Publications.

Harris, R. (1997) *The collected speeches of Margaret Thatcher*, London: HarperCollins.

Henderson, A. and McEwen, N. (2005: forthcoming) 'Do shared values underpin national identity? Examining the role of values in national identity in Canada and the UK', *National Identities*.

Hood, N. and Paterson, C. (2002) 'The growth and development of new firms', in N. Hood, J. Peat, E. Peters and S. Young (eds) *Scotland in a global economy*, Houndmills: Palgrave Macmillan, pp 237-57.

Hroch, M. (1985) *Social preconditions of national revival in Europe*, Cambridge: Cambridge University Press.

Mackintosh, J.P. (1974) 'The new appeal of nationalism', *New Statesman*, vol 88, 27 September.

McEwen, N. (2002) 'State welfare nationalism: the territorial impact of welfare state development in Scotland', *Regional and Federal Studies*, vol 12, no 1, pp 66-90.

McEwen, N. (2003) 'The depoliticization of national identity? Scottish territorial politics after devolution', in E. Longley, E. Hughes and D. O'Rawe (eds) *Ireland (Ulster) Scotland: Concepts, contexts, comparisons* (Belfast Studies in Language, Culture and Politics 7), Belfast: Queen's University Belfast.

Mitchell, J. (1990) *Conservatives and the union*, Edinburgh: Edinburgh University Press.

Mitchell, J. and Bennie, L. (1996) 'Thatcherism and the Scottish question', *British elections and parties yearbook 1995*, London: Frank Cass.

Mitchell, J., et al (2003) 'Third year, third First Minister', in R. Hazell (ed) *The state and the nations 2003*, Exeter: Imprint Academic, pp 45-76.

Nairn, T. (1977) *The break-up of Britain, crisis and neo-nationalism*, London: New Left Books.

Renan, E. (1882) 'What is a nation?', Reprinted in K. Bhabha Homi (1990) *Nation and narration*, London: Routledge.

Smith, A.D. (1998) *Nationalism and modernism*, London: Routledge.

Star, J. (2002) 'Scotland's economy and benchmarks', in N. Hood, J. Peat, E. Peters and S. Young (eds) *Scotland in a global economy*, Houndmills: Palgrave Macmillan, pp 49-67.

Yack, B. (1999) 'The myth of the civic nation', in R. Beiner (ed) *Theorizing nationalism*, Albany, NY: State University of New York Press, pp 103-18.

SEVENTEEN

Decline of religion

Nicole Bourque, Vernon Gayle and Robert E. Wright

Introduction

There is general agreement among academics, religious leaders and the media that religion is becoming less important in British society (see, for example, Brierley, 1991, 1995; Smith, 1992; Bruce, 1995a, 1995b, 1995c, 2002; Jenkins, 1996; Brown, 1997, 2001; Gill et al, 1998; Bruce and Glendinning, 2002a, 2002b; Denholm, 2002; Kerevan, 2002; Reid, 2002a, 2002b; Swanson, 2002; Wormsley, 2002). Most measures of 'religiosity', such as church membership, church attendance and religious attitudes, are trending downwards, with the decline being particularly sharp since the early 1960s. However, there is less agreement concerning what factors are responsible for this decline. A recent review (Bourque and Wright, 2002) of empirical studies that have attempted to model such factors reached three main conclusions. The first is that the rate of decline varies by observed characteristics such as age, gender, socioeconomic status, marital status, presence of dependent children, denomination and geographic location. The second is that research in this area has been hampered by a paucity of high quality data and by the application of relatively unsophisticated modelling techniques. The third is that on aggregate this empirical research has not added greatly to the understanding of the causes of the decline.

It is our view that much can be learned about the factors causing this decline by comparing England with the devolved territories of Scotland and Wales. In this chapter, we restrict the focus to a comparison between Scotland and England using data from the British Household Panel Survey (BHPS). The remainder of this chapter is organised as follows. The second part describes what variables relating to religion are included in the BHPS. The third part examines Scottish–English differences in these variables. In the fourth part of this chapter, logit regression models are estimated in an attempt to control for observed and unobserved factors that might 'explain' what appears to be a large

Figure 17.1: Religion (%)

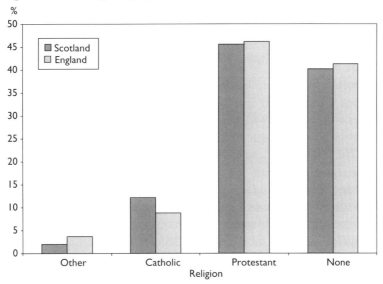

little difference with respect to the percentage who report having 'no religion' (40.2% for Scotland versus 41.3% for England). The Protestant shares are also similar (45.6% for Scotland and 46.2% for England). However, the Catholic share is larger in Scotland (12.2%) than in England (8.8%). Likewise, the share of 'other' religions (which includes such groups as Muslims, Hindus, Jews and Sikhs) is lower in Scotland (2.0%) compared to England (3.7%).

There are differences between Scotland and England with respect to religious group membership and activity. With respect to membership, in Scotland 16.1% of respondents report being members of a religious group or church organisation. The rate for England is lower at 11%. With respect to activity, in Scotland 13% of respondents are 'currently active' in a religious group or church organisation. Again, the rate for England is lower at 10.7%. Based on these two measures, it appears that religious group membership/activity is higher in Scotland than in England.

Further evidence in support of this claim is shown in Figure 17.2. This figure shows the frequency of attendance at religious services or meetings, which we shall term 'church attendance' for short. In Scotland, 14.9% of respondents report attending church at least once a week. The figure for England is significantly lower at 10.1%. Likewise, 8.3% of Scottish respondents and 6% of English respondents report attending church once a month. Therefore, almost 25% of Scottish respondents

Figure 17.2: Church attendance (%)

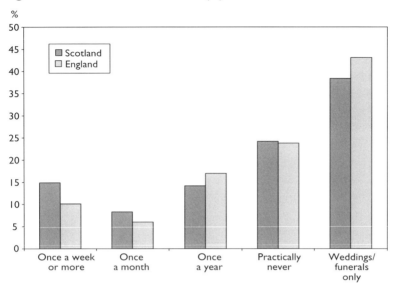

report attending church *at least* once a month compared to only 16.1% of English respondents.

Finally, Figures 17.3-4 show the distributions on the two religious attitude variables. Figure 17.3 is for the 'religion makes a difference' variable. There is little difference between Scotland and England with respect to the percentage who report that religious beliefs make 'no difference' (48.2% for Scotland and 47% for England). However, 17.1% of Scottish respondents, compared to 14.6% of English respondents, report that religious beliefs make 'a great difference'. Figure 17.4 shows the distribution for the 'Bible is God's word' variable: 15.4% of Scottish respondents, compared to 19% of English respondents, 'strongly disagree' with this statement. At the other end of the distribution, 7.1% of Scottish respondents, compared to 5.6% of English respondents, 'strongly agree'. Scottish responses on this question are clearly more skewed to the 'agree' end of the distribution compared to English responses.

This descriptive evidence suggests that 'religion' appears to be more important in Scotland than in England. The rates of religious group membership, religious group activity and church attendance are higher and religious attitudes appear to be more favourable towards religious beliefs. In the remainder of this chapter, the focus will be on church attendance. More specifically, we will focus on church attendance of at least once a week. This does not imply that we believe that this is the 'best' measure of religiosity. In fact, there are many well-known

Figure 17.3: 'Religion makes a difference to life' (%)

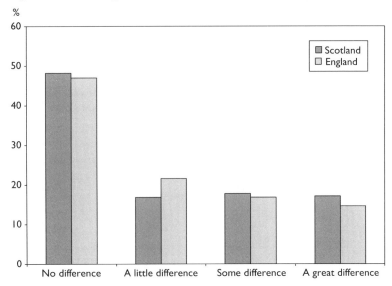

Figure 17.4: 'The Bible is God's word' (%)

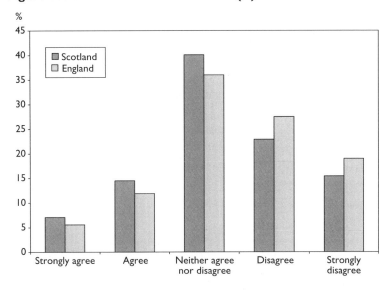

weaknesses with it (see Bruce, 1995a; Brown, 1997, 2001). However, given declining church attendance is leading to church closures, it seems to be a useful starting point.

Figure 17.5 shows the trend in weekly church attendance rates for Scotland and England based on the six waves of the BHPS that include this variable (waves 1, 3, 4, 5, 7 and 9). Two points about this figure are

Figure 17.5: Church attendance: 'Once a week or more' (1991-2000) (%)

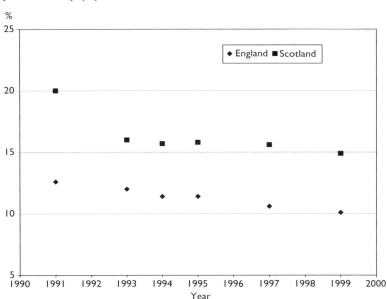

worth noting. The first is that the trend confirms what others have found: that church attendance has declined sharply in the 1990s. The second is that church attendance is considerably higher in Scotland than in England. At the beginning of the 1990s, about 20% of Scottish adults attended church at least once a week; this compares to 13% for English adults. By the end of the decade, these rates had declined to about 15% and 10%, respectively. In other words, at the end of the decade the Scottish church attendance was about 50% higher than the English rate.

Figure 17.6 shows church attendance rates by age. It is clear that for individuals aged 45+ church attendance rates are much higher in Scotland than in England. The evidence is less clear-cut for the younger age groups. However, grouping all individuals aged 44 and younger together yields a church attendance rate for Scotland of 8.3%. This is higher than the 5.7% rate observed for England. It appears that church attendance increases with age. Although more information relating to church attendance among younger people is needed, it is not unreasonable to suggest that church attendance appears to be higher in Scotland than in England across the age distribution.

It is worth mentioning at this point that one hypothesis that has been put forth for what appears to be higher church attendance in Scotland compared to England relates to observed differences in the

Figure 17.6: Church attendance: 'Once a week or more', age-specific rates (1999-2000) (%)

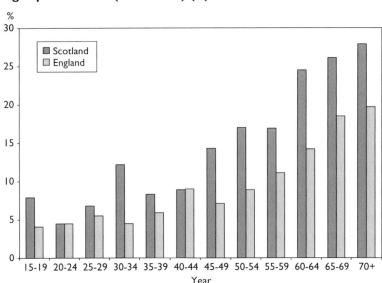

religion distributions of the two nations (Bruce 1995a; Brown 1997). More specifically, it is argued that Scotland's larger share of Catholics (who generally have higher attendance rates) explains Scotland's overall higher rate (Figure 17.1). In order to explore this idea, we 'standardised' the 1999-2000 Scottish church attendance rate using the religion distribution of England. This adjustment leads to a 'standardised' rate for Scotland of 14.5%, which is only slightly lower than the observed rate of 14.9%. In other words, a difference in the religion distribution does not close the observed gap between Scotland and England.

The above discussion is based on cross-sectional variation in the BHPS. Figure 17.7 summarises some of the longitudinal variation in the data, and illustrates the unique way in which the BHPS can be used to examine changes in church attendance. The figure is based on wave 1 individuals who attended church in 1991 at least once a week and were re-interviewed in the five other waves that collected information about church attendance. Therefore, the church attendance rate for this 'cohort' in 1991 is 100%. The figure then shows the church attendance rates for this cohort in each of the subsequent waves separately for Scotland and England.

This cohort indicates that there is a clear cohort-specific decline in church attendance during the 1990s. This has been noted by other researchers such as Brown (2001) and Bruce and Glendinning (2002a).

Figure 17.7: Church attendance: 'Once a week or more', 1991 BHPS cohort (%)

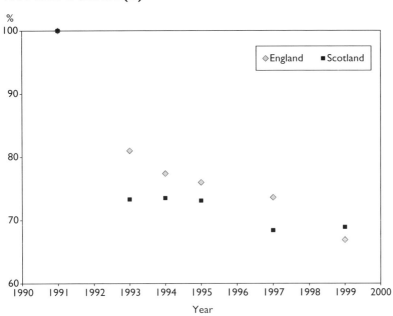

However, their data do not show that the sharpest rate of decline occurred between 1992 and 1994. By 1994, only 81% of the English cohort were still attending church once a week or more. The decline in Scotland was even more marked, with only 73% of the cohort regularly attending. After 1994, the decline continues, but at a more gradual rate. By 2000, the rate declined to 67% in England and 69% in Scotland. It is worth noting that, in spite of a sharper rate of decline in Scotland from 1992 to 1994, by 2000 a higher percentage of the Scottish cohort remained regular churchgoers. These results emphasise the importance of the BHPS in comparison to non-longitudinal data and suggest that the period 1992-1994 merits more research.

Regression analysis

In this section, regression models are estimated in an attempt to control for observed and unobserved factors that might 'explain' the difference in the church attendance rate between Scotland and England. The model is a logit regression, where the dependent variable is a dummy variable coded '1' if the individual attends church at least once a week and coded '0' otherwise. In the literature, there is some agreement on what factors affect church attendance. The factors that we consider are age, gender, education, marital status, presence of dependent children, employment status and social class.

The model is estimated by pooling together data from the six waves of the BHPS that collected information on church attendance. This generates a dataset consisting of 56,760 observations. Generally, standard regression techniques are not appropriate for the analysis of pooled data, the main reason being that repeated observations likely to violate the key assumption that the observations are independent. If this is the case, then parameter estimates are likely to be biased.

One potential way of dealing with this problem is to include in the specification an individual-specific error. More specifically, the model that we estimate is a 'logistic mixture model' (Heckman and Willis, 1977). The model is fit using the software package SABRE developed at the University of Lancaster (Barry et al, 1998). The model is essentially a logit regression that includes an individual-specific normally distributed random error term. More generally, this estimator is a 'Random Effects' model where the key assumption is that the individual-specific errors are not correlated with the included regressors (the so-called 'Fixed Effects' model does not require this assumption). This model explicitly takes into account the dependence across individuals and should help control for unobserved factors persistent across individuals.

A dummy variable, SCOT, is coded '1' if the individual resides in Scotland and coded '0' if the individual resides in England. The individual's age is included as a quadratic (AGE and AGE2) in order to test for a non-linear relationship between age and church attendance. The dummy variable for the individual's gender, FEMALE, is coded '1' if female and coded '0' if male. Marital status consists of five categories: (1) single (never married); (2) divorced/separated; (3) widowed; (4) cohabiting; (5) married. Four dummy variables representing the first four categories are included in the model, SINGLE, DIVORCE, WIDOW and COHAB, with the excluded category being married. Presence of dependent children, KIDS, is measured by a dummy variable coded '1' if there are dependent children in the household and coded '0' if not. Employment status is captured by a dummy variable, WORK, coded '1' if the individual is employed and '0' if not. Education consists of three categories: (1) no qualifications beyond basic school leaving; (2) university education; (3) qualifications between basic school leaving and university education. Two dummy variables, UNI and HS, are include in the model to represent the latter two education levels, with the excluded category being no qualifications beyond basic school leaving. The individual's social class,

CLASS, is measured using the so-called 'Cambridge Scale'. Since this variable can only be calculated for individuals who have held a job some time in their life it needs to be adjusted for individuals who have never worked. In order to do this, a variable, EVERWORK, was created. This variable is coded '0' if the individual has never held a job and coded '1' otherwise. This variable is interacted with CLASS, and both this interaction and EVERWORK are included in the model. Finally, dummy variables are included for each of the waves with the excluded category being wave 1 (that is, WAVE3, WAVE4, WAVE5, WAVE7 and WAVE9).

The parameter estimates of the logit models are shown in Table 17.2. Column A are the parameter estimates for the simple logit model while Column B are the estimates for the logit model that attempts to control for unobserved heterogeneity. Turning first to Column A, the estimates suggest that even after controlling for a series of variables, church attendance is higher in Scotland than in England. The parameter (b = 0.483) of SCOT variable is positive and highly statistically significant (b/se = 12.8). The point estimate indicates that the probability of church attendance is about 50% higher in Scotland after these other factors are held constant. This is very similar in magnitude to the differential observed in the 'raw' data (Figure 17.5). In other words, differences between Scotland and England in observed characteristics, such as age, marital status, and so on, do *not* 'explain' why church attendance is higher in Scotland.

It is worth noting that all the variables included in the model are statistically significant at conventional threshold levels. Age appears to be important. Both the linear and quadratic terms are statistically significant, with positive and negative signs respectively. Solving this implied inverted U-shaped relationship for its 'turning point', gives a value of 164 years, which is well outside the observed range of age in the data (that is, the oldest person is 95). Therefore, the probability of church attendance increases with age but at a slightly diminishing rate. Females have higher probabilities, as do individuals with higher levels of education. There are clear differences with respect to marital status. Compared to married individuals, the probability of church attendance is higher for single and widowed individuals and lower for individuals who are cohabiting or divorced/separated. The presence of children in the household increases the probability of attendance, while being currently employed lowers it. Being 'ever employed' lowers the probability of church attendance but this negative effect diminishes as social class rises. Finally, the wave dummies reaffirm that church attendance has declined sharply in the 1990s.

Table 17.2: Logit estimates of church attendance

Model Heterogeneity control?	(A) No	(B) Yes
SCOT	0.483[a]	1.446
	(12.8)	(10.4)
AGE	0.038	0.077
	(7.6)	(4.8)
AGE^2	−0.0001	−0.0003
	(2.4)	(1.8)
FEMALE	0.374	0.779
	(12.9)	(7.2)
SINGLE	0.248	−0.039
	(5.1)	(0.2)
DIVORCE	−0.389	−0.642
	(6.2)	(4.1)
WIDOW	0.132	0.573
	(2.7)	(3.6)
COHAB	−1.258	−1.736
	(13.4)	(8.4)
KIDS	0.160	0.284
	(4.1)	(2.4)
WORK	−0.308	−0.303
	(8.6)	(3.3)
HS	0.219	0.549
	(6.0)	(4.7)
UNI	0.451	0.616
	(7.9)	(3.4)
EVERWORK	−0.982	−2.036
	(14.8)	(9.2)
CLASS	0.017	0.021
	(18.6)	(7.6)
WAVE3	−0.118	−0.431
	(2.5)	(4.7)
WAVE4	−0.179	−0.608
	(3.8)	(6.5)
WAVE5	−0.175	−0.618
	(3.6)	(6.5)
WAVE7	−0.206	−0.837
	(4.4)	(8.9)
WAVE9	−0.270	−1.089
	(5.9)	(11.4)
Intercept	−3.322	−7.734
	(24.0)	(17.3)
θ	−	4.491[b]
		(67.5)

Notes: [a] Ratio of parameter to its standard error in parentheses.

[b] θ is the standard deviation of the (normal) mixing distribution.

The estimates that try to control for unobserved heterogeneity (Column B of Table 17.2) suggest that unmeasured factors are likely important in the explanation of church attendance. This effect is captured by the term 'θ' (the standard deviation of the mixing distribution), which is highly statistically significant. If this parameter was not statistically significant, then one could conclude that the included variables capture most of the variation and any remaining variation is due to random factors. The literature on the decline of religion in Britain, offers some suggestions as to what these unmeasured variables might be. Bruce (1995a, 1995c, 2002) links the decline of religiosity to the 'modernisation' of Britain, which entails:

- a rise in individualism;
- a loss of group identity as a result of urban migration;
- an increase in the number of different denominations and faiths.

As Bruce (1995a, p 10) notes, "it is easy to believe that a religion is right in every detail when there is no alternative ... it is not a matter of belief, it is a reflection of how things are". Brown (2001) continues with this theme. He claims that real decline in religiosity in Britain came as Christianity stopped becoming part of people's daily discourse and hence, part of their daily lives.

The 'θ' factor aside, what is more important is the impact that controlling for unobserved heterogeneity has on the magnitudes and statistical significance of the included variables. Again, the parameter ($\beta = 1.446$) of SCOT variable is positive and highly statistical significant ($\beta/se = 10.4$). However, its magnitude is about three times larger than in the simple logit model (that is, $\beta = 0.483$). This suggests that when both observed and unobserved factors are 'held constant', the 'Scottish effect' is even larger. It is also worth pointing out that the remaining variables in this model reveal a pattern of effect that is broadly similar to what was found in the simple logit model. Some of the parameters are smaller while others are larger, but the description is the same. There is, however, one glaring difference. The parameter of the marital status variable SINGLE is now essentially zero, while in the simple logit it was positive and highly statistically significant. It is unclear why these parameters are so different. Marital status aside, after age, gender, socioeconomic status, education levels and the presence of dependent children are factored out, it is clear that some other variables must be at work in Scotland. Brown (2001) offers a possible explanation, which is worth further investigation: perhaps Scotland is more religious because religion is more frequently discussed in the media or experienced on a daily basis due to sectarianism and/or football.

Conclusion

The purpose of this chapter was to demonstrate that the BHPS can be used to examine religiosity differences between Scotland and England. The results presented here are clearly preliminary and suggest areas where more research is needed. It is unfortunate that questions relating to religion were not included in wave 10, the second wave of the enhanced survey that includes a much larger sub-sample of Scottish households. However, these questions will be included in subsequent waves. Therefore, in the future, it will be possible to analyse with more rigour actual changes in behaviour by tracking the same individuals. Nevertheless, the analysis in this chapter does suggest that there are religiosity differences between Scotland and England. The challenge of course will be to try to explain why this is the case, and much can be learned on this front through the longitudinal analysis of the BHPS.

References

Argue, A., Johnson D.R. and White, L. (1999) 'Age and religiosity: evidence from a three wave panel analysis', *Journal for the Scientific Study of Religion*, vol 38, pp 423-35.

Barry, J., Francis, B., Davies, R.B. and Stott, D. (1998) *SABRE software for the analysis of binary recurrent events – A user's guide*, Lancaster: Centre for Applied Statistics, University of Lancaster.

Bourque, L.N. and Wright, R.E. (2002) *The decline of religiosity in Scotland and Great Britain*, Manuscript, Glasgow: Department of Sociology and Anthropology, University of Glasgow.

Brierley, P. (1991) *Prospects for the nineties: Trends and tables from the English Church Census*, London: MARC.

Brierley, P. (1995) *Prospects for Scotland 2000: Trends and tables from the 1994 Church Census*, Edinburgh: National Bible Society of Scotland.

Brown, C. (1997) *Religion and society in Scotland since 1707*, Edinburgh: Edinburgh University Press.

Brown, C. (2001) *The death of Christian Britain: Understanding secularisation 1800-2000*, London: Routledge.

Bruce, S. (1995a) *Religion in modern Britain*, Oxford: Oxford University Press.

Bruce, S. (1995b) 'The truth about religion in Britain', *Journal for the Scientific Study of Religion*, vol 34, pp 417-30.

Bruce, S. (1995c) *Religion in the modern world: From cathedrals to cults*, Oxford: Oxford University Press.

Bruce, S. (2002) *God is dead: The secularisation of the West*, Oxford: Blackwell.

Bruce, S. and Glendinning, T. (2002a) 'Scotland is no longer a Christian country', *Life and work: The magazine of the Church of Scotland*, June, pp 12-15.

Bruce, S. and Glendinning, T. (2002b) 'Religion and the supernatural', Manuscript, Aberdeen: Department of Sociology, University of Aberdeen.

Denholm, A. (2002) 'Kirk has to turn tide of history', *The Scotsman*, 21 May.

Gill, R., Hadaway, C.K. and Marler, P.L. (1998) 'Is religious belief declining in Britain?', *Journal for the Scientific Study of Religion*, vol 37, pp 507-16.

Heckman, J.J. and Willis, R. (1977) 'A beta-logistic model for the analysis of sequential labour force participation by married women', *Journal of Political Economy*, vol 85, pp 27-58.

Jenkins, T. (1996) 'Two sociological approaches to religion in modern Britain', *Religion*, vol 26, pp 331-42.

Kerevan, G. (2002) 'Shrinking Kirk must search its soul for a mission to fill pews and secure future', *The Scotsman*, 11 May.

Laurie, H.M. and Wright, R.E. (2000) 'The Scottish Household Panel Survey', *Scottish Journal of Political Economy*, vol 47, pp 337-9.

Reid, H. (2002a) *Outside verdict: An old Kirk in a New Scotland*, Edinburgh: St Andrew Press.

Reid, H. (2002b) 'Kirk in crisis', *The Scotsman*, 26 May.

Smith, I. (1992) *The economics of church decline: The case of the church of Scotland*, Discussion Paper Series no 9210, St Andrews: Department of Economics, University of St Andrews.

Swanson, I. (2002) 'Is Kirk turning off Scottish Christians', *The Scotsman*, 22 May.

Wormsley, T. (2002) 'Kirk debates decline in churchgoers', *The Scotsman*, 25 May.

EIGHTEEN

Volunteering and organisational participation

Jeanette Findlay and Patricia Findlay

Introduction

Interest in volunteering and participation in voluntary organisations and activities has a long history. Considerable benefits arise at an organisational and societal level from the efforts of those who commit their time and energy, without compulsion or personal financial gain, to a huge variety of causes and activities from philanthropy through to self-help and campaigning. In recent years, increased attention to the forms and effects of social capital has stimulated further interest in voluntary activities and organisational membership as indicators of the degree of social capital within communities and societies (Putnam, 1995, 2000). While some measures of social capital rely on attempts to measure the degree of trust relations, and some the existence of reciprocal networks of activity, others focus upon the extent to which individuals are members of voluntary organisations, or participate in voluntary activities. The economic value of formal volunteering in the UK has been calculated to be in the region of £40 billion per year (Hill, 2002). In this chapter, we define the concept of volunteering widely to include not only conventional volunteering, for example working without pay for a charity, but also to include other forms of voluntary civic or community engagement, such as joining a residents' association or a pensioners' club, or being active in a trades union (Findlay and McKinlay, 2002). Individuals may contribute to local social capital by establishing networks of information, communication and trust through their participation in a range of organisational activities.

The launch of the Active Community Initiative by the Prime Minister in January 1999 signalled a clear commitment to support the work of "those of us who believe in the power of community" (Scottish Executive, 2000) by encouraging people to volunteer and to involve themselves in community action. This initiative has also been strongly supported by the Scottish Executive who view voluntary activity as a key component in promoting and developing active citizenship and in addressing issues of exclusion.

> Indeed volunteering and community action may be viewed as a barometer of a healthy, inclusive and democratic society. (Scottish Executive, 2000)

Themes and issues in volunteering research

For many years, attempts to understand the individual rationale behind formal voluntary activity have tended to focus on altruism or self-sacrifice as an explanation. Indeed, volunteers themselves consistently list service to others as their most important reason for volunteering (Pearce, 1993). Thus, models of individual instrumentalism or rationality derived from the world of economics can be contrasted with models of altruistic individual behaviour derived from the field of psychology. However, even within psychological approaches, altruism can be criticised as an explanation of volunteer activity (Pearce, 1993). More helpfully, psychologists have focused on the idea of pro-social behaviours, whereby individuals behave in ways that maintain or promote the well-being of others without any restriction in returns to themselves (Rushton and Sorrentino, 1981). Thus, in addition to the social, economic and organisational benefits of voluntary activities, it is now recognised that individuals may derive considerable benefits from engaging in voluntary organisational activities. These are not simply related to enhanced self-esteem arising from engaging in actions that benefit others. In recent years, it has become increasingly recognised that volunteering and organisational membership may have direct learning and economic benefits for the individuals involved. Indeed, this has been explicitly recognised in discussions of social networks and social capital. As such, there is a growing interest within economics in the area of voluntary activity and participation. By recognising the potential for voluntary or discretionary activities to generate individual benefits, information on and analysis of such activities can be linked to policies for lifelong learning and the social economy, as well as contributing to local economic development.

In addition, more conventional employing organisations also have an interest in understanding 'voluntary' or additional efforts, either outside or within the workplace. We have seen greater attention to employer-sponsored volunteering as an element of good corporate citizenship (see, for example, Lee and Higgins, 2001). This may generate not only reputation benefits for the organisation, but also assist the organisation in terms of learning and skills transfer. In addition, a better understanding of volunteers and voluntary activities can be more directly linked to outcomes in employing organisations, as the literature on organisational citizenship behaviours suggests (Bolino et al, 2002).

Individuals engage in voluntary activities for a mixture of altruistic and self-interested reasons. The Institute for Volunteer Research (IVR, 2003a) has identified a number of key personal benefits from volunteering: enjoyment of activity; meeting of one's own needs and those of family and friends; satisfaction of seeing results; meeting people; and a sense of personal achievement. Among younger volunteers, the benefits of volunteering are more likely to be described in terms of instrumental benefits – the opportunity to learn new skills, to get a qualification, and to achieve a position in the community (IVR, 2003b). Some commentators have raised concerns over these personal returns to volunteering. Cater (2002) refers scathingly to "commitment-light CV filling graduates", and suggests that volunteering is a "hopelessly confused concept, its definition stretched from self-sacrificing generosity through to self serving paid jobs" (Cater, 2002). Nevertheless, the fact that individuals as well as voluntary organisations obtain benefits from the process may well alter the nature of the exchange between the two parties, with voluntary organisations able to make greater demands on volunteers in terms of skills, training, efficiency, quality and commitment.

While issues of motivation have been accorded considerable attention in research on voluntary or discretionary organisational participation, an important strand of the existing literature focuses on the question of who volunteers, in terms of demographic and other characteristics, the organisations that individuals volunteer to, and the type of activities that volunteers undertake. The literature on the determinants of volunteering for non-profit organisations is highly complex, and no conceptual model has received general support (Govekar and Govekar, 2002). Much of the traditional literature on volunteering is focused on identifying the demographic or personal characteristics of volunteers, their socioeconomic status, their interpersonal networks and their personality traits (Pearce, 1993). Clearly, much of the literature on volunteering proceeds from an individualist focus, reflecting its roots in social psychology. However, from an organisational perspective, an important literature has developed that analyses the organisational behaviour and contributions of volunteers (Pearce, 1993). While outside the immediate scope of this chapter, it is clear that any rigorous assessment of voluntary activity in terms of public policy requires its assessment from both an individual and an organisational perspective.

Data and methods

The British Household Panel Survey (BHPS) provides a useful (although not perfect) source of data to analyse volunteering in Scotland. It allows us to consider the extent of volunteering, the characteristics of volunteers, and the focus of voluntary activity and participation. It also enables us to compare voluntary activity in Scotland and England. This is of interest, given the widely held perception that Scotland is a more collectivist or cooperative society than England.

> Within Scotland, cooperative values run deep. We are in very many ways a caring society.... Scots have been engaging in grass roots and civic participation for many years. (Scottish Executive, 2000)

There is some evidence to suggest that in Scotland, more people give more in donations to voluntary organisations than elsewhere in the UK (Scottish Executive, 2000).

Of the two waves that contain a boosted Scottish sample (waves 9 [1999] and wave 10 [2000]) the richest set of questions are found in wave 9. Fortunately, however, many of the questions that are of most interest will be reinstated in wave 11. One useful question that does appear in wave 10, however, relates to levels of trust and some comments on this are dealt with later in this chapter.

It may therefore be the case that there is a stronger base in Scotland from which to inspire greater numbers to be involved in volunteering and community action. It has been suggested that an appropriate baseline survey is required to provide information against which to measure the success of the Active Community Initiative (Scottish Executive, 2000). We suggest that the BHPS provides a more appropriate baseline than alternatives such as the Scottish Household Survey (SHS) from 1999 and 2000 due to the broader definition of voluntary activity and participation used therein (although we acknowledge the intention to broaden the definition of voluntary activity in future Scottish Household Surveys).

The BHPS questions in wave 9 (1999) ask respondents separately about whether they are *active* in any one of a large number of specific organisations (or types of organisations) or whether they are *members* of those same organisations. This is important in that there may well be groups of people (women for example) who tend to downplay their involvement in activities. Such people may be unwilling to say that they are active in an organisation but will agree that they are members. It is also important in terms of the volunteering literature, which does not focus specifically on the 'active' but on people who join groups. In the tables in this chapter we present figures for those who say they are 'active' in any of the listed groups. In that sense, they may well underestimate the true extent of volunteering and social involvement as this is in some sense a 'stricter test'. In wave 9, respondents were asked how much time they spent when they 'attended local groups' while in wave 10 they were asked how often they 'do voluntary work'. Neither of these questions are, in themselves, ideal but they give some indication of the depth of individuals' volunteering activity. The 1999 SHS asked respondents:

> Do you give up any time to help as a volunteer or as an organiser for any charities, clubs or organisations, these days (I mean in an unpaid capacity)?

The interviewer goes on to list some 20 or so types of organisation and asks the respondents to indicate which is closest to the one in which they are involved. This is, however, too narrow a focus in that such a question is likely to lead to an underestimate of real activity and involvement for the reasons outlined earlier.

The 2000 SHS question is much broader:

> Thinking back over the last 12 months, have you given up any time to help any clubs, charities, campaigns or organisations (I mean in an unpaid capacity)?

It is also followed up by questions about the type of activity, for example, fundraising, help with administration, or help with campaigning. In that sense, it provides a better indication of the amount of social involvement of the respondents. However, as we indicate later on, the panel nature of the BHPS means that it is likely to be a much more useful tool for extensive analysis of individual volunteering activity in Scotland in the years to come.

The BHPS dataset does, however, have significant limitations. It does not allow us to consider the motivations behind volunteering. There are attitudinal variables in the BHPS relating to trust, collectivism, mutuality, and social networks but, as indicated earlier in this chapter, there is only one wave in which they have been asked for a sufficiently large Scottish sample. The dataset as a whole does suggest, however, that such an analysis for Scotland would be fruitful in the future. To illustrate, if we look at wave 10 (2000) figures for the UK as a whole, we can see a clear association between voluntary activity and levels of trust in others, in that volunteers are significantly more likely than non-volunteers to say that most people can be trusted (47.5% compared with 34.3%).

1999 BHPS results[1]

The extent of volunteering

Most survey figures focus on formal volunteering, although rates of informal voluntary activity tend to be higher (IVR, 2003a). In 1997, around 22 million adults, 48% of the adult population in the UK, took part in formal volunteer activity (IVR, 2003a). While this represented a slight fall over the preceding six years of 3% (or one million people), volunteers in 1997 devoted more time to volunteering on average than they had previously. Informal volunteer activity attracted 74% of the adult population. Eighty-eight million hours were formally volunteered in 1997, an increase from 62 million hours from 1991 (IVR, 2003a).

Using the BHPS wave 9, we see that in 1999 43.7% of the UK sample participated in one of a range of listed organisations, including civic or community groups, religious groups and more conventional voluntary service organisations. Similar proportions, 46.7% and 46% respectively, were active in Scotland and England. As indicated earlier in this chapter, the wave 9 data do not have a satisfactory question on the time spent in voluntary activities.

Who volunteers?

The question of who volunteers can usefully be addressed using Pearce's (1993) categorisation of volunteers in terms of their demographic/personal characteristics, their socioeconomic status, their interpersonal networks and their personality traits. The BHPS does not allow us to look in detail at interpersonal networks for the Scottish sample as indicated earlier, nor is there a particular focus on personality traits, although we attempt to relate voluntary activity to related proxy variables in the next section. It does, however, allow us to consider the first two of these categories. Thus, we can consider the composition of the volunteer group in terms of their gender, marital status, age, religion, ethnicity, education and qualifications, occupational status, income and home ownership. In so doing, we will highlight any national differences between the Scottish and English data.

Gender and marital status

While women have long been associated with traditional forms of voluntary activity, concerns have been raised in recent years over the effect of women's increasing participation in the labour market and the level of their voluntary or discretionary activities. Recent UK surveys have found that women and men were equally likely to volunteer, with 48% so doing (IVR, 2003a). However, looking at the 1999 BHPS data at UK level, we see that women are considerably more likely (54%) to undertake voluntary activity than men (48%) are. This difference is not a feature of the Scottish data, with no significant differences emerging between the 49.3% of Scottish men and 44.4% of Scottish women who engage in voluntary activity. The propensity to volunteer is, however, significantly higher for English men (47.9%) than English women (44.3%).

If we combine the range of marital status categories to reflect whether or not respondents live singly or as part of a couple (see Table 18.1), we find no significant difference in activity within the listed organisations, with 47.9% of respondents who live as couples and 44.8% of respondents who live singly engaging in voluntary activities. No significant differences emerged between Scotland and England in this regard, with the exception of cohabiting couples, who were the least likely of all categories of marital status to undertake voluntary activity, and were significantly less likely to do so in Scotland than in England.

Table 18.1: Those active in any of the listed organisations by marital status (%)

Marital status	Scotland	England
Married	49.6	48.0
Living as a couple	37.1	40.2
Widowed	43.8	45.3
Divorced	52.2	39.6
Separated	48.4	47.1
Never married	42.8	44.6

Age

It is well established that volunteering tends to peak in middle age, with a tailing off after retirement, although older people may contribute more hours to voluntary activity (Scottish Executive, 2001). However, since 1991 there has been some evidence of an increase in participation by those aged 65+ (sometimes referred to as the 'third age'), and a sharp decline in involvement by young people (IVR, 2003a). In the US, a different pattern has emerged in which older people have become less likely to engage in voluntary activity due to the decline or demise of the 'long civic' generation born between 1910 and 1940 (Putnam, 1996). Clearly, a decline in volunteering by young people is a cause for some concern. If this is occurring, it is important to know whether this represents a rejection of voluntary activity in principle, or lower activity levels stemming from the nature and form of voluntary activity (IVR, 2003b). The most recent research from the IVR suggests the latter is of particular significance.

In future, the BHPS data will enable some consideration of the involvement of Scottish young people in voluntary activity over time.

In overall terms, there were no significant differences between the Scottish and English samples in terms of the link between volunteering and age. However, if we look within each country sample (see Table 18.2), we find a number of interesting distinctions. In both countries, there was no significant tailing off of voluntary activity in the oldest age group, which would be consistent with recent findings of increasing participation by people in this age group. In addition, the youngest age group in Scotland were no less likely than their older counterparts to take part in voluntary activity, in sharp distinction with young people in England, who were significantly less likely than older people in England to engage in voluntary activity.

Religion

Research on volunteering behaviour has consistently found a positive relationship between religion and volunteering (for example, Park

Table 18.2: Those active in any listed organisation by age (%)

Age at time of interview	Scotland	England
16-25	41.2	40.9
26-45	47.8	47.2
46-65	48.6	48.8
66+	47.3	44.3

Table 18.3: Those active in any listed organisation by religious denomination (%)

Religious denomination	Scotland	England
No religion	39.2	40.8
Church of England	60.7	45.9
Roman Catholic	43.7	51.6
Church of Scotland	52.4	54.0
Christian	58.3	62.1
Other	55.6	61.0

Table 18.4: Those active in any listed organisation by attitude to religion (%)

Attitude to religion	Scotland	England
Religion makes no difference to my life	39.4	38.1
Religion makes a little difference to my life	50.0	44.5
Religion makes some difference to my life	48.9	52.3
Religion makes a great difference to my life	62.7	66.6

and Smith, 2000). Religious participation not only exposes individuals to collective values, it also involves them in established and enduring social networks. The BHPS data (see Table 18.3) confirm this to be the case for both Scotland and England for most organised religions (certain denominations including major religious groupings such as the Jewish and Muslim faiths were excluded due to the very small numbers appearing in the Scottish sample).

In addition, the degree of attachment to religion or faith of any kind is positively associated with a propensity to volunteer in both Scotland and England (see Table 18.4). Any religious commitment, even a little, is associated with a significantly increased propensity to volunteer.

Ethnicity

A priori, ethnicity is likely to exhibit some association with voluntary activity due to differing cultural norms and patterns of social networks. Concerns have been raised about the under-participation of minority communities in the community and voluntary sector in Scotland (BEMIS, 2000; CEMVO, 2001; Scottish Executive, 2000; Sullivan, 2002). Information on ethnicity is contained in the dataset but it is only collected on the first entry of a respondent into the survey. It therefore has to be extracted for each individual from the first wave in which they appear. Fortunately there are plans for the responses to such one-off questions to be collected into a single file and this will be released from wave 11 onwards.

Education and qualifications

Formal volunteering has been established elsewhere as being positively related to human capital (Wilson and Musick, 1997).The data presented here indicate that this relationship holds equally in both Scotland and England.Those with no qualifications are significantly less likely in both countries to undertake voluntary activity, while those with graduate qualifications are the most likely to do so (see Table 18.5).

Occupational status

There is consistent evidence that volunteering is more likely to be done by those with higher occupational status. The BHPS dataset indicates that this holds in both Scotland and England. What is of particular interest, however, in looking at the raw frequency data, is the activity level among unskilled workers in Scotland, which appears out of line with the established pattern of relationships. This result should be treated with caution, however, given the small numbers in the sample.

Table 18.5: Those active in any listed organisation by qualifications (%)

Qualifications	Scotland	England
No qualifications	31.2	35.9
School qualifications	47.9	43.4
Non-academic qualifications	51.3	42.9
Professional qualifications	52.4	54.1
Graduate	63.3	61.4

Table 18.6: Those active in any listed organisation by RG social class (%)

RG social class	Scotland	England
Unskilled	50.0	29.8
Partly skilled	42.5	43.5
Manual skilled	46.6	43.1
Skilled non-manual	41.7	44.4
Managerial and technical	52.6	55.1
Professional	69.8	63.2

Table 18.7: Those active in any listed organisation by income (%)

Household income	Scotland	England
Less than £6,000	37.3	31.5
£6,001-£20,000	42.2	39.0
£20,000 and over	50.5	47.7

Table 18.8: Those active in any listed organisation by tenure (%)

Tenure	Scotland	England
Homeowner	50.9	47.1
Shared owner	57.1	33.3
Renter	37.2	35.1

Income

Levels of volunteering are positively correlated with levels of household income (Pearce, 1993; Scottish Executive, 2001). There is clearly a potential link between the effect of qualifications, occupational status and income in terms of their impact on volunteering, with some analyses suggesting that the most influential factor is education (Pearce, 1993). In both Scotland and England, those on the lowest incomes were least likely to participate in voluntary activity, although those on middle-ranged incomes in Scotland (£6,001-£20,000) were significantly more likely to be active than their counterparts in England (see Table 18.7).

Home ownership

As in the literature more generally (for example, Babchuk and Gordon, 1962), homeowners in the sample are more likely to undertake voluntary activities than non-homeowners in both Scotland and England. In Scotland, however, homeowners are significantly more likely to report such involvement (see Table 18.8).

Enablers to volunteering

It is useful to consider the participation of individuals in voluntary or discretionary activities in relation to their opportunities to undertake such activity. There are clearly barriers to volunteering, and we have already considered two important potential barriers – income and education/qualifications. Another important issue is time. For example, Putnam questions the impact of the time spent commuting and watching television on civic or community participation (Putnam, 1996). Employment and family responsibilities represent an important potential time constraint, and we look here at their impact on voluntary activity.

In addition, and relating back to Pearce's (1993) summary of the volunteering literature, certain personality traits are associated with a propensity to volunteer, and hence these act as enablers to voluntary activity. Volunteer activity has been associated with gregariousness, confidence and high self-esteem. In the absence of psychological measures of this nature in the BHPS, we have attempted to relate voluntary activity to relative satisfaction with a number of aspects of an individual's life, such as their jobs, leisure time and health.

Employment

Volunteering involves a time commitment; therefore, we might expect that people with more time are more likely to volunteer. Ironically, however, a number of surveys have established that those in work are more likely to volunteer. For example, research from the Institute for Volunteering Research (IVR) (2003a) confirms that those in work are most likely to volunteer, with rates of involvement among unemployed people falling from 50% in 1993 to 38% in 1997 (part of which may be related to changes in the system of welfare benefits). Similarly, the 2000 SHS illustrates that volunteers are more likely to be busy people, employed full (26%) or part time (34%), or self-employed (37%), as opposed to unemployed (17%) (Scottish Executive, 2001). Similar relationships are found in the BHPS data, with higher activity levels in both Scotland and England among the employed, self-employed and retired than among the unemployed (see Table 18.9). Perhaps worryingly, those who are unemployed in Scotland are significantly less likely than their counterparts in England to participate in discretionary organisational activities. The higher levels of participation by the unemployed in England seem to be across a range of organisational activities, although they report greater participation

Table 18.9: Those active in any listed organisation by employment status (%)

Employment status	Scotland	England
Employed	49.8	47.8
Self-employed	45.3	49.1
Retired	48.3	44.4
Unemployed	19.3	34.7

particularly in sports clubs, social groups, and parents' associations, and lower participation rates in political and religious organisations.

Family responsibilities

Family responsibilities have an interesting relationship with voluntary activity. On the one hand, the presence of children in a household undoubtedly has implications in terms of the discretionary or personal time available to adult household members. On the other, however, the presence of children may also expand the number and type of voluntary activities available to related adults, and involve adult household members in additional social networks, for example, relating to schools and youth organisations. According to Wilson and Musick (1997), formal volunteering is positively related to the presence of children within the household. To gauge the impact of this in the sample, we considered the presence or absence of a child aged under 12. However, no such relationship was identified in either Scotland or England.

Satisfaction with leisure time

Individuals face competing demands on non-work or leisure time, with evident consequences for voluntary activities (Putnam, 1996). A priori, one might expect that a precondition to undertaking voluntary activity would be some level of satisfaction with available leisure time. Yet no obvious pattern to support such a hypothesis could be established from the BHPS data (see Table 18.10). Those respondents in the English panel exhibiting least satisfaction with the amount of leisure time available to them volunteer in significantly higher proportions than Scots in the same category. However, this pattern is not repeated consistently throughout the scale.

Table 18.10: Those active in any listed organisation by attitude to amount of leisure time (%)

Satisfaction with amount of leisure time	Scotland	England
1 Not satisfied at all with amount of available leisure time	22.9	33.1
2	43.0	41.9
3	44.2	42.0
4	42.4	44.8
5	51.8	47.5
6	54.0	50.8
7 Completely satisfied with amount of available leisure time	46.8	48.0

Table 18.11: Those active in any listed organisation by health (%)

Perceptions of own health	Scotland	England
Excellent health	54.8	52.8
Very good health	49.4	48.9
Good health	47.1	44.8
Fair health	35.0	41.8
Poor health	33.8	28.6

State of health

It is useful to hypothesise that an important enabler to voluntary or non-essential activity is relative good health and well-being (although there is an important issue arising from the direction of causation between perceptions of health and voluntary activities). It is clear from the data that those who perceive their health as poor are significantly less likely to participate in voluntary organisational activity in both Scotland and England (see Table 18.11).

Satisfaction with job

There are competing perspectives on the possible link between voluntary activity and other forms of organisational involvement. On the one hand, those who are satisfied with their work lives may be more likely to undertake additional voluntary activities in other organisations. On the other hand, however, voluntary activity within non-work organisations may be an important avenue for diversion or source of satisfying activity for those who are unfulfilled or unsatisfied in their working lives. Given this reasoning, it is perhaps no surprise that no clear pattern emerged in the voluntary participation rates of those who were more or less satisfied at work.

Where do people volunteer?

As indicated earlier in this chapter, people engage with a broad range of organisations and activities on a voluntary basis. It is a legitimate criticism of much large-scale survey data in this area that it focuses on formal group or organisational participation at the expense of identifying more informal and disparate voluntary activity. This may result in a significant underestimate of voluntary activity in some circumstances. However, the additional difficulties of measuring less formal discretionary activities must be acknowledged.

According to the 2000 SHS, the most popular groups or organisations that attract volunteers are those connected with church or religious activities (16%), and activities and organisations working with young people and children (15%). The next most popular are those working in health-related projects (11%), and sporting activities (12%). Those working with disabled people account for 9% (Scottish Executive, 2001). In the BHPS data, the most popular groups identified are sports clubs, followed by religious organisations and social groupings. Due to the numbers involved, it was not possible to distinguish between the support for particular types of organisation in Scotland and England.

There is an established relationship between gender and the type of organisations to which voluntary activity is offered. According to IVR, women were three times more likely than men to volunteer in schools, and also more likely to be involved in social welfare groups, while men were twice as likely to be involved in sports groups (IVR, 2003a). From the BHPS data, we see that men in both Scotland and England are twice as likely to undertake activity in sports clubs, social groups and professional organisations as women are. Women in Scotland and England are twice as likely to undertake discretionary activities within religious organisations as men are, and almost three times as likely to participate in parents' associations. Again, these figures must be treated with caution given the small numbers involved in each category.

Gender has also been linked elsewhere with particular activities within the voluntary sector. For example, while women are more likely to be volunteers, and more likely to be involved in fundraising, men are more likely to hold management committee positions (IVR, 2003a). Similarly, young people have a distinctive profile in terms of the particular voluntary activities they undertake (IVR, 2003b). Unfortunately, the BHPS data do not provide information on what activities are undertaken by volunteers within voluntary organisations. This limitation means that the dataset cannot be used to contribute to discussions of the rise of 'professional' volunteering, where individuals contribute the same skills set in a voluntary as in a work context (see Table 18.12).

Statistical analysis

One obvious way to analyse the data further is to carry out a statistical procedure designed to estimate the change in the odds of an outcome taking place. A logistic regression is estimated, which looks at the effect of a number of the variables above on the probability that one is

Table 18.12: Activity by country and gender (%)

Type of group	Scotland	England	Scottish men	Scottish women	English men	English women
Environmental group	1.6	1.5	1.9	1.3	1.6	1.5
Other civic or community group	1.8	1.6	1.4	2.0	1.5	1.8
Parents' association	3.7	4.9	1.3	5.9	2.6	7.0
Pensioners' group	2.3	2.0	1.45	3.0	1.3	2.6
Political party	0.9	1.1	1.3	0.6	1.1	1.2
Professional organisation	4.2	3.3	5.5	3.2	4.6	2.1
Religious group	12.8	10.6	8.7	16.5	7.5	13.5
Scouts or guides	1.7	1.9	1.0	2.4	1.6	2.2
Social group	6.4	8.5	8.9	4.0	11.5	5.6
Sports club	19.8	18.0	27.4	13.0	23.9	12.7
Tenants' or residents' group	3.2	4.4	2.9	3.5	4.3	4.5
Trades union	3.8	2.3	5.0	2.7	2.9	1.7
Voluntary service organisation	4.3	3.8	3.2	5.2	2.9	4.6
Women's group	0.9	0.4	0	1.6	0	1.7
Women's institute	1.5	1.7	0.2	2.2	0.1	3.2
Other organisation	4.4	6.1	5.1	3.7	5.7	6.5

Table 18.13: Impacts on odds of *not* being active in any voluntary organisation: logistic regression results

Variable	B	SE	Sig	Exp(B)
Male	−0.109	0.308	0.004*	0.896
Marital status				
Child under 16	−0.797	0.366	0.029	0.451
Married	−0.055	0.053	0.295	0.946
Living as couple	0.213	0.075	0.005*	1.237
Widowed	0.034	0.089	0.706	1.034
Divorced	0.208	0.092	0.024	1.231
Separated	−0.091	0.147	0.533	0.913
Attitude to religion: religion makes a difference to life				
Not answered	−0.555	0.299	0.064	0.574
A little difference	−0.305	0.046	0.000*	0.737
Some difference	−0.606	0.050	0.000*	0.546
A great difference	−1.248	0.056	0.000*	0.287
Living in Scotland	0.025	0.060	0.682	1.025
Age	0.004	0.001	0.002*	1.004
Income	0.000	0.000	0.000*	1.000
Constant	0.614	0.078	0.000*	1.848

Notes: *significant.

The default variables are respectively being female, never married, living in England and taking the view that religion makes no difference to your life.

not active in any of the listed (voluntary) organisations contained in the dataset.

The results are shown in Table 18.13, and they appear to confirm much of what is commonly held in the literature. Men are more likely to volunteer; living as a couple makes you less likely to volunteer; and those on higher incomes are more likely to volunteer. The most notable result is having any religious views at all makes you far more likely to volunteer, with the most religious being the most likely to volunteer. It is interesting to note that the age variable appears to suggest that being older makes you less likely to volunteer and this does not accord with the notion outlined earlier of the older generation being part of the 'civic generation'.

Conclusion

A particular concern has been raised in the Active Community Initiative to promote social inclusion by identifying and removing barriers to involvement in volunteering and community action experienced by particular individuals and groups (Scottish Executive, 2000). To do so, we must be able to identify in some detail the composition of the volunteer group. The BHPS allows us to make considerable progress in this regard. Our analysis in this chapter has raised some positive issues in the Scottish context: in Scotland, voluntary activity is equally shared between the sexes and no significant age differences emerged. The latter is of particular importance given that learning to volunteer at a young age is likely to be positively associated with propensity to volunteer later in life. However, certain areas of concern have been identified. In both Scotland and England, an important influence on voluntary activity is religious belief, yet participation in organised religion continues to decline, with possible implications for voluntary activity. In both countries, those people without qualifications are largely excluded from voluntary activities. Worryingly, there appear to be lower levels of voluntary participation among unemployed people in Scotland than in England. However, there are indications that taking part in work in Scotland, even in an unskilled capacity, is more likely to precipitate voluntary activity than in England.

Identifying barriers to participation in voluntary or civic activities is also of great importance in avoiding systematic exclusion of particular groups, and it would be of great use if future surveys were to include questions relating to the reasons why people either participate or do not participate in voluntary activities.

Future use of the BHPS data

Returning to our discussion at the beginning of this chapter, it has become increasingly important to acknowledge the benefits that individuals might obtain through voluntary activity, given that six out of 10 volunteers say that volunteering gives them an opportunity to learn new skills (IVR, 2003a). One very interesting possibility for the future is to use the BHPS to track the development of human capital among volunteers in Scotland.

Note
[1] All tables are derived from weighted data for wave 9 (1999). Cross-sectional weights were used throughout.

References

Babchuk, N. and Gordon, C.W. (1962) *The voluntary association in the slum*, University of Nebraska Studies, New Series no 27, Lincoln: University of Nebraska Press.

BEMIS (Black and Ethnic Minority Infrastructure in Scotland) (2000) *Listening to the Voice: Feasibility Report*, Edinburgh: BEMIS.

Bolino, M.C., Turnley, W.H. and Bloodgood, J.M. (2002) 'Citizenship behaviour and the creation of social capital in organisations', *Academy of Management Review*, vol 27, no 4, pp 505-22.

Cater, N. (2002) 'Hidden costs of free time and talent', *Guardian Unlimited*, 9 May (www,society.guardian.co.uk/comment/story/0,7884,712035,00.html).

CEMVO (Council for Ethnic Minority Voluntary Organisations) (2001) *Sensing the scene*, Report on BME Voluntary Organisations in Scotland.

Findlay, P. and McKinlay, A. (2002) 'Bargaining alone: social capital and new unionism', *Renewal*, vol 10, no 2, pp 21-9.

Govekar, P.L and Govekar, M.A. (2002) 'Using economic theory and research to better understand volunteer behaviour', *Nonprofit management and leadership*, Fall, vol 13, no 1, pp 33-48.

Hill, N. (2002) 'Volunteering: the issue explained', *Guardian Unlimited*, 5 June (www.society.guardian.co.uk/volunteering/story/0,8150,1425530,00.html).

IVR (Institute for Volunteering Research) (2003a) '1997 national survey of volunteering in the UK', National Centre for Volunteering (www.ivr.org.uk/nationalsurvey.htm).

IVR (2003b) 'What young people want from volunteering', National Centre for Volunteering (www.ivr.org.uk/youngresearch.htm).

Lee, L. and Higgins, C. (2001) 'Corporate volunteering: ad hoc interaction or route to dialogue and partnership?', *Journal of Corporate Citizenship*, vol 4, pp 79-90.

Park, J.Z. and Smith, C. (2000) 'To whom much has been given: religious capital and community involvement among church going Protestants', *Journal for the Scientific Study of Religion*, vol 39, no 3, pp 272-86.

Pearce, J.L. (1993) *Volunteers: The organisational behaviour of unpaid workers*, London: Routledge.

Putnam, R.D. (1995) 'Bowling alone: America's declining social capital', *Journal of Democracy*, vol 6, pp 65-78.

Putnam, R.D. (1996) 'The strange disappearance of civic America', *The American Prospect*, vol 7, no 24, pp 7-24.

Putnam, R.D. (2000) *Bowling alone: The collapse and revival of American community*, New York, NY: Simon and Schuster.

Rushton, J.P. and Sorrentino, R.M. (eds) (1981) *Altruism and helping behaviour: Social, personality and developmental perspectives*, New Jersey, NJ: Erlbaum.

Scottish Executive (2000) 'Supporting active communities in Scotland: a draft strategy for volunteering and community action', Report by the Scottish Active Communities Working Group (www.scotland.gov.uk/library2/doc11).

Scottish Executive (2001) *Volunteering in Scotland: Evidence from the Scottish Household Survey 2000*. Edinburgh (www.scotland.gov.uk/library3/society/vis.pdf).

Sullivan, W. (2002) 'Communities within community: ethnic minority networks and civil society in Scotland', *Renewal*, vol 10, no 2, pp 30-4.

Wilson, J. and Musick, M. (1997) 'Who cares? Towards an integrated theory of volunteer work', *American Sociological Review*, vol 62, no 5, pp 694-713.

NINETEEN

Conclusion

John F. Ermisch and Robert E. Wright

The comparative studies in this book help provide a 'baseline' for analysing the impacts of subsequent differential developments in policy arising out of Scottish devolution. They allow us to address the question of whether Scots behave differently despite similar policy regimes in Scotland and the rest of Britain, or the same, despite some pre-existing differences in policy. The identification of these differences is important for policy formulation by the Scottish Executive. it allows the Executive to identify policy issues that are distinctive to Scotland and helps it to formulate policies aimed at narrowing those differences that represent 'disadvantage'. We summarise some of the policy questions raised by the findings under each theme.

Families and households

- What, if any, are the implications of the tendency of parents in Scotland, particularly lone parents, to monitor the behaviour of their adolescent children less than parents in England?
- What are the implications for policies relating to social welfare, housing and social care of more independent living by Scottish young people and older Scots? What institutions and policies are responsible for this tendency toward more sole person and unrelated person households in Scotland than England?
- What hinders residential mobility by non-employed Scots?
- What policy measures best address the greater degree of 'fuel poverty' in Scotland?

Inequalities

- Why do negative life circumstances, such as smoking and unemployment, produce worse health outcomes in Scotland than England, and positive ones better health outcomes? What are the implications for poor health prevention policies?

- What lessons can we learn from the smaller increase in income inequality in Scotland than England?
- What are the policy implications of rising income inequality among the Scottish elderly population?

Labour market issues

- Why is earnings instability greater in Scotland, and does it matter?
- Does a smaller gender pay gap in Scotland have lessons for elsewhere, or is it just a product of poorer earning opportunities for Scottish men?
- Why are the returns to further and higher education higher in Scotland, and what are the implications for policy (for example, for the expansion of the further education sector) and future levels of skills and inequality?
- Why are Scottish older workers more likely to retire, but also more likely to subsequently re-enter work? How can policy help keep a larger proportion of older Scottish workers in employment?

Social and political behaviour

- Given the finding that the Scottish Parliament appears to be primarily an expression of the country's national identity, will it make a difference to the quality of public policy formulation and implementation in Scotland?
- Will the greater importance of religion in Scotland affect policy formulation and implementation?
- How can more people be encouraged to involve themselves in community action and other voluntary activity, particularly in light of the decline in religious belief?

The future

This book has provided a baseline of behaviour and outcomes at the beginning of the Scottish Parliament using the British Household Panel Survey (BHPS) booster sample for Scotland and the ongoing BHPS for the rest of Britain. The annual waves of the BHPS continue: two (2001-02) have already become available since the analysis in these chapters was completed. Using these data, it will be possible to study the extent to which behaviour and outcomes in Scotland change relative to the rest of Britain in response to distinctive policies adopted by the devolved Scottish government. Two examples of these are the so-called 'free personal care for elderly' programme and the firm commitment not to introduce tuition fees in the higher education sector for Scottish students. Others will follow. The baseline established in this book and the stream of BHPS data will help us evaluate the effects of these policies in the future.

Index

Page references for tables and figures are in *italics*; those for notes are followed by n

Also available from The Policy Press

Exploring social policy in the 'new' Scotland
Edited by Gerry Mooney and Gill Scott

"This is a timely volume on social policy under devolution, based on informed critical analyses. It does not make comfortable reading for those seeking simple governance solutions alone, but offers ideas and visions of an alternative social strategy of relevance and transferability to other devolved territories." *Mike Danson, Centre for Contemporary European Studies, University of Paisley*

Exploring social policy in the 'new' Scotland is the first book specifically aimed at students that integrates the description and analysis of social policy in Scotland since devolution in 1999. It has been designed to support the delivery of social policy and related courses in Scotland itself but also to appeal to students on social policy, politics, sociology, public policy and regional studies courses across the United Kingdom, on which devolution and its impact are examined.

Paperback £19.99 US$29.95 ISBN 1 86134 594 1
Hardback £55.00 US$75.00 ISBN 1 86134 595 X
240 x 172mm 288 pages June 2005
INSPECTION COPY AVAILABLE

Taking stock
Scottish social welfare after devolution
John Stewart

"A much needed and valuable contribution to the analysis of social welfare in Scotland and to emerging debates about social policy diversity within nation states. The book serves an important purpose in raising the profile of diversity within the UK and the distinct nature of social policy in Scotland." *Dr Sharon Wright, Department of Applied Social Science, University of Stirling*

This topical book examines social welfare in Scotland since devolution. In particular, it focuses on the politics of welfare during and after the devolution process; poverty and inequality; and the two single most important powers devolved to the Edinburgh Parliament, education and health. It is the first work to attempt such a synthesis.

Paperback £19.99 US$32.95 ISBN 1 86134 523 2
234 x 156mm 176 pages September 2004

People and places
A 2001 Census atlas of the UK
Danny Dorling and Bethan Thomas

"... a compendium of facts that will have anyone interested in policy flipping through, manically, as well as wagging their fingers at their friends demanding 'did you know…?' From the precipitate rise of single living in London,

Nottingham and Glasgow to the nation's unshakeable addiction to commuting by car - it is all here." *Audacity*

People and places: A 2001 Census atlas of the UK provides an at-a-glance guide to social change in the UK at the start of the new millennium. It is the first comprehensive analysis of the 2001 Census and offers unique comparisons with the findings of the previous Census a decade ago. Over 500 full-colour maps covering 125 topics clearly illustrate the state of UK society today and how it is changing.

Paperback £29.99 US$45.00 ISBN 1 86134 555 0

Hardback £59.99 US$89.99 ISBN 1 86134 586 0

240 x 303mm 224 pages August 2004

Developing locally
An international comparison of local and regional economic development
Edited by Andrew Beer, Graham Haughton and Alaric Maude
"... adds interesting material to the evidence base and provides an accessible contribution to the literature on the role of local and regional development organisations within a developed economy setting for undergraduates, postgraduates and local and regional development policy-makers and practitioners. The references at the end of the book provide a useful way into the literature for undergraduates in particular - and, unlike many contemporary texts on local and regional economic development issues, the price of this paperback edition also makes the book affordable." *Local Government Studies*

Throughout the developed world governments have invested substantial sums in local and regional economic development. This is the first book to provide a cross-national comparison and evaluation of regional development strategies, institutions and agencies.

Paperback £22.99 US$32.50 ISBN 1 86134 485 6

Hardback £50.00 US$65.00 ISBN 1 86134 546 1

234 x 156mm 208 pages November 2003

To order further copies of this publication or any other Policy Press titles please visit **www.policypress.org.uk** or contact:

In the UK and Europe:
Marston Book Services, PO Box 269,
Abingdon, Oxon, OX14 4YN, UK
Tel: +44 (0)1235 465500
Fax: +44 (0)1235 465556
Email: direct.orders@marston.co.uk

In the USA and Canada:
ISBS, 920 NE 58th Street, Suite 300,
Portland, OR 97213-3786, USA
Tel: +1 800 944 6190 (toll free)
Fax: +1 503 280 8832
Email: info@isbs.com

In Australia and New Zealand:
DA Information Services, 648 Whitehorse Road
Mitcham, Victoria 3132, Australia
Tel: +61 (3) 9210 7777
Fax: +61 (3) 9210 7788
E-mail: service@dadirect.com.au

Further information about all of our titles can be found on our website.